MULTICULTURA

JAMES A. BAN

First Freire: Early Writings in Social Justice Education
CARLOS ALBERTO TORRES

Mathematics for Equity:
A Framework for Successful Practice
NA'ILAH SUAD NASIR, CARLOS CABANA, BARBARA SHREVE, ESTELLE WOODBURY, AND NICOLE LOUIE, EDS.

Race, Empire, and English Language Teaching:
Creating Responsible and Ethical Anti-Racist Practice
SUHANTHIE MOTHA

Black Male(d): Peril and Promise in the Education of African American Males
TYRONE C. HOWARD

LGBTQ Youth and Education: Policies and Practices
CRIS MAYO

Race Frameworks:
A Multidimensional Theory of Racism and Education
ZEUS LEONARDO

Reaching and Teaching Students in Poverty:
Strategies for Erasing the Opportunity Gap
PAUL C. GORSKI

Class Rules:
Exposing Inequality in American High Schools
PETER W. COOKSON JR.

Teachers Without Borders? The Hidden Consequences of International Teachers in U.S. Schools
ALYSSA HADLEY DUNN

Streetsmart Schoolsmart:
Urban Poverty and the Education of Adolescent Boys
GILBERTO Q. CONCHAS AND JAMES DIEGO VIGIL

Americans by Heart: Undocumented Latino Students and the Promise of Higher Education
WILLIAM PÉREZ

Is Everyone Really Equal? An Introduction to Key Concepts in Social Justice Education
ÖZLEM SENSOY AND ROBIN DIANGELO

Achieving Equity for Latino Students: Expanding the Pathway to Higher Education Through Public Policy
FRANCES CONTRERAS

Literacy Achievement and Diversity:
Keys to Success for Students, Teachers, and Schools
KATHRYN H. AU

Understanding English Language Variation in U.S. Schools
ANNE H. CHARITY HUDLEY AND CHRISTINE MALLINSON

Latino Children Learning English: Steps in the Journey
GUADALUPE VALDÉS, SARAH CAPITELLI, AND LAURA ALVAREZ

Asians in the Ivory Tower: Dilemmas of Racial Inequality in American Higher Education
ROBERT T. TERANISHI

Our Worlds in Our Words: Exploring Race, Class, Gender, and Sexual Orientation in Multicultural Classrooms
MARY DILG

Culturally Responsive Teaching:
Theory, Research, and Practice, Second Edition
GENEVA GAY

Why Race and Culture Matter in Schools:
Closing the Achievement Gap in America's Classrooms
TYRONE C. HOWARD

Diversity and Equity in Science Education:
Research, Policy, and Practice
OKHEE LEE AND CORY A. BUXTON

Forbidden Language:
English Learners and Restrictive Language Policies
PATRICIA GÁNDARA AND MEGAN HOPKINS, EDS.

The Light in Their Eyes:
Creating Multicultural Learning Communities, 10th Anniversary Edition
SONIA NIETO

The Flat World and Education: How America's Commitment to Equity Will Determine Our Future
LINDA DARLING-HAMMOND

Teaching What Really Happened:
How to Avoid the Tyranny of Textbooks and Get Students Excited About Doing History
JAMES W. LOEWEN

Diversity and the New Teacher:
Learning from Experience in Urban Schools
CATHERINE CORNBLETH

Frogs into Princes: Writings on School Reform
LARRY CUBAN

Educating Citizens in a Multicultural Society, Second Edition
JAMES A. BANKS

(continued)

MULTICULTURAL EDUCATION SERIES, *continued*

Culture, Literacy, and Learning:
Taking Bloom in the Midst of the Whirlwind
CAROL D. LEE

Facing Accountability in Education:
Democracy and Equity at Risk
CHRISTINE E. SLEETER, ED.

Talkin Black Talk:
Language, Education, and Social Change
H. SAMY ALIM AND JOHN BAUGH, EDS.

Improving Access to Mathematics:
Diversity and Equity in the Classroom
NA'ILAH SUAD NASIR AND PAUL COBB, EDS.

"To Remain an Indian": Lessons in Democracy from a Century of Native American Education
K. TSIANINA LOMAWAIMA AND TERESA L. MCCARTY

Education Research in the Public Interest:
Social Justice, Action, and Policy
GLORIA LADSON-BILLINGS AND WILLIAM F. TATE, EDS.

Multicultural Strategies for Education and Social Change:
Carriers of the Torch in the United States and South Africa
ARNETHA F. BALL

We Can't Teach What We Don't Know:
White Teachers, Multiracial Schools, Second Edition
GARY R. HOWARD

Un-Standardizing Curriculum: Multicultural Teaching in the Standards-Based Classroom
CHRISTINE E. SLEETER

Beyond the Big House:
African American Educators on Teacher Education
GLORIA LADSON-BILLINGS

Teaching and Learning in Two Languages:
Bilingualism and Schooling in the United States
EUGENE E. GARCÍA

Improving Multicultural Education:
Lessons from the Intergroup Education Movement
CHERRY A. MCGEE BANKS

Education Programs for Improving Intergroup Relations:
Theory, Research, and Practice
WALTER G. STEPHAN AND W. PAUL VOGT, EDS.

Walking the Road:
Race, Diversity, and Social Justice in Teacher Education
MARILYN COCHRAN-SMITH

City Schools and the American Dream:
Reclaiming the Promise of Public Education
PEDRO A. NOGUERA

Thriving in the Multicultural Classroom:
Principles and Practices for Effective Teaching
MARY DILG

Educating Teachers for Diversity:
Seeing with a Cultural Eye
JACQUELINE JORDAN IRVINE

Teaching Democracy:
Unity and Diversity in Public Life
WALTER C. PARKER

The Making—and Remaking—of a Multiculturalist
CARLOS E. CORTÉS

Transforming the Multicultural Education of Teachers: Theory, Research, and Practice
MICHAEL VAVRUS

Learning to Teach for Social Justice
LINDA DARLING-HAMMOND, JENNIFER FRENCH, AND SILVIA PALOMA GARCIA-LOPEZ, EDS.

Culture, Difference, and Power
CHRISTINE E. SLEETER

Learning and Not Learning English:
Latino Students in American Schools
GUADALUPE VALDÉS

The Children Are Watching:
How the Media Teach About Diversity
CARLOS E. CORTÉS

Multicultural Education, Transformative Knowledge, and Action: Historical and Contemporary Perspectives
JAMES A. BANKS, ED.

First Freire

EARLY WRITINGS IN SOCIAL JUSTICE EDUCATION

Carlos Alberto Torres

Foreword by
Moacir Gadotti

Teachers College
Columbia University
New York and London

Published by Teachers College Press, 1234 Amsterdam Avenue, New York, NY 10027

Chapter 1 was adapted from Moacir Gadotti and Carlos Alberto Torres, "Paulo Freire: Education for Development." *Journal Development and Change*, November 2009, *40*(6), 1255—1267. Journal published by Blackwell Publishing on behalf of the Institute of Social Studies, The Hague. © 2009 by the Institute of Social Studies. Used with permission.

The poem "A Little More Than a Year Ago (for Paulo Freire)" was originally published in Spanish in Carlos Alberto Torres, *Poesía perdida al atardecer*, 2004. Valencia, Spain, Editorial Germania. Translated into English by Dr. Peter Lownds. Used with permission.

Library of Congress Cataloging-in-Publication Data

Torres, Carlos Alberto.
First Freire : early writings in social justice education / Carlos Alberto Torres ; foreword by Moacir Gadotti.
pages cm. — (Multicultural education series)
Includes bibliographical references and index.
ISBN 978-0-8077-5533-4 (pbk. : alk. paper)
ISBN 978-0-8077-5534-1 (hardcover : alk. paper)
ISBN 978-0-8077-7289-8 (ebook : alk. paper)
1. Freire, Paulo, 1921–1997—Criticism and interpretation. 2. Education—Philosophy. 3. Social justice—Study and teaching. 4. Critical pedagogy. I. Title.
LB880.F732T673 2014
70.11'5—dc23 2014007431

ISBN 978-0-8077-5533-4 (paperback)
ISBN 978-0-8077-5534-1 (hardcover)
ISBN 978-0-8077-7289-8 (eBook)

Printed on acid-free paper
Manufactured in the United States of America

21 20 19 18 17 16 15 14 8 7 6 5 4 3 2 1

For Carlos Alberto, Pablo Sebastián, Laura Silvina and Ian, caminantes de la utopia.

For Mónica Mignone, María Marta, and César Lugones, friends who were disappeared by the Dictatorship for practicing liberatory education in Argentina.

For my grand-daughter Madeline Lia

For Ana Elvira, meu amor.

Contents

Series Foreword

Carlos Alberto Torres was a friend, colleague, and "first critic" of Paulo Freire. In this astute and rigorous book, Torres provides an extensive and insightful analysis of Freire's early writings and a discerning and contextualized account of Freire's intellectual and political journeys. This book explicates how and why Freire made seminal contributions to critical and constructivist pedagogy. It also describes Freire's significant role in the construction of the idea that education is the practice of freedom. Torres's descriptions of his personal relationship and interactions with Freire enrich this book and make it a unique contribution to the literature on Freire. The major concepts and themes in Freire's early writings—such as social justice education, democracy, and citizenship—amplify and extend the themes, concepts, and theories in the other publications in the Multicultural Education Series.

This book will help educators to acquire the knowledge and insights needed to implement critical pedagogy in their classrooms and schools and to deconstruct what Freire called "the banking concept of education," in which students are "receptacles" that are filled with information that teachers narrate and the students regurgitate. Freire believed that education should help students develop critical consciousness and that teachers and students should think critically in joint discourses and deliberations. Freire also believed that students must be active learners in order to be educated for freedom and liberation. This book also provides educators with innovative ideas about ways to conceptualize and implement interventions and teaching strategies that will enable their students to experience cultural freedom and recognition in their classrooms and schools. Reforming the structure of schools to make them more culturally empowering will greatly benefit students from the diverse racial, ethnic, cultural, linguistic, and religious groups that are rapidly increasing in the nation's schools.

American classrooms are experiencing the largest influx of immigrant students since the beginning of the 20th century. Almost 14 million new immigrants—documented and undocumented—settled in the United States in the years from 2000 to 2010. Less than 10% came from nations in Europe. Most came from Mexico, nations in Asia, and nations in Latin America, the Caribbean, and Central America (Comarota, 2011). A large but undetermined number of undocumented immigrants enter the United States each year. The U.S. Department of Homeland Security (2010) estimated that in January 2010, 10.8 million undocumented immigrants were living in the United States, which was a decrease from the estimated 11.8 million who resided in the United States in January 2007. In 2007, approximately 3.2 million children and young adults were among the 11.8

million undocumented immigrants in the United States, most of whom grew up in this country (Perez, 2011). The influence of an increasingly ethnically diverse population on U.S. schools, colleges, and universities is and will continue to be enormous.

Schools in the United States are more diverse today than they have been since the early 1900s when a multitude of immigrants entered the United States from Southern, Central, and Eastern Europe. In the 20-year period between 1989 and 2009, the percentage of students of color in U.S. public schools increased from 32% to 45% (Aud, Hussar, Kena, Bianco, Frohlich, Kemp, & Tahan, 2011). If current trends continue, students of color will equal or exceed the percentage of White students in U.S. public schools within one or two decades. In 2010–2011, students of color exceeded the number of White students in the District of Columbia and in 13 states (listed in descending order of the percentage of ethnic minority students therein): Hawaii, California, New Mexico, Texas, Nevada, Arizona, Florida, Maryland, Mississippi, Georgia, Louisiana, Delaware, and New York (Aud, Hussar, Johnson, Kena, Roth, Manning, Wang, & Zhang, 2012). In 2009, children of undocumented immigrants made up 6.8% of students in grades kindergarten through 12 (Perez, 2011).

Language and religious diversity is also increasing in the U.S. student population. The 2012 American Community Survey estimated that 21% of Americans aged 5 and above (61.9 million) spoke a language other than English at home (U.S. Census Bureau, 2012). Harvard professor Diana L. Eck (2001) calls the United States the "most religiously diverse nation on earth" (p. 4). Islam is now the fastest-growing religion in the United States, as well as in several European nations, such as France, the United Kingdom, and The Netherlands (Banks, 2009; Cesari, 2004). Most teachers now in the classroom and in teacher education programs are likely to have students from diverse ethnic, racial, linguistic, and religious groups in their classrooms during their careers. This is true for both inner-city and suburban teachers in the United States, as well as in many other Western nations such as Canada, Australia, and the United Kingdom (Banks, 2009).

The major purpose of the Multicultural Education Series is to provide preservice educators, practicing educators, graduate students, scholars, and policymakers with an interrelated and comprehensive set of books that summarizes and analyzes important research, theory, and practice related to the education of ethnic, racial, cultural, and linguistic groups in the United States and the education of mainstream students about diversity. The dimensions of multicultural education, developed by Banks (2004) and described in the *Handbook of Research on Multicultural Education* and in the *Encyclopedia of Diversity in Education* (Banks, 2012) provide the conceptual framework for the development of the publications in the Series. The dimensions are content integration, the knowledge construction process, prejudice reduction, an equity pedagogy, and an empowering institutional culture and social structure.

The books in the Series provide research, theoretical, and practical knowledge about the behaviors and learning characteristics of students of color, language minority students, low-income students, and other minoritized population groups, such as LGBT youth (Mayo, 2014). They also provide knowledge about ways to improve academic achievement (Au, 2011; Gay, 2010; Lee, 2007) and race relations in educational settings (Howard, 2006; Stephan & Vogt, 2004). Multicultural education is consequently as important for middle-class White suburban students as it is for students of color who live in the inner city. Multicultural education fosters the public good and the overarching goals of the commonwealth.

When the Arizona legislature voted to ban the Mexican American Studies program in the Tucson Unified School District in 2010, the critics of the program objected to the use of Freire's *Pedagogy of the Oppressed* in it. Most social justice educators strongly embrace Freire's publications and the concepts they explicate. However, individuals who are committed to maintaining the status quo in society and the schools often harshly criticize his ideas and publications. The clashing views on Freire's work are salient indications that the quest for social justice is an unfinished journey and that Freire's publications are still significant, contentious, timely, and powerful.

James A. Banks

REFERENCES

Au, K. H. (2011). *Literacy achievement and diversity: Keys to success for students, teachers, and schools.* New York, NY: Teachers College Press.

Aud, S., Hussar, W., Johnson, F., Kena, G., Roth, E., Manning, E., Wang, X., & Zhang, J. (2012). *The condition of education 2012* (NCES 2012-045). Washington, DC: U.S. Department of Education, National Center for Education Statistics. Retrieved from http://nces.ed.gov/pubsearch

Aud, S., Hussar, W., Kena, G., Bianco, K., Frohlich, L., Kemp, J., & Tahan, K. (2011). *The condition of education 2011* (NCES 2011-033). U.S. Department of Education, National Center for Education Statistics. Retrieved from http://nces.ed.gov/programs/coe/pdf/coe_1er.pdf

Banks, J. A. (2004). Multicultural education: Historical development, dimensions, and practice. In J. A. Banks & C. A. M. Banks (Eds.), *Handbook of research on multicultural education* (2nd ed., pp. 3–29). San Francisco, CA: Jossey-Bass.

Banks, J. A. (Ed.). (2009). *The Routledge international companion to multicultural education.* New York, NY, and London, UK: Routledge.

Banks, J. A. (2012). Multicultural education: Dimensions of. In J. A. Banks (Ed)., *Encyclopedia of diversity in education* (Vol. 3, pp. 1538–1547). Thousand Oaks, CA: Sage Publications.

Camarota, S. A. (2011, October). *A record-setting decade of immigration: 2000 to 2010*. Center for Immigration Studies. Retrieved from http://cis.org/2000-2010-record-setting-decade-of-immigration

Cesari, J. (2004). *When Islam and democracy meet: Muslims in Europe and the United States*. New York, NY: Pelgrave Macmillan.

Eck, D. L. (2001). *A new religious America: How a "Christian country" has become the world's most religiously diverse nation*. New York, NY: HarperSanFrancisco.

Gay, G. (2010). *Culturally responsive teaching: Theory, research, and practice* (2nd ed.). New York, NY: Teachers College Press.

Howard, G. R. (2006). *We can't teach what we don't know: White teachers, multiracial schools* (2nd ed.). New York, NY: Teachers College Press.

Lee, C. D. (2007). *Culture, literacy, and learning: Taking bloom in the midst of the whirlwind*. New York, NY: Teachers College Press.

Mayo, C. (2014). *LGBTQ youth and education: Policies and practices*. New York, NY: Teachers College Press.

Perez, W. (2011). *Americans by heart: Undocumented Latino students and the promise of higher education*. New York, NY: Teachers College Press.

Stephan, W. G., & Vogt, W. P. (Eds.). (2004). *Education programs for improving intergroup relations: Theory, research, and practice*. New York, NY: Teachers College Press.

U.S. Census Bureau. (2008, August 14). *Statistical abstract of the United States*. Retrieved from http://www.census.gov/prod/2006pubs/07statab/pop.pdf

U.S. Census Bureau. (2012). *Selected social characteristics in the United States: 2012. American community survey 1-year estimates*. Retrieved from http://factfinder2.census.gov/faces/tableservices/jsf/pages/productview.xhtml?pid=ACS_12_1YR_DP02&prodType=table

U.S. Department of Homeland Security. (2010, February). *Estimates of the unauthorized immigrant population residing in the United States: January 2010*. Retrieved from http://www.dhs.gov/files/statistics/immigration.shtm

Foreword: Paulo Freire's First Critic

I met Carlos when Paulo Freire visited my house in São Paulo in January 1987. Paulo introduced us with the following sentence: "This is my friend Carlos. You will like him. He is the first critic of my books."

Paulo Freire "didn't kick balls out of bounds," as the saying goes. Everything he said had weight, meaning, and intention. He often spoke to us of friendship and of criticism—two things that ordinarily do not appear to go together, except with Paulo. He wanted to let me know that I was not the first person to critique his writing. Carlos had gotten there before me. In 1979, I had translated and introduced Paulo's book *Education and Change*. In the preface, I had made some critical comments about Paulo's use of the phrase *pedagogy of dialogue* instead of *pedagogy of conflict*. It became clear to me that Paulo's take on dialogue stressed unity rather than dialectical opposition, which is another of its component parts. In 1985, Paulo and I edited a book together that discussed this theme: *Pedagogy: Dialogue and Conflict*.

In presenting Carlos to me by saying that he had been Paulo's first critic, Paulo Freire was thinking of the context of this debate that we had introduced some years before. He wanted to let me know that Carlos had critiqued his work as early as 1975 (*Lectura Crítica de Paulo Freire*) and 1976 (*Diálogo con Paulo Freire*) (see Torres Novoa, 1978a, 1978b, 1978c) *[Editors note: Torres Novoa is how the author of this book was credited in these works]*.

It was not Paulo's style to deviate from a theme. He valued words too much, both spoken and written. He wrote, always in longhand, with extreme care, and he rarely changed one word for another in his texts. He made sure that, even in the first draft, the words he chose were the most appropriate ones. Before his thoughts materialized as words on paper, they were subject to intense mental scrutiny. He would express thoughts and ideas that he carried in his mental archives in dialogue with many people before he stated his conclusions.

In this brief Foreword, I want to speak about friendship and criticism, in that order—the same order that Paulo Freire used.

We know we have friends when we miss them. That is what I am feeling as I write this because Carlos and I have traveled together on quite a long road. Ours is a friendship that has grown stronger over the years throughout the world.

Some years after we met, in 1991, we imagined the creation of the Paulo Freire Institute on a beautiful spring afternoon at the University of California in Los Angeles.

I was very moved when I read Carlos's dedication of his book *Freirian Studies,* published in Argentina in 1995: "For Moacir Gadotti, intimate friend." Who else would dare to speak of intimacy in friendship? Only those who are profoundly "intervolved." Shortly after Paulo introduced us, we discovered that we had been born on the same day and had the same kind of typewriter and tape recorder, with which we were writing the same book. We even began to dream the same dreams. Carlos is one of the founders of the Paulo Freire Institute, dedicated to reinventing Paulo's work throughout the world, connecting kindred spirits with his emancipation projects. Paulo considered Carlos a great scholar, the one who has best studied him and his work.

As often happens with friends who are authors, Carlos wrote prefaces to several books of mine, including for *Reading Paulo Freire: His Life and Work* (Torres, 1994d) and *Pedagogy of Praxis: A Dialectical Philosophy of Education* (Torres, 1996a). We have coedited various books: *Estado e educação popular na América Latina* (1992), *Educación popular: Crisis y perspectivas* (1993), *Educação popular: Utopia latino-americana* (1994), and *Paulo Freire: Uma bio-bibliografía* (2001).

Carlos was born and raised in Argentina and has lived in the United States for many years. He has a very strong sentimental relationship to Brazil, a country he knows very well. I am happy and proud to be one of his friends, who are legion and spread throughout the world, as is always apparent when we travel together, even in the company of Paulo Freire. After Paulo's first wife, Elza, died in 1986, I wrote to Carlos to ask why he thought Paulo had such a weakness for tangos. He sent me a long letter in response in which he claimed that the tango expressed the dreams of generations of immigrants—their anguish and also the social pressure on those at the bottom of the ladder. The tango is a form of social criticism that Paulo Freire understood and with which he surely agreed.

Carlos gradually discovered the enormous affect hidden by his enormous intellectual labor. There was a sleeping poet inside him who did not want to be awakened. The first poem he wrote was in memory of our common friend, Paulo Freire, shortly after Paulo passed, on May 2, 1997. Carlos writes:

> Paulo, friend and master, you are no longer among us. Your heart which loved so much stopped beating and you went. And you left us very much alone. With you went the voice of the poor, of the dispossessed, of the oppressed, of those with no voice. With you went the consciousness of Latin America and also a large part of our dignity. . . . And now you have gone, but you left us your pedagogy of the oppressed and of hope. You left us your limitless spirituality as well as your humanity. You left us your scruples, your old warrior's testament without concessions to capitalism, injustice, to the lack of democracy, to oppression, to indifference, and to the last of the demons that you tried to exorcize, neoliberalism. You left us with an invitation not to celebrate you or repeat you, but to reinvent you.

This work of continuing and reinventing Paulo Freire was taken up by Carlos together with the Paulo Freire Institutes, diffusing it throughout the world. As Paulo used to say, poetry is a way of remembering and healing at the same time. I think that Paulo Freire's death impacted the poetry of Carlos. He shows us that art—in his case, poetry—is the best way to express emotion.

As I mentioned, I very much like to dedicate books. Written in the heat of the moment, dedications reveal what is going on deep within the soul. I was in Buenos Aires when Carlos handed me *Reading Paulo Freire* (1994), my first book published in English. I asked him to write me something celebrating our encounter. Here's what he wrote: "To write is also to die a little, drop by drop, letter by letter, in the agony of expression and the pleasure of creation. This book, which I so enjoyed reading, has the passion of life, the eros of desire, and the anguish of tanatos (death). With great affection. Plaza de Mayo, June 8, 1994."

That is how friendship is. A lot of communication in a few words. Suddenly, we feel closer to our friends than to our blood relatives. Carlos appeared in my life and I did not need much time to be sure that I would learn much from him, suffer with him, share my intimate self with him, and that we would dream together. Our history had already been amalgamating for some time. All we needed to seal it was to meet.

To learn to value the presents life gives us is fundamental to our existence. What privileged beings have passed, are passing, or will pass through our history? In what ways will they change our trajectory? How will we give them value and reveal this value to other people, especially the young? Yes, I can say that I made friends. Some became brothers. Among them, Carlos Alberto Torres, brother and friend.

Carlos Alberto Torres was Paulo Freire's first critic. His first critique was written more than 30 years ago, in 1975, in Buenos Aires, during a shocking period in Argentine life. A year earlier, Carlos had received his bachelor's degree in sociology.

The link to Freire was made through utopian practice. Soon after finishing his sociological studies, Carlos moved to Patagonia, in the south of Argentina, with the dream of creating a rural freedom school in Freirean style. It was during this period of a little more than a year and a half that he read Paulo Freire and wrote his first critique, at a time when there was little freedom of expression because of the repression unleashed by the military junta that controlled the state beginning in March 1976. Carlos finished the book *Lectura crítica de Paulo Freire* (Torres Novoa, 1978b) in Patagonia, publishing it in Mexico in 1978 (Torres Novoa, 1978c) and in Brazil in 1980 (Torres, 1981a). Political conditions in his own country made it impossible to publish there.

I will not advance the analysis that Carlos made of Paulo Freire in his books. Like all analyses, it is contextualized and Carlos did not stop thinking, researching, and writing in 1975. He followed closely the trajectory Paulo traveled through the world until Carlos became Paulo's great Latin American biographer, demonstrated by the book that I organized with him, *Paulo Freire: Uma biobibliografia* (Gadotti, Araújo Freire, Ciseski, Torres, et al., 1996). Carlos coordinated a vast investigation about Paulo Freire's actions as São Paulo's municipal secretary of education (1989–1991), which was first published in English (Westview Press, 1998) and, later, in Portuguese, by the Paulo Freire Institute in collaboration with Cortez Publisher under the title *Educação e Democracia: A praxis de Paulo Freire em São Paulo,* with coauthors Maria del Pilar O'Cadiz and Pia Lindquist Wong. It is the most complete work, both theoretical and empirical, about the Paulo Freire educational administration in the city of São Paulo. O'Cadiz, Torres, and Wong (1998) provide the best analysis of our attempt to construct an interdisciplinary curriculum based on the Freirean principle of generative themes as the crucial point of the examination.

In the 1970s, Carlos Alberto Torres brought Freire and Piaget together with Marx. They were the reference points that enabled him to make a constructive critical reading of Freire. They also happened to be three authors who were banned in Argentina by the military junta. *Educación como práctica de la libertad* and *Pedagogía del oprimido* were translated into Spanish. Carlos participated in Catholic Church base community groups oriented by Liberation Theology. He could have been one of the *desaparecidos* of the Argentine military dictatorship if he had not listened to the great Uruguayan philosopher and Protestant pastor, Julio Barreiro, who advised him to leave the country. This he did at the end of 1976, with his first wife and three children. Julio Barreiro was a friend who saved his life.

Carlos Alberto Torres was studying Freire's work before the publication of *Lectura crítica de Paulo Freire* (Torres, 1981a), trying to understand it within the Hegelian tradition. As a result of these studies, he published an article in the review *Síntese* Edições Loyola (Rio de Janeiro) (Torres, 1976a) in April 1976, showing that the difference between the Hegelian dialectic and the Freirean dialectic is rooted in the concept of the subject, which is idealistic in Hegel and historical in Freire. Paulo Freire is inspired by the slave–master dialectic, but he performs a "historictomy" and extracts from it the consequences for a consciousness-raising education. Self-consciousness projecting itself toward liberation. Freire tries to integrate the consciousness of self (Hegel) within the consciousness of the other when posing the problems of the Latin American anthropological universe.

After *Lectura crítica de Paulo Freire* and *Diálogo con Paulo Freire,* Carlos published *Consciencia y historia: La praxis educativa de Paulo Freire* (Mexico City: Ediciones Gernika, (Torres Novoa, 1978a, 1978b, 1978c), dedicating part of the book to his selection of Freire's as-yet-unedited texts. So we are exposed for the first time to "*Tercer mundo y teología: Carta a un joven teólogo;*" (Torres Novoa, 1978a, pp. 99–105), "*Conscientizar para liberar: Nociones sobre la palabra conscientización*" (Torres Novoa, 1978b, pp. 107–120); "*Desmitificación de la conscientización*" (Torres Novoa, 1978b, pp. 121–137); and "*Investigación y metodología de la investigación del tema generador*" (Torres Novoa, 1978b, pp. 139–172).

The next year, he published *Paulo Freire: Educación y concientización* (Torres, 1980b), where he demonstrates the relationship between Freire's pedagogy and its importance in the social transformation of Latin America. In this book, Carlos analyzes the anthropological foundations of Freirean pedagogy and their relationship with the indispensable process of conscientization toward liberation.

In *Lectura crítica de Paulo Freire*, Carlos Torres showed, in the first half of the 1970s, the growing importance in Latin America of Freire's theoretical, philosophical, pedagogical, and political thinking, illustrated by some of Freire's still-unpublished texts. He contributes one of the first biographies of Freire along with texts of fellow devotees such as Rosiska Darcy de Oliveira, Pierre Dominicé, José Luis Fiori, Fausto Franco, and Martha B. Bardaro, most of whom were dealing with philosophical themes and the adult education methods of Paulo Freire.

I also highlight a work translated into various languages and first published in 1994 (Torres, 1994b): *Freirean Studies.* In this book, translated into Portuguese under the title *Pedagogia da Luta: Da pedagogia do oprimido à escola pública popular* (1997), Carlos Torres again takes up the Freirean theme of the alliance between theory and practice, between technical competence and political commitment. It is an evocative and provocative book in a neoliberal age. He discusses the essence of Paulo Freire's legacy: At a time of violence and wars, we need his dialogical, comprehending pedagogy.

Always dedicated to the study and investigation of the work of Paulo Freire, Carlos has published dozens of articles about Freire, discussing the philosophical currents that have enriched his philosophy, his educative praxis, and his literacy methodology, and maintaining constant personal dialogues with him. At the Paulo Freire Institute, I have a letter that Paulo wrote to Carlos on February 1, 1989, inviting him "as my personal adviser" to accompany him and evaluate his work as São Paulo's municipal secretary of education. Carlos accepted the challenge and, as a result of his constant tracking of the Freire administration, published the aforementioned book, with O' Cadiz and Wong, *Education and Democracy: Paulo Freire, Social Movements, and Educational Reform in São Paulo.*

Carlos Alberto Torres once confessed that, in the terrible days of 1970s Argentina, Paulo Freire was like "a soft breeze" during a torrid summer, an alternative way of thinking that went beyond the era's infinitely orthodox socialist visions. Paulo Freire's thought became increasingly important to Carlos Torres's *oeuvre.* Paulo Freire was like a giant's shoulder that enabled Carlos to look further into history. Today, Carlos Torres's work represents one of the most outstanding Latin American contributions to universal social and educational thinking. And it all began with a "critical reading." We honor authors not by reproducing them but, rather, by critically reinventing them. That is what Carlos Torres did in relation to Paulo Freire. And that is why this book is important—because it carried Carlos Torres well beyond its boundaries. It was a long road on which political and human dimensions crossed, where utopia and the quotidian embraced in what Paulo Freire would call "rationality wet with emotion."

Since that memorable encounter in 1987, I have been in permanent contact with my friend Carlos. Together with other colleagues such as José Eustáquio Romão, Francisco Gutiérrez, and Walter Garcia, and with Paulo Freire we created the Paulo Freire Institute in São Paulo. I have two thick files of correspondence with Carlos in the first years after the Institute's founding. We had the opportunity to travel to many places together, as voyagers of the Freirean utopia, attempting to create a contribution to that "other possible world." This has been a very gratifying and enriching experience for me.

Carlos Torres was, from 1995 until 2005, the director of the Latin American Center of the University of California, Los Angeles. He is a point of reference as a scholar and researcher of the great Latin American themes and dilemmas, having written more than 60 books and hundreds of articles. He also directs the Paulo Freire Institute in Los Angeles, whose agenda today includes an ongoing investigation about the planetary impact of globalization in education, being done in conjunction with Unifreire (Universitas Paulo Freire, Brazil). His most recent studies have to do with the relation between Habermas and Freire.

I consider my friend Carlos a great intellectual. He has an enormous capacity for work and an immense amorousness. I admire his ability to synthesize and analyze, to criticize and to love. Carlos rapidly intuits situations and facts that take me a while to understand. Moreover, it is just as easy for him to create a poem as it is to write a critical text or map out a pedagogical project. Carlos is a very creative human being. His intelligence is equaled only by his ability to love. That is why he is a happy person. His happiness is uncompromising. He is happy because he is always attempting to "be more." To be his friend is a great honor.

—Moacir Gadotti,
Founding director of the
Paulo Freire Institute,
and emeritus professor of education at
São Paulo University, São Paulo, Brazil,
May 2, 2013, a day when we remember,
with saudades, the death of Freire.

Preface: Consciousness and Revolution—The First Freire

> *I am not impartial or objective; not a fixed observer of facts and happenings. I never was able to be an adherent of the traits that falsely claim impartiality or objectivity. That did not prevent me, however, from holding always a rigorously ethical position. Whoever really observes, does so from a given point of view. And this does not necessarily mean that the observer position is erroneous. It's an error when one becomes dogmatic about one's point of view and ignores the fact that, even one is certain about his or her point of view, it does not mean that one's position is always ethically grounded.*
>
> *(Freire, 1998a, p. 22)*

The work of Paulo Freire is exemplary in linking theory and research, producing frameworks for educating global citizens, including building community and mutual respect, creating social responsibility, instilling an appreciation for diversity, and promoting multiple literacies and conflict-solving approaches within the framework of social justice education.

This book explores some of the meanings of Freire's early writings, or what I will call, for lack of a better term, the *first Freire*—that is to say, the work of Paulo Freire in the 1950s, 1960s, and early 1970s, well represented in his earlier books, articles and interviews, which greatly impacted the world of pedagogy and politics.

Freire wrote his magnum opus, *Pedagogy of the Oppressed*, between 1967 and 1968 while he was exiled in Santiago, Chile, and this book—translated into English and published in English, Spanish and Portuguese in 1970 and by now in more than 40 languages—was an instantaneous success.[1] He was 49 years old, and just in a few years after his first books, with the growing importance of *Pedagogy of the Oppressed* in the world of pedagogy, Paulo Freire became what the Swiss educator Pierre Furter (1985) called "a myth in his own lifetime" (p. 301). What this book attempts to do is trace the origins of Freire's thought and his struggle to give meaning and relevance to his analytical framework around *Pedagogy of the Oppressed*, tracing at the same time the roots and the origins of the thought of the first Freire.

I developed an intellectual biography that is at the same time a generational biography of the 1960s and 1970s struggle for freedom in Latin America. I document in some detail the insights of the impact of this "first Freire" in Argentina, my native country. This is not, however, an intellectual biographical analysis of Freire and the reception and impact of his work in the world, which I have accomplished elsewhere with other colleagues (Gadotti, Araújo Freire, Àntunes Ciseski, Torres, et al., 1996[2]). Nor is this book an attempt to reconstruct the key concepts of the Freirean narrative, which have been successfully accomplished in a Freirean dictionary available in English (Danilo Streak et al. editor, 2013). An additional and important recent book is Daniel Schugurensky's *Paulo Freire* (2011).

This period of Freire's life is important also for the connections between research, literacy, praxis, and policy. His early experiments on literacy training in the 1960s and 1970s were conducted within the movement of popular culture. Anthropologist and early participant in the Freirean experiments Carlos Rodrigues Brandão insightfully describes this period.

Freire's early work on education took place in Brazil within a model of socioeconomic development and social transition and within the ideological framework of the Instituto Superior de Estudos Brasileiros (ISEB) (Higher Institute of Brazilian Studies), which predicated a developmentalist approach as has been analyzed in a controversial book by Vanilda Paiva (1980). Paiva's book argues that Freire's perspective was eminently populist, and related to the developmentalist nationalism that prevailed in the João Goulart administration.[3] Paiva's analysis relies heavily on a limited understanding from a fairly orthodox Marxist perspective of the notion of Russian populism, and is coupled with a dissatisfaction with Freire's Christian philosophical and anthropological roots.[4]

The ISEB was a most important institute of higher education in Brazil before the coup d' état of 1964. The ISEB sought to develop a nationalist ideology that would contribute to the process of social modernization supported by the government of João Goulart. Along with other intellectuals—Helio Jaguaribe, Roland Corbisier, Alvaro Viera Pinto, Vicente Ferreira da Silva, Guerreiro Ramos, Durmeval Trigueiro Méndes—Paulo Freire was a participant in the intellectual atmosphere produced within the workshops of ISEB and these authors were extensively quoted in Freire's dissertation (1959, 2001). Among the most influential authors for the ISEB's theoreticians was Karl Mannheim. Also influential was the German anthropology of the 1930s—Spengler, Alfred Weber, and Max Scheller—the philosophy of Existence—M. Ortega y Gasset, J. P. Sartre, M. Heidegger and K. Jaspers—and historical-sociological sources—Max Weber, Alfredo Pareto, and Arnold Toynbee (C. N. de Toledo, 1977; Paiva, 1980).

Yet, it is in Chile in the late 1970s where Freire became more conversant with contemporary social theory (particularly Marxism and the work of Gramsci, because the first Spanish translations of the *Prison Notebooks* were already available in Spanish since the early 1960s) (Aricó, 1988). It was also there that he worked politically and professionally, conducting full-time educational research. *Pedagogy of the Oppressed* represents Freire's learning and his goal to produce a critique of the banking education that he identified as the hardcore educational and cultural project of authoritarian and also populist regimes. *Pedagogy of the Oppressed* represents his attempt to create a model of conscientization as cultural action for freedom (Freire, 1970, 1972b) that will help social transformation.

One of Freire's central concepts was to study the mutual contributions of democracy to education in the context of the turbulent 1960s and 1970s period of Latin American history. Yet the concept of democracy has different meanings to different people. It has become a "sliding" signifier. Therefore, it is important to ask what is to become of democratic education. I focus on the connections between democracy, citizenship and education highlighting the importance of civic virtues (Torres, 1998a, 1998b).

I am talking about key virtues such as hope, honesty, courage, friendship, self-respect, trust, decency, self-esteem—virtues that we need as individual citizens in a flourishing democracy if we hope to prosper in a peaceful environment, both at the local and global level. Many of us, following the inspiration of Freire, have drawn from classical philosophical work to explore how these civic virtues can contribute to citizenship socialization in multicultural, multilingual, and conflict-prone societies.

As James Banks (2003, 2004) has argued, effective citizenship education helps students acquire the knowledge, skills, and values they need to function effectively within their cultural communities, nation-states, regions, and the global community. It also helps students acquire the cosmopolitan perspectives and values needed to attain equality and social justice for people around the world. This was exactly Freire's perspective in linking social justice education with democracy and citizenship.

Yet political machinations in the United States, such as those responsible for Arizona's toughest law on undocumented immigration, have linked ethnic studies schools and universities to Freire's *Pedagogy of the Oppressed*. Some Republican activists are objecting to the incorporation of *Pedagogy of the Oppressed* in the curriculum and are ultimately challenging the existence of ethnic studies altogether. This resembles to me what happened in the middle of the Argentinean dictatorship. *Pedagogy of the Oppressed* was one of the books prohibited in the schools and higher education institutions, and the teachers who used these texts ran great risks of being kidnapped, tortured, disappeared, and killed.

Although one may not expect the tragedy of the Argentinean dictatorship to be repeated in the context of the U.S. democracy, the parallels between the narratives are definitely frightening, underscoring the challenges conservatives, neoconservatives, and neoliberals are making to all forms of scholarship associated with social justice education (Lewin, 2010).

Social justice education is a social construct that a large cadre of critical and radical educators and communities as well as social movements have developed to question the way the capitalist state has used education and schooling more as a form of social control and political legitimation than as a model of political, social, and cognitive empowerment. Moreover, as in many other places in the United States, we are using this social construct in our teacher-training program at UCLA, and it is beginning to make a most serious impact on the way we address cognitive and moral education in Los Angeles and elsewhere.

Writing a book like this one is not only an intellectual but also an existential exercise. It was José Luis Borges (1999) who said countless times that we only write one book—that is, we write our own biography in the context of talking about the biographies of others: "A man sets himself the task of portraying the world. Over the years he fills a given surface with images of provinces and kingdoms, mountains, bays, ships, islands, fish, rooms, instruments, heavenly bodies, horses and people. Shortly before he dies he discovers that this patient labyrinth of lines is a drawing of his own face" (p. 143).

The reader may, however, ask this simple question: What was the overall project of the first Freire? I address this question in this book, but particularly in Chapter 10. Yet at the outset I will argue that it was a most ambitious project, well beyond the literacy training that made Freire famous. To define in one sentence what Freire wanted to do, one might say he wanted to exploit the possibilities of education to reconstruct the public sphere in Brazil and elsewhere. It was his concern with "the public" and the contributions of culture and education to make the public possible in colonial, authoritarian, and burgeois societies the leitmotif that articulates the overall project: the Paulo Freire System.

I hope that these pages, discussing the insights provided by the "first Freire," will contribute to the dialogue about social justice education and provide a better understanding of the connections between democracy and education. But before I end this Preface, I would like to add a very personal note to the understanding of Freire's scholarship, life, and work.

MY LAST CONVERSATION WITH PAULO FREIRE[5]

I was traveling, at the end of April 1997, to Madrid from Los Angeles, where I have lived for 2 decades, to participate in a conference organized by the Universidad Complutense and the University of California.

On the way to the airport, I had a sudden impulse to call Paulo Freire. I cannot recall why I felt such urgency, but we had been planning to write a book together about new educational challenges at the threshold of the 21st century. The book had a tentative title: *Education and the Possible Dream*.

We wanted to update the discussion about some of Paulo's great theses and think about ways to implement them in classrooms of the advanced capitalist world. We wanted, to use a phrase dear to Paulo, to "reinvent and not to repeat Paulo Freire."

I called him from my cellphone on the way to the airport. Paulo answered the phone in his house in São Paulo and, after the customary greetings, I told him that I was flying to Europe and wanted to know when and where we could meet to work on the book. He told me that he would be giving a course at Harvard that fall and perhaps it would be easier for me to travel to Cambridge than to São Paulo to work with him. Cambridge would provide us a more tranquil workplace than São Paulo, without the enormous demands that the academic, political, and educational life of Brazil imposed on Paulo's agenda.

I asked him if he had been thinking about the overriding themes we would be addressing. His response was not only direct but seemed almost laconic: "Carlos, we have to criticize neoliberalism. It's the new demon of the world today." At that moment, silence fell at the other end of the telephone, which let me know that we had lost our connection. I was arriving at the Los Angeles International Airport, and the power of the communications systems in the area might have interfered with our call.

I hesitated to call him back. My boarding time was near and, of course, a cellphone call is always costly. I decided to call him on my way back from Paris, where I would work for a few days after the meeting in Madrid. I started to think about an academic meeting at the Catholic University of São Paulo with retired cardinal Paulo Evaristo Arns, who had been one of the foremost Brazilian representatives of the Theology of Liberation, along with Paulo Freire. The title of this meeting was "The Diabolic and the Symbolic," and it seemed to me a good one because, theologically speaking, the symbolic is the antithesis of the diabolic. The interrupted conversation with Freire stayed with me as I pondered the theme.

I never imagined that, while I was in Paris, I would learn of Freire's sudden death, on May 2, 1997, of a heart attack soon after an operation on his coronary arteries. Paulo died alone while he was recovering from the operation in the intensive care unit of a São Paulo hospital.

One of the great masters of Latin America—with his prophetic gestures, white beard, and eyes that reflected the dedicated authenticity of his words, who captivated readers and listeners alike with his logic and his poetry—was dead. An enormous piece of the history of our cherished and conflictive continent died with him. Freire was one of the 20th century's most important political philosophers of education.

I want to end this Preface by paying homage to Paulo Freire, the critical conscience of Latin America, with a poem I wrote on the first anniversary of his death.[6]

A Little More Than a Year Ago (for Paulo Freire)

A little more than a year ago, your magic was still strolling these streets.
Like a troubadour, you were singing songs of freedom.
The faces of children, youths, adults and old people were still practicing

All possible vowel combinations: be bi ba, bo, bu.
Curiosity was, once again, the basis of epistemology
And your generosity was challenging power.

A little more than a year ago, hope and wisdom still bore your name,
And utopia too,
Amid rancorous outcries, rows and popular knowledge
Wet with oppression but tempered
By amorous encounters of unknown intensities.

A little more than a year ago, your words were still shaping hymns,
Destroying palaces, crumbling temples,
Inviting us to an immoderate revolution,
And an impatiently patient struggle.

A little more than a year ago, Latin America was still full
of contagious optimism,
Borders, barbed wire and bayonets were being erased
Like the indistinguishable characters of an extinct past while
Circuses, carnivals and processions were gathering, in their splendor,
The legacy of tradition and rupture.
Men and women were looking to politics
For truth, justice and liberty.

A little more than a year ago, we still had you here, among us.
Today, in your infinitely suffocating death, you still live within us.

A little more than a year ago you ascended in a sonorous vocal choir
of words repeated
But reinvented as well,
Of traditional but not antiquated teaching,
Of prophecies where love is the fair measure of all things,
And where ethics and smiles are the banners and shields of
an ancestral battle,
Like your lessons, teacher, friend who continues among us.

Acknowledgments

This book has been in the making for many years, and it will not have reached its publication without the contributions of many friends, family and colleagues. I would like to thank James Banks for asking me to prepare a book for his series in Teachers College Press. Brian Ellerbeck, senior editor in Teachers College Press, has been invaluable source of advice for many years. Tara Tomczyk did a great job of copyediting the manuscript, and Aureliano Vazquez Jr. did a masterful job in the design and production of the book.

I have written several parts of this book in Spanish which required expert translation by some of my former students. My thanks to Dr. Peter Lownds, Dr. Jaana Flávia Fernandes Nogueira and Dr. Meredith Wegener. Joaquin Noguera helped securing bibliographical information.

My wife Ana Elvira Steinbach Silva Raposo Torres not only provided love and emotional support but also technical assistance with Portuguese translations and intercultural understanding. She has been the first critic of the ideas of this book.

Among my colleagues and friends at UCLA a special note of thanks to John Rogers with him I understood the philosophy of John Dewey better; Pat Mcdonough whose knowlege of Pierre Bourdieu and her powerful intelligence has illuminated my own work over the years; Robert Rhoads, with whom we explored how to apply Critical Theory to the study of higher education; Concepción Valadez, who was the first Freirean whom I encountered when I arrived to UCLA and has been an example in the struggle for social justice education; and Megan Franke whose research on teachers training and mathematics education is embedded in the radicalism of social justice education. Graduate School of Education and Information Studies Distinguished Professor and Dean Marcelo Suárez-Orozco and Chair of Education Louis Gomez provide the intellectual leadership that is needed in a school deeply committed to theory, research and practice in social justice education.

My students at UCLA have been a most important source of inspiration, criticism and learning. The founding members of the UCLA Paulo Freire Institute and research associates, particularly Dr. Peter Lownds, Dr. Chitra Golestani, Dr. Aly Juma, Dr. Liliana Olmos, Dr. Chen-Wei Chang, Dr. Peter Hoffman-Kipp (in memoriam), Dr. Lucas Arribas Layton, Dr. Sung-Sang Yoo, Dr. Peter Weldon, Dr. Julie Thompston, Dr. Jaana Flávia Fernandes Nogueira, Dr. Meredith Wegener, Dr. Greg Misiaszek, Dr. Lauren I. Misiaszek, Dr. Octavio Pescador, Dr. Rich Van

Heertum, Dr. Hyung-Ryeol Kim, Dr. Armando Alcantara, Dr. Jevdet Rexhepi, Ms. Inês Sachetti, Ms. Fang Tzu Hsu, and Mr. Jason Dorio provided insightful critiques and suggestions to my ideas since the creation of the institute in 2002.

A special thanks to the friends and colleagues of the Instituto Paulo Freire in São Paulo, Brazil, particularly his director and dear friend Moacir Gadotti. Access to Paulo Freire's library holdings over the many years of research has proven to be quintessential in bringing this book to fruition. Needless to say that the multiple meetings in which I have participated in Brazil for more than three and a half decades, and particularly conversations with the Brazilian founding directors of the IPF, Moacir Gadotti, José Eustaquio Romão, and Walter Garcia have enlightened my understanding of liberation education beyond any measure or expectations. Dialogues with distinguished Freirean scholars Daniel Schugurensky and Peter Mayo have been influential for the development of my analysis since our early work at the University of Alberta, Edmonton, Canada in the eighties.

Finally, I would like to recognize learning and knowledge production in the context of social movements. My participation in the social movement of the Paulo Freire Institutes in the world, the dialogues and debates with *compañeros* and *compañeras* have helped my understanting of Freire's work and the importance of pedagogies of liberation, truly reinforcing my commitment to social justice education. My heartfelt thanks to the colleagues of the Paulo Freire Institutes, Ângela Antunes, Paulo Roberto Padilha, Alexandre Munck, Francisca Pini, and Sonia Couto (Brazil), Pep Aparicio, José Beltrán and Francesc J. Hernàndez i Dubon (Spain), Luiza Cortesão and Antonio Teodoro (Portugal), Silvia Manfredi and Piergiorgio Reggio (Italy), Penny Jane Burke (United Kingdom), Liliana Olmos, María Inés Lucca, and Cristina Catano (Argentina), Ivor Baajtes (South Africa), Afzal Hossain (India), Chen-Wei Chang (Taiwan) and Sung-Sang Yoo and Hyung-Ryeol Kim (South Korea).

ONE

Freire's Education for Development: Past and Present

Moacir Gadotti and Carlos Alberto Torres

Brazilian philosopher and pedagogue Paulo Reglus Neves Freire (1921–1997) came of age in the turbulent years of transition from authoritarian conservative government to authoritarian populist government in Latin America. This historical transition was interrupted in the 1970s by a series of dictatorships, resulting in a perverse cycle of authoritarianism and a lack of democracy in the region (Torres, 2004). Freire was born into a middle-class family in Recife, the capital of the Brazilian state of Pernambuco, on September 19, 1921. The experiences of his family during the Great Depression, which started in 1929, set the tone for his later concern for the poor and influenced his perspective on education. Freire enrolled at law school at the University of Recife in 1943, where he also studied philosophy and the psychology of language. Rather than beginning a career in the law, however, he became a secondary school teacher of Portuguese. In 1944, he married Elza Maia Costa de Oliveira, a fellow teacher, with whom he had five children.

In 1946, Freire became director of the Department of Education and Culture in the Brazilian state of Pernambuco. It was in this role, working primarily with the illiterate poor, that Freire began to develop a nonorthodox philosophy of education and literacy. His original work in the 1950s and early 1960s was deeply connected to the question of education for socioeconomic and cultural development, and particularly how to link education and citizenship building.[1] Here, his work on literacy training was among his foremost contributions to educational science (Brown, 1978). In 1961, he became the first director of the Department of Cultural Extension of Recife University, and in the following years, he was able to put his theories to the test: Three hundred sugarcane workers were taught by Freire, his team from the university and university students to read and write in just 40 hours, using "circles of culture," in which the students were encouraged to learn through dialogue with the educators. The success of this experiment led to the creation of thousands of circles of culture across the country, a project that was supported by President Goulart. In 1964, however, a military coup overthrew the Goulart government, and Freire was arrested.

Freire was accused of being a communist and a subversive; he was jailed for 70 days and then offered exile instead of continued imprisonment. He did not return to Brazil until 1980. Thus exiled from his homeland, he moved first to Bolivia and then a few months later to Chile, where he worked for the United Nations; he later connected with the left wing of the Christian Democratic Party. In this period he earned his living by working as a researcher studying the process of agrarian reform in Chile, which led to his criticism of the notion of extensionism (see de Lima, 1981; Freire, 1979, 1991; Williamson, 1988). It was also in Chile that he wrote *Education, the Practice of Freedom* (first published 1967) and his most influential work, *Pedagogy of the Oppressed* (published in English, Portuguese and Spanish in 1970).

In his earlier work in Brazil, Freire had been exposed to the theoretical paradigm of popular education. The new theories of development and political theory that he encountered while in Chile completed his formative period (Gadotti & Torres, 1992; Torres, 1990), the foundation that would make him one of the most prominent popular educators in the history of the Latin American region. This formative experience extended to his early exposure to the nascent philosophy of Liberation in academic circles, and Theology of Liberation in Church circles.[2] In fact, it is this radical combination of theories that made his message so appealing at the time, and that made *Pedagogy of the Oppressed* his emblematic book, a classic that has now been translated into more than 40 languages, with sales of nearly a million copies in English alone. Freire's work moved in different directions during his exile; his contributions—as an advisor—to education for social and economic development in the emerging Portuguese-speaking African countries after their wars of liberation (such as Guinea-Bissau and São Tomé e Principe) were particularly intriguing (Harasim, 1983; Freire, 1977, 1980, 1981a, 1981b).

Freire was able to return to Brazil in 1980. On more than one occasion, when asked about his plans upon returning to Brazil, Freire responded that he had come back to relearn Brazil, and especially to listen to the Gramsci, which was being popularized in the favelas, shantytowns, and countryside. He joined as one of its founder the Partido dos Trabalhadores (PT) (Workers' Party) in the city of São Paulo, and acted as a supervisor for its adult literacy project from 1980 to 1986. After the PT won the municipal elections in 1988, Freire was appointed secretary of education for São Paulo. His wife, Elza, had died in 1986; Freire married educator and author Ana Maria Araújo Freire on August 19, 1988.

Freire never abandoned his concern for the connections between education and socioeconomic development. It was this, together with his concern for democracy and citizenship—although he did not renounce his class perspective—that articulated his work throughout his life. Yet he addressed the question of development not from the perspective of the economist, but rather from the perspective of the political and pedagogical scholar-activist trying to reinvigorate the question of ethics in education and its implication for citizenship building. Freire was first and foremost a Latin American *pensador*—a thinker, an intellectual (Freire & Torres, 1993; Torres, 1994c).

EDUCATION FOR DEVELOPMENT: THE FIRST FREIRE

Freire's first book, which made him a celebrity, particularly among the Christian educators in Latin America, and which was so influential in the writing of the Medellin documents of 1968[2] is entitled *Education, the Practice of Freedom* (Freire, 1967/1976b). It was connected with his doctoral thesis, defended at the University of Recife in 1959[3] (Freire, 2001). Yet it was his second book, *Pedagogy of the Oppressed*, that catapulted him to international fame.

The underlying thesis of his historical analysis is that the roots of Brazilian democratic inexperience are found in the type of colonization that Brazil suffered. It was this "predatory colonization," involving the use of slave labor and the excessive utilization of power on the part of the dominant elite, that engendered the "muteness" of the Brazilian people, their apparent incapacity to speak for themselves. Therefore, "the democratic inexperience [is] rooted in truly cultural complexes" (Freire, 1967/1976b, p. 60). Moreover, Freire (1967/1976b) presents the exploitation of slave labor as a fundamental characteristic of the kind of societal analysis he undertakes: "[slave labor] from which arose a series of obstacles and, simultaneously, the impossibility of forming a democratic mentality, a permeable consciousness, experiences of participation and of self-governance" (p. 67). This exploitation made the creation of "community life" impossible; the demographic dispersion that characterized the vast feudal landholdings of the great estates, together with the growth of urban nuclei and the unlawful use of power, gave rise to a marked individualism. The conclusion of Freire's analysis is that:

> Without a doubt, it is the exacerbation of power that has characterized our formation from the beginning. It was the strength of this power around which an almost masochistic lust to be all-powerful continued to grow. Submission was part and parcel of this exacerbated sense of power. From this submission was born a consequent adjustment; accommodation rather than integration. Accommodation requires a minimal dose of critique. Integration, on the contrary, demands a maximum of reason and consciousness. (Freire, 1967/1976b, p. 69)

Thus, the Brazilian people found themselves castrated from the start when it came to expressing themselves. Marginalized and devoid of civil rights, the common man and woman found themselves irredeemably alienated from any experience of self-government or dialogue: They were made constantly submissive, "protected," and the only way to react was by a clamorous outcry—the voice of those who are mute when they are faced with the growth of communities and never have the option of finding an authentic voice. This voice must be won by the people with the growth of new historical conditions that will provide the first attempts at dialogue (Freire, 1967/1976b).

Freire does not explain how the crisis of 1930 (the Depression) and the fall of the international stock market as well as the consequent transfer of monetary focus from livestock to industrial interests stimulated the rise of an urban bourgeoisie. There was a dominant proposal for a free market economy as a way to generate a workforce that would also act as internal market consumers, thereby beginning the "Europeanization" of Brazil. This process was made possible by the abolition of slavery in 1888. Democracy appeared, then, to be the kind of politics that would bring with it a great change in consciousness, but:

> Since it did not require the "decomposition" of the Brazilian society, allowing the established powers to participate, it had exactly the opposite result: the alienation of the people through "public welfare". In a general way, it can be said that, with few exceptions, the common people were either marginalized from all these processes or participated in them as a clamorous mob without a discernible voice. (Freire, 1967/1976b, p. 77)

To the establishment, this was absurd. How could a methodology, particularly one applied to poor people, assume that the students will grasp an understanding of the world's challenges while simultaneously achieving consciousness raising, self-reflection and practice in a single pedagogical and political process.

THE SECOND FREIRE: TO AFRICA AND THE REST OF THE WORLD

After being forced to leave Brazil in 1964, Freire went to Bolivia and then Chile, where he wrote *Education, the Practice of Freedom* and *Pedagogy of the Oppressed*. His influence in Latin America was illustrated by his teaching in the CIDOC—Center for Intercultural Documentation, organized by Ivan Illich in Cuernavaca, México. In 1969, Freire taught for a semester at Harvard University, which had offered him a visiting professorship, but the second phase of his exile began with his move to Geneva in 1970 to work as a special education advisor to the World Council of Churches. The following year, a group of Brazilian exiles created the IDAC (Instituto de Ação Cultural) (Institute for Cultural Action), and Freire, appointed president of the executive committee of IDAC, continued his work on conscientization (Freire, Ceccon, Darcy de Oliveira, Darcy de Oliveira, 1989).

In 1975, the minister of education of the republic of Guinea-Bissau, Mário Cabral, invited Freire and the IDAC team to collaborate on the reconstruction of the country after the end of colonial control. This raised the question of what language to use to teach literacy—after all, Portuguese was the language of the colonizer—and how to organize a process of literacy training in a country that had been devastated by a war of liberation. From this experience, and from Freire's immersion in postcolonial projects in Africa, arose a number of wonderful and important books that demonstrated the radicalization of Freire's thought, but also its applicability in contexts beyond Latin America (Freire, 1980, 1981a, 1981b; Scocuglia, 2010).

EDUCATION FOR SOCIAL CHANGE: FREIRE RETURNS TO BRAZIL

Cultural invasion is a central theme in Freire's work. As he states in his book *Extensão ou comunicação?* (1979): "now that we recognized that all the agrarian engineers, the so-called extensionists, created a cultural invasion, it is impossible to ignore the ostensible cultural invasion of the term *extensão*" (p. 43). He concludes on the same page that the extensionist agronomist "transforms all his specialized knowledge, all his techniques into something static, materialized, and mechanically extends them to the persons, indisputably invading their culture, their view of the world" (p. 43). Freire understands cultural invasion as the penetration, in any society, of a foreign culture that imposes its ways of seeing the world: "[Cultural invasion] is the penetration of the invaders in the context of the invaded, without respecting their potentiality to be, imposing their view of the world, breaking their creativity, and inhibiting the expansion of the invaded people" (Freire, 1983, p. 178, our translation). In criticizing extensionism, Freire was very concerned with the role of education in socioeconomic development.

Freire is clear about the basic objectives that an "education for development" should attempt to achieve. It should "provide students with the necessary instruments to resist the deracinating powers of an industrial civilization" (Freire, 1968, p. 82). Here, Freire pauses in his reflection, apparently to examine the meaning of work, of the social organization of work and the risks that exist in an industrial society. Education for development should be an "education that makes it possible for people to fearlessly discuss their problems" (Freire, 1968, p. 84), "that is situated in dialogue" (p. 85), and that "makes it susceptible to a kind of rebelliousness" (p. 85). Freire seems to focus on how individuals struggle to affirm their ethics in the face of all these risks. The source of his reflection seems to be the biblical texts, and their emphasis on the importance of freedom and liberation from all forms of oppression and evil. Hence the importance of rebellion in the life of people.

Freire seems to focus on how individuals struggle to affirm their ethics in the face of all these risks. The source of his reflection seems to be the biblical texts, and their emphasis on the importance of freedom and liberation from all forms of oppression and evil. Hence the importance of rebellion in the life of people. This popular rebelliousness, usually very naïve and emotional, should be transformed, for the lack of a better formulation, into models of "social engineering" for social transformation. Freire insists that his "education for development" "is identified with scientific methods and processes" (p. 85). Furthermore, education should orient people in their lives. It should "help people reflect about their ontological vocation as subjects" (Freire, 1973e, p. 52).

Freedom, democracy, and critical participation are key ideas that initially constituted the core of Freire's pedagogy. He rejects the teacher–student dichotomy, suggesting that a deep reciprocity should be inserted into our notions of teacher–student and student–teacher relationships. He rejects the school in favor of the more flexible arrangement of the "circle of culture." He rejects the role of teacher as "factotum" in favor of an animator or coordinator of the pedagogical experiences inside the circle. He rejects prescribed curricula and proposes instead a program created in and with the people. The essential dimension of all this pedagogical process is dialogue. Freire concludes that "critique is the fundamental note of the democratic mentality" (Freire, 1973e, p. 52).

THE LAST FREIRE: ECO-POLITICAL PEDAGOGY AND THE CITIZEN SCHOOL

In an interview with the *Revista Veja* of São Paulo (April 19, 2000), Thomas Skidmore, a noted Brazilianist, argued that Brazil was wrong to try to copy models from the outside, and that it should seek its own path. He cited Paulo Freire for creating a pedagogy that provides an appropriate solution to Brazilian problems:

> Brazil seems to believe that there are no other possibilities to discover new roads. And this is the country that produced the Paulo Freire Method of Literacy Training that has been studied and become famous all over the world. This method was left aside, and instead of using the popular culture to improve education, as proposed by Paulo Freire, Brazil reaches out to foreign formulas that do not always help.[4] (*Revista Veja*, 2000)

A year earlier, the famous American futurologist Alvin Toffler was invited by the Ministry of Education of Brazil to speak about education and new methodologies of information. To the surprise of the Brazilian hosts, he presented the Paulo Freire method, unequivocally stating that it was the most appropriate method to teach informatics. Alvin Toffler said that 50 years earlier Paulo Freire had created a methodology that is still used by the youth today; they spontaneously create "circles of culture" to teach one another and to learn how to use computers. In just a few days they transform themselves into "professors" of informatics, which demonstrates the efficacy of Freire's global method.

These two curious and recent experiences in Brazil give us an indication of the currency and recognition of Freire's in the twenty-first century, as it is discussed in Chapter 11. In the last years of his life, Freire dealt with debates and themes that he had not addressed in earlier books, including ecology and the environment (Gadotti, personal communication). On April 17, 1997, just a few days before he passed away,[5] Freire was talking about eco-pedagogy. In an interview at the Paulo Freire Institute, he talked of his love for the Earth, the animals, the plants: "I want to be remembered as somebody who loved the men, the women, the plants, the animals, the Earth," he said on that occasion. In one of his last books, *A Sombra desta Mangueira* (literally, *In the Shadow of this Mango Tree*, but published in English as *Pedagogy of the Heart* [1998a]), he speaks of the pleasure of breathing pure air, the joy of entering a river that has no pollution, of stepping on grass or the sand on the beach. He criticized the capitalist logic that gives no value to those free pleasures, and substitutes for them the pleasure of profit. Capitalism substitutes the free happiness of satisfying human needs for happiness that can be bought or sold, but above all, for satisfying the needs of capitalism—not human needs, but needs imposed upon human beings by the search for profits. Freire did not separate human needs from the needs of the planet. When he died, Freire was writing a book about ecology. The book was published posthumously by his widow, Ana Maria Freire, in 2000. In it, Freire argues:

> It is urgent that we assume the duty to fight for the ethical principles of respect of life of human beings, life of other animals, the life of birds, the life of the rivers and the life of the forest. I do not believe in the love [*amorosidade*] between human beings if we cannot become capable of loving the world. Ecology is gaining a fundamental importance at the end of the century. Ecology has to be present in every radical practice, be that critical or libertarian. . . . In this sense it seems a regrettable contradiction to make a radical progressive discourse, a revolutionary discourse and to have a practice that negates life—the practices of polluting the oceans, the waters, the fields, the devastation of the forest, and those which threaten the animals and birds. (pp. 66–67)

Another concept highlighted in the last years of his life was the *escola cidadã* (citizen schools). The concept of *escola cidadã* is very strongly linked to the movement of popular and communitarian education, which in the 1980s resulted in the movement for a public popular school, as a model to be implemented in various regions of Brazil. The concept of popular education is the most important contribution of Latin American educationists to universal pedagogical thought. The *escola cidadã* is a new type of school that does not simply impart knowledge, but creates and administers knowledge. It is an eco-political and pedagogical project; that is to say, it is an eminently ethical project, an innovative school, constructing meaning while it is intimately connected to the world. In an interview Freire gave to the TV Educadora do Rio de Janeiro on March 19, 1997 (Paulo Freire archives [Sao Paulo]), he defined *escola cidadã* as a social and political-pedagogical space which becomes a center of rights and responsibilities, and therefore citizenship building takes place. A public and popular school system, one in which people from all walks of life, but particularly those who are discriminated and marginalized, find ways to express themselves, to learn about themselves, the world and the cultural domains. Freire's conscientization is a way to work towards new models of social transformation of both social relationships and productive forces in a given society.

Escola cidadã is a center of rights and responsibilities, where citizenship is created. It cannot be an *escola cidadã* in itself and for itself: It is an *escola cidadã* insofar as it facilitates the building of citizenship among those citizens who use its space. An *escola cidadã* is a school that is consistent with freedom, and with its formative and liberating discourse. It is a school that is struggling for itself, and for all those who educate and are educated, so that they can be themselves. And because people cannot be themselves alone, an *escola cidadã* is a school of the community, of camaraderie (*companheirismo*). It is a school where knowledge and freedom are produced in common, all together. It is a school that can never permit a kind of cavalier licentiousness; similarly, it can never allow authoritarianism. It is a school that lives the tense experience of democracy.

The curriculum of the *escola cidadã* is considered the space of sociocultural relationships. It is not only the space of knowledge but also the space of debates about human and social relationships; the space of power, of work, and of caring; the space of respectfully living together (*convivência*). This is the link with ethics, with the notion of sustainability[6] (Gadotti, 2008a),with the question of violence. The curriculum and the eco-political and pedagogical project of the school are inseparable realities. The curriculum reveals the political-pedagogical trajectory of the school, its successes and failures. If the school will be ready to facilitate the achievement of the possible dreams and desires of all their members—teachers, employees, students, and community—then the curriculum has to be intimately related to the life project of each one of them. That is why the curriculum needs to be constantly evaluated and reevaluated. The project of an *escola cidadã* is considered, in terms of process and context, an institutional and individual life project.

Education for citizenship is at the same time an education for a sustainable society. *Escola cidadã* and eco-pedagogy sustain the principle that all of us, since we are children, have the fundamental right to dream, to make possible our projects, to invent. As Marx and Freire have argued, we all have the right to decide our own destiny, including the children defended by the distinguished Jewish-Polish educator Janusz Korczak who refused to be set free and stayed with his orphan students when the institution was sent from the Ghetto to Treblinka extermination camp, accepting to die in the Nazi gas chambers jointly with his students. Yet, the issue is not to reduce the school and pedagogy today to *tabula rasa* and build on its ashes the ideal *escola cidadã* and eco-pedagogy. We are not talking about an alternative school and pedagogy in the sense that these would have to be constructed separately from today's existing schools and pedagogy. Rather, this new pedagogical and political model is starting from the school we have and the pedagogy we actually practice, in order to dialectically build other possibilities without destroying what already exists. The future is not the annihilation of the past, but its improvement.

On the basis of the intuition[7] of Paulo Freire, the Paulo Freire Institutes continue to reinvent his legacy. Our current problems, including ecological problems, are provoked by our way of living; in many respects, school bears a great deal of responsibility for how we live. Our understanding of the world we live in and our way of life depends to a considerable extent on what the school does or does not teach, the values that are or are not transmitted, and the curriculum or the books that are taught or not taught.

We thus need to reorient education, starting with the principle of sustainability—that is, to redress education in its totality. This implies a revision of curricula and programs, educational systems, the role of the school and the teachers, and school organization. The notion of eco-pedagogy as developed by the Paulo Freire Institutes implies a reorientation of curricula to make us understand that we need to consider the planet a unique community and the Earth our mother, an organism that is alive and in evolution. We also need to build a new consciousness of what is sustainable, appropriate, and makes sense for our existence. We need to be gentle with the Earth as our home, our unique address, and to develop a sense of socio-cosmic justice, seeing the Earth as a victim of poverty and oppression. We need to promote life, communicate among ourselves, share, problematize, create new relationships, and live with enthusiasm. We need to "walk" daily in achieving these goals. And finally, we need to develop an intuitive rationality, and an affectionate, not instrumental, form of communication. As Frei Beto, the spiritual advisor of President Luiz Inácio Lula da Silva, argued at the moment of the latter's electoral triumph, the Brazilian people elected Lula not for the work of Marx but for the work of popular education and the presence of Paulo Freire. This, we believe, is another lasting legacy of the creator of Pedagogy of the Oppressed.

THE GLOBAL IMPACT OF PAULO FREIRE

It is a fitting conclusion to this chapter to briefly discuss the impact of Paulo Freire in international settings. The MOVA-Brazil, a social movement for literacy training that emerged during and continued after Freire's time as secretary of education in the municipality of São Paulo, has extended its work throughout Brazil, and its example is also reaching the neighboring countries of the Southern Cone (Gadotti, 2008b). However, Freire's pedagogical approach has been taken up well beyond Brazil or Latin America. His method and theories were introduced into the world as a revolution of adult learning. His impact on literacy training, in particular, has stood the test of time, and is reflected in a multitude of initiatives, programs, and documents. Most recently, his contributions to adult learning have been highlighted as an inspiration by UNESCO (2009) in the Global Report of Adult Learning and Education (GRALE), used as a resource document in the VI CONFINTEA (Sixth International Conference on Adult Education, May 2009, Belem, Brazil)—the most important decennial conference on adult education, attended by the majority of the world's ministers and secretaries of education, as well as other government officials and members of NGOs and social movements around the world (Torres, 2011a).

At a more generic level, Paulo Freire is considered the originator of the theoretical model of Critical Pedagogy that has influenced the educational training of teachers, particularly in the United States, but also in several other advanced industrial societies. The work of Paulo Freire and especially his *Pedagogy of the Oppressed* reflects the quintessential nature of comparative and international education. Freire's critique of "banking" education; the idea of education for freedom; the fact that his theoretical framework can be used to study the relations between class, race/ethnicity, gender, and the state in education; and Freire's critique illuminating the intricate relationship between politics and education through the paradigm of popular education—all of these have meant that Freire's message has made a deep and lasting impact on educational models, including Critical Pedagogy. The movement for popular education in Latin America, Africa, and Asia owes a great deal of its theoretical foundations, methodology, and praxis to the work of Paulo Freire and the pedagogues of liberation. After the crisis of neoliberalism, with the failure of the different models of structural adjustment in Latin America and in light of the current global financial situation, these models of popular education have acquired renewed energy in the context of counteracting the crisis of capitalism, and are being used by social movements in new and original ways. The influence of Freire on contemporary scholars and practitioners has been well documented and the number of studies and doctoral dissertations show that research on Freire's epistemology, theory, and methods has burgeoned.[8] Freire has been linked by some with the Swiss Argentine psychologist Enrique Pichón-Rivere. He has been compared by others to the Polish educator Janusz Korczak (1878–1942) who as we already mentioned died together with 200 of his students in a Nazi gas chamber. Other comparisons have been made to Eduard Claparéde, Pierre Bovet, Célestin Freinet, Bogdan Suchodolski, the new European sociologists of education, the American psychologist Carl Rogers with his model of student-centered learning, the work of Ivan Illich and his proposal of deschooling (with which Freire disagreed), as well as Lev Vigotsky and John Dewey.

Paulo Freire's pedagogy of the oppressed, his notion of constructivist pedagogy, and his interdisciplinary approach have impacted many disciplines and practices across the world. Although his theories have crossed the borders of disciplines and sciences, his reflections have deepened the theme that he pursued his whole life: education as the practice of freedom. His theories spilled over into different fields of knowledge, from education to health, from pedagogy to politics, from sociology to social work. His work took root in many places, from the shantytowns of Latin America to the *burakinin* communities of Japan. His contributions to the field of education could be compared to the efforts of those working on AIDS prevention, or to therapists working on ways to liberate human consciousness from early childhood traumas or personality disorders. There is no question that Paulo Freire's border-crossing perspective in the 1960s resulted in a transdisciplinary approach that has gained even more recognition in the new century.

TWO

Paulo Freire: An Itinerant Thinker of Praxis

The useful task of the historian is to keep the memory green.
(John Kenneth Galbraith)

If you scratch a theory, you find a biography.
(Troy Duster, cited in Carlos Alberto Torres, 1998d)

THE HISTORICAL SPACE AND LOCATION OF THE WRITING

These two epigraphs illuminate the spirit of this chapter. The great Keynesian economist, John K. Galbraith, reminds us that the most useful task of the historian is to keep the memory alive. In the same manner, Professor Troy Duster (1998d) of the University of California, Berkeley, whom I cited in one of my books, pointed out in one of his classes that when one "scratches a theory, one finds a biography."

The tone of this chapter is, at the same time, biographical and theoretical. It is biographical insofar as it concerns the author and his circumstances while also serving as a testimonial, probably partial and idiosyncratic, of the experience of an entire generation of Argentineans in Diaspora. Although biographical, this is also a theoretical text that reviews the arguments that made the work of Freire and a generation of pedagogues for liberation relevant 45 years after *Pedagogy of the Oppressed* was published. This reanalysis involves a theoretical construction and reconstruction of their premises from the perspective of current educational and political circumstances and challenges. Through all of this, we come to understand Freire's theories and politics as the work of a thinker of praxis, an itinerant thinker, and a universal thinker.

When I wrote my first book on Freire, I was only 25 years old and had just completed a degree in sociology and been hired as a sociology professor at la Universidad del Salvador in Buenos Aires, Argentina.

The first book in the three-book series, *La Praxis Educativa de Paulo Freire*, was written in Esquel, Chubut, a province of Argentinean Patagonia, from mid-1975 to March 1976, at the request of Julio Barreiro, who was Paulo Freire's editor at Tierra Nueva, a publishing house connected to the World Council of Churches that had started in Montevideo, Uruguay, and moved to Buenos Aires after the Uruguayan military coup.[1]

Julio Barreiro wanted a critical approach to Freire's perspective. After a seminar he gave about Paulo Freire's thinking at the institute Estudio de la Ciencia Latinoamericana (ECLA) that I organized in my role as the Institute's general secretary, Julio Barreiro asked me to put together a book that would include a descriptive and critical essay on Freire's political philosophy and pedagogy. It is worth mentioning that, by the mid-1970s, Freire was beginning to be known but did not yet enjoy the worldwide renown he would achieve in the 1980s, which lasted until his death (Torres, 2002; Torres & Morrow, 2002b[2]).

On May 1, 1975, having resigned my position at ECLA, I moved to Patagonia with the dream of starting a school of farming and animal husbandry under the auspices of the bishopric of Esquel, a project that never got off the ground. Still in Patagonia, and after having reviewed and studied a lot of material, I decided to include in the book I was writing some of Freire's unpublished texts in Spanish.

I will get back to Barreiro, a friend to whom I may owe my life, in a little while. But, for the moment, I would like to look at what else was happening at that time and place—the background action, as it were—bearing in mind that it is more or less by historical accident that I wrote the second and third Freire books in Mexico while studying for my master's degree in political science at FLACSO (Facultad Latinoamericana de Ciencias Sociales [Latin American Faculty of Social Sciences[3]]).

The end of the 1960s and the beginning of the 1970s were a turbulent time in Argentina and in Latin America as a whole. These were years of very intense class struggle and apparently irresolvable political conflict. Argentina was deeply damaged by widespread political conflict wherein the armed forces, characterized by their anti-Peronism, were confronting a national popular movement of the working classes, known as Peronism or Justicialism, that saw, in the mythical figure of Perón, a heroic national savior whom they were trying to reinstate almost 20 years after he had been deposed and exiled by the military coup of 1955.

A majority of Argentineans believed in Perón's return. Two words—*Perón Vuelve*—were scrawled on all unguarded walls and billboards and passed from mouth to mouth as a fervent murmur in streets and homes throughout the land. Perón's return was seen as an antidote to all the nation's ills. On March 11, 1973—soon after its proscription had terminated in 1972—the Justicialist Party, an electoral instrument and part of the FREJULI (Frente Justicialista de Liberación) alliance of political parties organized by Perón, won the national election with a formulaic leader, Dr. Héctor J. Cámpora, Perón's personal representative in Argentina. The party's campaign slogan was "Cámpora governs; Péron's in power!" These were the first democratic elections authorized by the military dictatorship commanded by General Lanusse, who shortly before the electoral process had subscribed to a treaty that included all the active-duty generals but one, a commitment to respect any government that would be voted in (a commitment of the generals in active duty to agree not to overthrow any government democratically elected at least until 1977) (Gregorich, 1983). Cámpora resigned and called for new elections that made Péron's return from Spanish exile possible. Juan Domingo Perón won the September 1973 election under the banner of Socialismo National (Socialism for a Nation), which most young people considered the necessary answer for those times—although some of us felt it was not enough to solve the contradictions of Argentina's economic and political development. Perón's Argentine socialism was very quickly converted to National Socialism, a rightist model of traditional Peronist syndicalism allied with sinister figures in Argentine politics such as José López Rega, Perón's personal secretary and head of the Ministry of Social Security in the Cámpora government, who initiated paramilitary groups known as the Triple A, or the Argentine Anticommunist Alliance. This organization was responsible for many acts of violent vandalism that paved the way for a military intervention—the most methodical project imaginable for Third World fascism like that implemented by the Military Junta of Argentinean Process after 1976. It was a project that sought to physically eliminate its political opposition. Thus began a new chapter in the history of human rights, with the figure of the political *desaparecido* (disappeared person), tortured and assassinated in Argentina, from the middle period of the Peronista government until its paroxysm with the installation of the military dictatorship on March 24, 1976.

Of course, this confrontation was not just ideological. It also manifested in class warfare in the streets—in Buenos Aires, Córdoba, Rosario, and other principal cities there were civil disturbances in the years preceding the democratic restoration. The middle and working classes, timid at first, were radicalized into political activism, which ended in armed conflict and the senseless bloodshed of guerrilla war.

It was an era simultaneously utopian and violent, but the options were not limited to a dispute between alternatives that advocated violence of any form. There were many other options besides taking up arms or accepting the complex and limited logic, given the conditions in Argentina, of formal democracy. These options gradually faded with the loss of the democracy, which was evident soon after the crisis of 1975,[4] but were in no way the announcement that not everything would end in the barrel of a gun. Perhaps this period was best captured by the title of a book by Luis Suárez, a Spanish Republican journalist exiled in Mexico, who defined the way we lived in Latin America during the 1970s as "*entre 'el fusil y la palabra'* " ("between 'the rifle and the word' ") (Suarez, 1980).

The not-so-distant echoes of the Cuban revolution kept offering—together with the already universally mythical figure of Ernesto "Che" Guevara—a revolutionary alternative to the models of economic and social development inspired by the American spirit of democracy and the prevalence of the United States, not only as one of the two hegemonic world powers but also the one that intended to control Latin America (pejoratively referred to as its "backyard") at any price. The Cuban embargo—euphemistically called a "quarantine" because it did not stem from a formal declaration of war—which has now lasted over 50 years, was another indication of the arrogance of American interventionism in the region, which insisted on obtaining by force what it could not achieve through reason or negotiation.

But as I said, there were other options. One of these, in which I participated as a member of the nascent Theology of Liberation, was the base communities. These existed in different forms. Some were utopian socialist communities that were taking shape as low-walled monasteries in the midst of poor and lower-middle-class neighborhoods. I got married and went to live in one of these communities with other young people, the majority of them university students, who wanted to inspire social change from within, starting from the interstices of life, both urban and suburban, and in a gradual manner. Partly as a celebration of justice, partly as a celebratory act of love, we were looking to change reality by example, with our words, with our work, and with our prayers.

Ours was a community politically committed to the country's social transformation. Not for nothing had we painted in my community, in blue on a whitewashed wall and large enough for it to be seen from the street, a phrase of the Cuban poet Miguel Barnes's collected in the emblematic book of the Nicaraguan poet Ernesto Cardenal, *Ernesto Cardenal en Cuba*: "Revolution, between you and me a heap of contradictions that, together, make me fearful enough to build you with the sweat of my brow."

This seemed to be the leitmotif of a community crossed by the country's ideological contradictions, especially by those of the distinct militant factions of revolutionary *Peronistas* and socialist *Marxistas*.

There were utopian residential communities of different cultural and political stripes. They were not necessarily linked to Liberation Theology, but they were clearly linked to one countercultural model and option or another.[5] Some European experiences at the time, like the one sponsored by Lanza del Vasto. Lanza del Vasto was a disciple of Gandhi, preaching non-violence, and founding communities in Europe, the best well known is called Comunidad del Arca. He was Italian and his real name was Giuseppe Giovanni Luigi Enrico Lanza di Trabia. He was born on 29 September 2001 and died 5 of January 1981. He also impacted our imagination, perhaps much more than the communal experiments of American hippies. Some of these communities in Argentina had had their day and were now very established, like the one inspired and led by the architect Claudio Caveri, in the Moreno district of Buenos Aires Province, which tried to unite an architectonic project of constructing sheet-metal houses in a very economical and particularly functional way, with home industries in carpentry and organic gardening.[6] Other, younger communities had a certain anarchist style and taste, without mixing families or experimenting with a hippie-style model where everything that happened in the community was the construction of one big family.

Such communities coincided in a clear option of struggle against the established authority, a constant critique of power. They sought means of production, distribution, exchange, and consumption that were different from those capitalism had to offer. Of course, they were also looking for a new solidarity, a collaboration of people who were willing to build a radical democracy starting with families. At this time in Argentina, the benefits of feminist proposals for a much more democratic family interaction than that offered by traditional patriarchal models were not yet well known. Paradoxically, we were also interested in the construction of a new state and new forms of solidarity, despite our disdain for the state we had. Among these were initiatives for voluntary labor that had been impelled in the first months of the Frente Justicialista de Liberación (FREJULI) government and the enormous interest released in Dr. Allende's Chilean experiment in democratic socialism.

Argentina was a country in ferment—very fertile territory for the development of anticolonialist and postcolonial thinking that was celebrating the independence of African countries, especially Guinea-Bissau, Mozambique, and Angola. The process of independence of Portuguese African societies provided the opportunity to Freire, who was exiled in Switzerland, to engage in a new chapter of his political and pedagogical agenda.[7] Certainly, the anti-Peronista campaign of the establishment, civic education model and official knowledge prevalent in the schools system create a narrative erasure. Thus an important part of Argentine history disappeared from the textbooks (Perón's name was all but erased from the official record and, when mentioned, was accompanied by the words *fugitive tyrant*) and impacted a generation that had neither the theory nor the civic practice necessary to understand the dilemmas of the democracy and the country's actual history.

Perhaps it happens in every country that the constrution of hegemony requires a systematic action of historical reading and rereading of the past. These readings and rereadings go hand in hand with the era's transformations and social conflicts. Two historiographies marked the 20th century Argentinean life. The writing of Argentinean history between the supporters of Bartolomé Mitre (perhaps much more tied to the unitary image of the predominance of Buenos Aires Province and the oligarchic politics of the great landholdings) and those of Juan Manuel de Rosas (a revisionism that saw in certain caudillos from the interior the expression of the federal country exploited by the Unitarians). This political and historical tension left its mark on the majority of disputes about the nation, the state, and the market and especially the understanding of Argentinean history. But it is also certain that there were other eloquent voices, although not necessarily widely published ones, such as the attempt to explain things from a Marxist point of view carried out by the illustrious Argentinean historian Rodolfo Puiggrós, who was rector of the University of Buenos Aires (UBA) during the Cámpora–Solano Lima government[8] the really suggestive books of the Trotskyite historian Milcíades Peña, or Juan José Hernandez Arregui's book *La Formación de la Conciencia Nacional* (1960) that influenced my generation as a revisionist book from a left-wing nationalist Peronista point of view that was read both in the academy and in the urban neighborhoods, by Peronista diehards and by people in the slums. This book consisted of an accelerated course in political and historical theory for a generation that lived through Argentina's history reading in the schools historical episodes that only reached to the middle of the 20th century, literally stopped by the time of the inception of Peronism in the country. This historiography was always descriptive, chronological, with interpretations of the official knowledge and very little room for a critical and independent reading of what had happened. An exemplary text of historical analysis is Tulio Halperin Donghi's *El espejo de la historia* (1987). A book with a very complete and elaborate systematization of Argentinean political models and ideologies is Juan José Sebreli's *Crítica de las ideas políticas argentinas* (2003).

If I learned anything politically at that time, it was that the past could not be expunged by an official decision. The figures of Perón and Evita lived on in a most vigorous way on the walls of the houses of Argentine Peronistas like my godfather, Bautista, who hung the graduation photo of his policy academy officers generation with General Perón on one of the walls of his humble home in the Haedo neighborhood next to another photo of Perón mounted on a white bay horse and, in another corner of the house, a photo of Evita, her blond hair blowing in the wind—in spite of the risks he ran because he was a police officer.

The cult of Perón was alive and well in family get-togethers. Some of craziest were in my family where there was a sector of uncles who were socialists amid a Peronista majority, which meant, especially after the typical libations that go along with a family party, that the political theme heightened the tone of the discussions, which were only held in check by respect for the owners of the house, the permanent solidarity of the women of the house who would remind everyone of the importance of consanguinity, and by the continuing necessity of cohabitation. History lives on in people's memories, even more so if it concerns a national popular movement of working people like Peronismo in 1970s Argentina.

Peronismo began in 1945 as a national popular movement of the people in the style of the writing of Antonio Gramsci in the Italian *Mezzogiorno*. Clearly, the shady episodes accompanying the installation of neoliberalism in Argentina under the guise of Carlos Saúl Menem's original Peronista government have demonstrated how even the oldest precepts of Justicialismo can be betrayed and can cast doubt on the very nature of Peronismo as a political regime. Peronismo has ceased to be the central voice of opposition to the capitalist and conservative political system, as it was from the overthrow of Perón in 1955 until the reestablishment of his political figure in 1973 and has been converted into a complex amalgam of orientations, groups, caudillos, and ideologies that recall the "one governing party" style of the Partido Revolucionario Institucional (PRI) in Mexico, but less disciplined and clearly playing a part in the "smorgasbord" of Argentinean politics. The experience of the four Kirchner governments (Néstor and Cristina Fernández de Kirchner) marks the approximation of traditional Peronism to a model of defense of human rights and a social democratic model—though with a heavy dose of democratic centralism—that departed drastically from the neoliberal model of Carlos Saúl Menem's, President of Argentina in the period 1989–1989, Peronism.

WHY PAULO FREIRE IN ARGENTINA? AN ITINERANT THINKER

I know All the Tales
I don't know many things, it's true
I can only say what I've seen.
And I've seen:
That people's cradles are rocked with tales . . .
That people's anguished cries are stifled with tales . . .
That they drown people's weeping with tales . . .
That they bury people's bones with tales . . .
And that people's fear
has invented all the tales.
I don't know many things, it's true.
But I have slept with all the tales . . .
And I know all the tales.

(León Felipe)

This põem of the Spanish Republican poet Léon Felipe, who died in exile, illuminates my own understanding of publishing a book about Freire addressing the context of class warfare in Argentina. As I have already mentioned, I finished the first book of the planned trilogy a few days before the military coup of March 24, 1976, in Esquel, Chubut. Two students from my classes at the University of Patagonia typed the manuscript in triplicate with carbon paper and, armed with these copies, I boarded a plane to Buenos Aires to give the book to Julio Barreiro.

Julio greeted me in his office on Diagonal Norte Street, in the center of the now Autonomous City of Buenos Aires, with tremendous affection, took the materials that I handed him, and told me, "I will read them with an editor's eye, but I'm afraid I will not be able to publish them in Argentina under current conditions. Perhaps we can do it in Italy and in Italian."

This sentence was like a pail of cold water being poured over me. After having spent so many hours on it, writing most of it in a boarding house on a small farm near the town of Trevelin, a Welsh settlement a few kilometers from Esquel, I had such high hopes that my first book would be published. My family and I had been lent this place without electricity so I had actually written most of the manuscript by candlelight or kerosene lantern while the imposing cold of the Patagonian night penetrated through all the chinks of the old house, which had not been inhabited for quite some time and whose only source of heat was a wood-burning stove that we also used for cooking. This stove was connected to the plumbing so we could have hot water; it would be scalding for the first 2 minutes and then lukewarm after that, which meant we had to take quick baths or we froze. I had made a great effort in my reading, doing bibliographical research in a small city that did not really have libraries except the private ones of some diehard readers. The National University of Patagonia's Esquel campus had just been created and had no bibliographical material whatsoever. Only the constant support of Julio Barreiro's office, which sent me materials by mail, had allowed me to revise the bibliography in a place that was extremely isolated from the country's cultural circles.

In the course of our conversation, Julio was able to understand my frustration and, changing the subject, asked me what I was able to do in Esquel during the year that had passed since I had moved to that city. I told him that I was teaching in different places, including the Costa Rica teacher's college, the University of Patagonia's Esquel campus, and a secondary school for adults that had evening classes, and that I had other part-time jobs as well—for example, I had been appointed a health-care sociologist in the Esquel hospital by the province's Peronista government. The need for multiple sources of income, typical of the Argentinean economy at that time, has not changed substantively since.

I noticed that Julio seemed agitated and asked me what I was teaching in my courses. I told him I was offering courses in philosophy, adult education, and business organization and administration, using texts by Freire, Marx, and Piaget. He stopped me with a peremptory and preoccupied tone: "Carlos, you have to return immediately, ask for your course outlines, destroy them, and replace them with others containing different bibliographies, ones that do not include Piaget, Freire, or Marx. The Secretary of Intelligence (SIDE) a National Agency of Security is inspecting educational establishments and, as these authors are banned, there can be very grave consequences for those who teach Freire, Marx, and Piaget."

In my naiveté, I asked Julio why the situation seemed so difficult to him; after all, we had had a number of military dictatorships before. He asked if I would join him in a cup of coffee, opened his desk drawer, and pulled out a news magazine that was very popular with the middle class. He handed me the magazine. There were two full pages in the middle that I recognized immediately as having to do with material connected to Paulo Freire. The left-hand page contained passages taken from *Educación como Práctica de la Libertad (*Education: the Practice of Freedom); the right-hand page had passages from *Pedagogía del Oprimido* (Pedagogy of the Oppressed). They were some of the most incendiary sentences from both books, taken completely out of context.

At the end of the "article," there was a statement that read something like this: "The Argentinean Revolution has been waged against this kind of Marxist education for our children." Julio closed the magazine, looked me straight in the eye, and said, "This is paid propaganda." He proceeded to tell me that we needed to be very careful at this particular time.

Julio had chosen to live in Argentina as a kind of exile after the Uruguayan military coup. He had been one of the first Latin American intellectuals to audaciously describe the allied effort at the annihilation of the political opposition that the armed forces of the Southern Cone had launched under the pretext of combating the guerrillas in what was later disclosed as an intercontinental operation coordinated with the approval of the United States, the Condor Operation. This fact is abundantly documented and not worth going into more extensively in this chapter.[9]

Suffice it to say that this conversation with Julio Barreiro changed my life and perhaps saved me and my family from a torturous future or even death. But this was not the first time that I had perceived something very difficult to explain in a country where violence defied the imagination. In October 1975 I had received a handwritten letter in Esquel from Dr. Emilio Mignone[10] who had been the director of ECLA and with whom I had worked in 1973 as general secretary of the organization. In this letter he went into some detail about the arrest of his daughter, Mónica Mignone, who had been taken from her Santa Fé Street apartment by a group of men who identified themselves as belonging to one of the armed forces' ominous Grupos de Tareas or Working Groups.[11]

That night they took Mónica Mignone, María Marta Lugones and César Lugones, friends whom we had talked to about joining our community for some time and were hoping would travel to Esquel with us to start the school. In fact, César Lugones, an agronomist, had come with another member of the community, architect Freddy Garay, and me to Esquel to explore the possibility of starting a new community there. After 2 months of fruitless attempts in which it became clear that the bishop's invitation was a fraud, César gave up and returned to Buenos Aires. As militants in the Peronist Youth movement and as people working with adult alphabetization following the Freirean model of popular education in a shantytown on the outskirts of Buenos Aires, Mónica, María Marta, and César were arrested and disappeared. We never heard from them again. They were some of the first victims of a veritable orgy of madness, violence, torture, blood, and death.

My conversation with Julio Barreiro put Dr. Mignone's letter in clearer perspective and led me to look for options that would allow me to leave the country. A few months after having obtained a scholarship from FLACSO, I left to study for my master's degree in Mexico.[12]

I want to reiterate that Julio Barreiro was one of the first people to perceive this drastic political situation with exceptional lucidity and to offer a prophetic critique of the growing tragedy in his notable book of essays, *Los molinos de la ira* (*The Anger Mills*), which won the publishing house Siglo XXI Editores prize in

1980. His title was inspired by the biblical phrase: "The mills of God grind slowly but surely." Without Julio Barreiro's orientation and the altruistic support of the erstwhile director of FLACSO–Argentina, Dr. Emilio Mignone, I am convinced that I would not be writing these lines today.

Another noteworthy contribution of Julio Barreiro was the publication of a book that was absolutely seminal in the understanding of popular education in the region: *Popular Education and the Process of Concientization in Latin America* (1974). Many of us cut our teeth with this book, understanding the different models and the intellectual as well as the political project in the connection between the movements of popular culture and the movement of popular education. As it happens, 35 years later I learned that this book was actually written in the midst of the Brazilian dictatorship (and perhaps during its harsher phase) by the distinguished Brazilian anthropologist Carlos Rodrigues Brandão—whom Freire indicated upon leaving the World Council of Churches was the best candidate to replace him, which shows the admiration that Freire felt for Rodrigues Brandão. Since the publication of the book and the author would have been at risk in Brazil, Julio Barreiro, who was editor of the publishing house Tierra Nueva, agreed to publish the book under his own name, covering up the fact that it was actually written by Rodrigues Brandão.

But let us go back to the Argentinean experience that forced my exile and that of a large number of other Argentineans and Latin Americans. The Postscript at the end of this chapter provides rich insights into this peculiar and original book's history.

EXILE AS LEARNING

My vision of the Argentina took on added clarity when, while living in Mexico City, I found myself surrounded by thousands of exiled Argentineans, Uruguayans, Chileans, Brazilians, Bolivians and Central Americans. The city, which hosted many institutes of higher education, had become a kind of Mecca for Latin American social scientists. The generous solidarity of Mexico, a country that I learned to appreciate and love dearly, preserved much of what today exists as Latin American social sciences by saving an important part of its human resources, who were then able to proceed with their studies and investigations. It also preserved research archives that would have been unthinkable in the Southern Cone countries suffering under violent dictatorships, and facilitating in its extraordinary institutions of higher education, such as UNAM, UAM, FLACSO, el Colegio de México, and so many others, an atmosphere of intellectual freedom and scientific rigor with libraries containing veritable bibliographic treasures,[13] exceptional intellectual ambience, and human resources that I had never experienced until that moment.

When I finished my master's degree at FLACSO in 1978, I decided not to return to Argentina. After a brief stint of work at the Secretariat of Statistics and Census, and thanks to the generosity of my great friend José Ángel Pescador Osuna who was successively a federal deputy, undersecretary of education, secretary of education, and undersecretary of government (Pescador & Torres, 1985), I was given a contract as a university professor and participated in the creation of the Universidad Pedagógica Nacional (UPN) or National Pedagogical University in 1978. After working at UPN and, then, as the director of the research office of the Directory General of Adult Education in the Secretariat of Public Education, at that moment directed by Maestro Pescador Osuna, I left, thanks to his support and counsel, to work on my doctorate at Stanford University in 1980, in the SIDEC program from which José Ángel himself had graduated in the early 1970s.

Having left Argentina in September 1976, I did not return until April 1984, shortly after the electoral victory of the radical government of Dr. Alfonsín, to spend a month with my father, who was dying of lung cancer.

Exiles of any kind will probably say that being exiled is like having one's soul fragmented, living a life of perpetual fragmentation. It is like riding two horses at the same time. One horse symbolizes the country you were forced to leave, even though in your spirit and imagination you never left, while the other horse symbolizes the new country that has received you, but you never become "one of them." It is as if we perpetually seek closure, knowing we will never get it. There are different kinds of exiles. I was part of an exile, or Argentinean Diaspora, responding to a violent authoritarian government, but today there are "approximately 214 million transnational immigrants, 15 million refugees, over 740 million internal migrants, and millions more of immediate relatives left behind, immigration defines our era" (Suárez-Orozco, Louie, & Suro, 2011, p. ix).

Clearly, many immigrants leave their country or their region in search of a better life for themselves and their families; thus one could speak of such immigrants as economic exiles. There is no question that when visiting "ethnic" neighborhoods in Los Angeles, New York, Toronto, London, or Paris, to name just a few global cities, one feels a sense of being in a place that is a "transplant" from some other place. Immigrants who are exiled from their souls try to reconnect and regain that spiritual, ethical, and political ethos by reinventing in the First World the barrios of the Third World. The aromas, sounds, words, language, style of dress, written advertisements, food, and music all resemble the place they left, thinking that one day they might go back. Alas, many more who remain living inside countries with authoritarian governments, in order to survive become "internal exiles" with many dramatic experiences akin to those who had to abruptly leave the country to survive.

Incompleteness is perhaps a good word to define these exiles of the soul. Academics are not exempt from this feeling and occasionally from uttering their own sense of loss, fragmentation, and belonglessness. One of the most distinguished Argentinean writers, Julio Cortazar, who died in Paris, used to say that he carried Buenos Aires tied to his body as one carries his tied-up shoes.

I cannot imagine a better description of exile and incompleteness than Cortazar's words. Yet we academics are privileged subjects, whether the exile of our souls is fully, partially, or not recognized at all. We work in the life of the mind and the spirit, in the realm of the imagination and discourse—but make no mistake, when this work is not merely self-congratulatory and/or idealist, we work with specific and practical concerns for social transformation and, hence, praxis is the ultimate goal.

Even considering the risks of alienation that all who manipulate symbols, living through rituals of symbolic performance or constructing and deconstructing discourses, may face, there is no question that the life of the mind and the spirit might eventually soothe this open wound of exile and incompleteness. Alas, this is a momentary reprieve. The longing for the "lost paradise" that never really was, will always watch us, like a ghost in the night.

Freire, like few exiled people that I meet, felt this longing daily—hence, his extraordinary happiness when he reencountered with his own Portuguese language with his consulting work with the decolonized countries in Lusophone Africa, or the excitement he had when invited to my house he will always expect and get beans, a staple in Brazilian cuisine.

Freire in a conversation with Frei Betto (1985) addressed what he considered the pedagogical experience of the exile. "For me, the exile was profoundly pedagogical. As an exiled, I took distance from Brazil, and began to understand myself and Brazil better. . . . In the moment that you say no to yourself, in any moment, to make value judgements, you begin to learn a virtue that I consider so fundamental in this country: the virtue of tolerance. Tolerance that teaches us, overcoming all preconcepts, how to live together with the different, for in the end, to better struggle with the antagonical" (p. 56–58).

For Freire the exile was a profound source of learning (Freire, Ceccon, Darcy de Oliveira, & Darcy de Oliveira, 1989) The ultimate proof is in his emblematic book *Pedagogy of the Oppressed.* Every writer knows that the two most difficult sentences to write in a book are the first and the last sentence. The first paragraph in *Pedagogy of the Oppressed* starts as follows: "The pages that follow and that we propose as an introduction to *Pedagogy of the Oppressed* are the result of our observations in this *five years of exile*" (Freire, 2002, p. 23, emphasis added).

Perhaps the fact that I shared with Paulo this feeling of incompleteness helped me to understand better what the role of education is in our contemporary world. The question, perhaps, is what philosophical stance to draw in the politics of liberation.

As a result of my studies of Freirean thinking, reflected in articles and books through the years, I am convinced that there are two books that mark the important developments of the philosophy of education in the 20th century. One is *Democracy and Education* by John Dewey (1916), and the other is Paulo Freire's *Pedagogy of the Oppressed* (1973e). My reading of Freire, which came long before my reading of Dewey (Feinberg & Torres, 1995; Torres, 2003), was a critical reading rather than a complacent one, as Paulo Freire told Moacir Gadotti when he introduced us.[14]

One only criticizes that which is worth criticizing, in the spirit of the Aufheben, to criticize, to conserve, and to overcome in the itinerary of the philosophy of negative reason as Marx and Marcuse (1967) have taught us. It was very much the same thing that Freire had in mind when he insisted that he did not want us to repeat him but, rather, to reinvent him.

POSTSCRIPT: THE CURIOUS STORY OF A HISTORICAL BOOK

I have cited a book in the history of popular education in Latin America, Julio Barreiro, *Educación Popular y Proceso de Concientización* (1974). It was a very important book in the discussion about Freire, popular cultures, and conscientization in Latin America. It is a very important book, particularly to understand the first Freire.

Many years after I read *Educación Popular y Proceso de Concientización*, I learned that Barreiro had donated his name as the author in order to protect Carlos Rodrigues Brandão, the Brazilian anthropologist who had written the book and asked Barreiro to publish it. Here is the story of the book narrated by Rodrigues Brandão (this is my translation of a personal communication via email from Rodrigues Brandão to Moacir Gadotti and me):

> Dear friends, Carlos and Gadotti. The fact the complete story is the following. Since 1969, in the middle of the dictatorship in Brazil, I began, jointly with some compañeros and compañeras some daredevil journey through Latin America in the name of the Ecumenical Center of Documentation and Information, affiliated to Iglesia y Sociedad en América Latina (ISAL). Those were trips to sow throughout Latin America the ideas of Paulo Freire, and his method of literacy training and popular education. I remember a meeting with militants in Equator, in the middle of the Andes, and with lack of air in my lungs, using a kind of school blackboard, less than 10 square feet, to unfold the "cards of discovery" (representations of) the generative words of the Paulo Freire Method.
>
> They requested that we write a paper to leave with the people. In my travels between Argentina and in Costa Rica I began to write documents that were mimeographed and distributed for every place we went. Then the idea emerged that these papers should be combined in a book. It was my responsibility, as a "political task" to write this book. Each chapter was rigorously revised by Beatriz Costa, Jether Pereira Ramalho, and Elter Dias Maciel. When the book was finished—and it was more work to correct the manuscript than to write it—we had a meeting in ISAL in Montevideo; I believe it was 1970 or 1971. They agreed that it was reckless to publish the book with my name, given the situation of Brazil. I suggested as a

pseudonym the name of a Chilean guerrilla fighter Manoel Rodrigues. The idea was not accepted because of the Argentine publishing laws (the book was going to be published by Tierra Nueva, in Buenos Aires). Because of this legal restriction Julio Barreiro, a brave Uruguayan Protestant theologian, made the "sacrifice" to become the author of our book. I say "our" because although it was written by me, it was read, reread, and revised by many people. It was finally published by Siglo XXI Editores. It was forbidden with the coup d'état of 1976. It was published with some editions in Mexico. Then it was published in Spain. The last time I visited Spain, the book was in its 15th edition. There is a Portuguese edition, and if I am not wrong (I must check this), a Cuban edition. Ten years later, when the repression diminished in Brazil, the book was published by Editora VOZES, and I was listed as translator of my own book. Later, another edition was published by Editora Sulina from Porto Alegre, where finally the story was told.

In Spanish, the book was published as *Educación Popular y Proceso de Concientización*. In Portuguese, it was published as *Educação Popular e Conscientização*. Julio Barreiro, a dear friend, passed away 3 years ago. This is the history (or story) of one of the most curious cases of book editions on education here in Latin America.

There is a tale in the folklore of the book that after the coup in Argentina an edition of 1,000 copies was destroyed. I will never know if this information is real.

THREE

Political Philosophy of Education

"There was a time during which I became impassionated with Hegel. And I tell you the following–I believe that Marx was absolutely correct when he sometimes revealed the accuracies of Hegel's thought. Essentially it is Hegel who first opens up the path for Marx. It is Hegel that discovers work as an element of the making of men and women."

(Freire in Torres, 1998d, p. 92)

Educators have very often wondered about the type of philosophy that Paulo Freire upholds. His writings, as opposed to those of other authors, refer us permanently, in his reference notes and bibliography, to such a broad series of currents of thought that it proves to be very difficult to identify in a reliable manner some preponderant current.

Moreover, Freire's thought is not circumscribed to a strict theme and style of reflection. On the contrary, his philosophical work constitutes a wide-ranging synthesis, very hard to grasp immediately. His style of reflection has distinct disciplinary levels that, when the reader is someone oriented in a sociological discipline, for example, make it troublesome to understand the strictly philosophical or didactic analyses in all their density, and vice versa.

Perhaps there exists a consensus on the existence of a "humanist" line of thought in Freire, especially in his first phase, but perhaps the role that philosophy plays in his educational practice is not seen as clearly. More concretely, in which of his articles or books does one find set out in a detailed way his philosophy of education?

In the 1970s, after Freire began to be internationally recognized, Latin American educators have been accustomed to associating Freire with his psychosocial method of adult literacy acquisition and to understanding it in the framework of a pedagogical concept: permanent education or continuing education.[1] But, likewise, they wonder: What is Paulo Freire's ideology? What is the ideological substratum of his thought?

This chapter starts out from the belief that Freirean thought is a theoretical amalgam of considerable scope in which—in its more useful and significant elements—different philosophical leanings complement one another in some cases, and confront and oppose one another in others (Torres, 1980a).

In the words of Fausto Franco (1973): "It seems to me important to indicate here something that powerfully grabs one's attention in the entirety of Freire's work. As one reads his works, the reader gets the impression that he is hearing familiar sounds; but at the same time one experiences in a lively manner that the result of the total harmony is new. For instance, upon studying the anthropological traits that form the base of his pedagogy we realize that the elements that appear are the common heritage of the personalist movement and the legacy of the humanist tendencies that have been continuously purged throughout the history of thought; and, nevertheless, the cables that Freire is throwing from those assumptions to concrete situations facing education, have all the force of evocative findings" (p. 20; quote translated from the Spanish).

Furthermore, it is understood that in Freire's work philosophy has the role of accompanying the pedagogical action reflexively and in a critical form, with the object of making explicit its philosophical foundations, its scope, and its limits. This philosophy is not found, explained, and analyzed at great length in any of his books, but instead is present in the entire context of his thought. Thus, we are obliged to consider panoramically Freire's entire intellectual output, with the object of comprehending it, without making explicit, in the present case, its different stages through time (Torres, 1981a).

On the other hand, the role of his philosophical reflection has a very precise dimension: to provide the elements for the constitution of an anthropology—specifically, a political anthropology of education. This political anthropology of education may explain how each human being is in a process of humanization. Let us not forget that Freire reserves for education the role of "helping man reflect on his ontological vocation of subject" (Freire, 1973e, p. 52).

Finally, all ideological thinking, all ideology, is committed thought. Ideology accompanies structures to support or modify them. It sees at the same time the partial phenomena and the global phenomena of a society, but it always sees this social reality as a concrete totality and tries to explain it. Freire is wholly aware of the presence of ideology in all thought and of the need to expose it, step by step, in the implementation of the educational action (IDAC, 1975).

This chapter seeks to lay the foundations for the philosophical tendencies that fertilize Freirean thought, as a contribution to an understanding of the philosophy of education—no longer only the philosophy of Freirean education but now what is known as liberating education in general. Yet I aim to provide an angle on the understanding of Freirean ideology in particular.

The philosophical confluences allow us to individualize four key philosophical streams: *existential thought* (human beings are as beings-in-the-process-of-building, always work in process); *phenomenological thought* (human beings build their consciousness as intentionality); *Marxist thought* (human beings live in the drama of the economic conditioning of the infrastructure and the ideological conditioning of the superstructure), or, in the words of Freire (1972a) himself: "To understand the levels of consciousness, we must understand the cultural-historical reality as a superstructure in relation to an infrastructure" (p. 57); and finally, *Hegelian philosophy* (human beings as self-consciousness, part of the common experience, until they raise themselves toward science, through dialectics, so that what is "in itself" comes to be "in itself and for itself."[2]

EXISTENTIAL THOUGHT: ITS INFLUENCE IN PAULO FREIRE

From the structure of language comes the explanation of why the human spirit is condemned to an odyssey.

(Habermas, 1992c, p. 15)

Paulo Freire's method places the person who is in the process of acquiring literacy in the condition to make the words that form his or her world re-existing in a critical manner: Human beings learn to "ad-mirare" (i.e., to look at) and to admire themselves. It is in this dialectic of admiration that a human being discovers the "other." For Freire, this critical path begins when humans, through their consciousness, come to perceive themselves as social existence; when, through their consciousness, they manage to grasp the historical determinants of their human behavior or human existent.

Now, what is this "human existent" (Dasein)? Naturally, the concept of existent is basic to the philosophy of existence. The Dasein possesses temporality as its fundamental structure. The phenomenological description that Heidegger[3] might carry out in search of existential analytics of the Dasein suggests that the Dasein is manifested as a being whose basic character is to-be-in-the-world, with its corresponding existential behavior. This behavior consists of the power to surrender itself to the world of things —an aptitude that the human existent has in order to absorb himself or herself in things.

In the more personalist criterion of Emannuel Mounier,[4] the surrendering of the self should not be understood as a rigid opposition between having and being, but, on the contrary, as two poles between which incorporated existence is spread. Having constitutes the density of being—but also its heaviness, its tightness. It speaks of the "expansion of personality," which implies, as "an interior condition, a renunciation of the self and of its goods which depolarizes egocentricity: For only in losing himself or herself can the person find himself or herself. His or her riches consist in what remains with him or her when is stripped of all his or her possessions—of what is still his or her in the hour of death" (Mounier, 1952, p. 40).

Three aspects complement the Heideggerian analysis of self-surrendering. Its first potentiality consists of intelligence or the prospective apprehension of its possibilities, capable of transforming its future. The second potentiality is a de facto situation revealing a past that has been imposed on it and that it must inescapably accept: With respect to the first potentiality or prospective attitude, this one manifests itself as a retrospective attitude. Finally, it should maintain itself—subordinate itself—in an attitude of servitude toward certain things of the present being.

The Dasein thus implies a continuous tension, as anticipation of the future, dependence on the past, and absolute necessity to be in contact with some present things. In sum, this whole analysis can be summarized in the hyphenated phrase, "to-be-in-the-world."

But, this being-in-the-world, as human experience, runs a great risk: *estrangement*—that is, alienation in a world that massifies (through functionalization, having, as a value for being, the loss of the sense of mystery). Consequently, and only by starting from experience as existence, is the communication of intersubjectivities possible, by means of dialogue which can only be elaborated as a compromise with the "challenges" of the world.

From an ontological perspective, this existing-in-the-world is equivalent to "existing-in-time." Existentialism has constantly insisted on considering human beings as a "being-in-the-world"—that is, human beings as existence, but also human beings as a "being-with-the-others," as an opening.

So the dialogue, which is possible only as compromise, expresses a compromise that reassesses fidelity and hope. In Heideggerian thought, the existent, upon having an advanced apprehension of his temporality, of his-being-for-death, in no way has any rational knowledge, but an experience consisting of a certain affective tonality.

This affective tonality can be expressed in the concept of anguish—the sliding of the totality of the existent toward the void, as Heidegger would have it—as if the last potentiality of the existent were the void. In regard to this existential orientation, the expression "existing-in-the-world" or "existing in the midst of the existent" does not mean necessarily and unavoidably an existing among other existents as though the latter were beings-placed-before-us.

It is on this point that existentialism paid the price of being a European thought that arose from a crisis, not only of thought but of daily life—let us not forget that it developed between the two World Wars—though it remained immersed in this critical cycle.

On the other hand, Freire, assuming this slope of a way of thought that thinks itself out, modifies it from the perspective of his optimism, the fruit of his Latin American environment as reality on the verge of blooming. He modifies it by incorporating all the Teilhardian (i.e., Teilhard de Chardin[5]) undercurrent of hominization and, basically, through the very significant recurrence—in its main features—of the personalist thought of Emmanuel Mounier, who is raised up as the great critic of existential thinking, all the while professing that very way of thinking.

Freire (1972a) shows that a human being "exists in and with the world" (p. 51). Freire begins by telling us that human beings are a being of relations and not only of contacts with the world (the human being as "situated and dated"—as expressed by Gabriel Marcel[6])—or being-in-a-situation—as Karl Jaspers[7] would put it, and as such admires (i.e., "looks at") that world, being, at once, a transformer of that world, of nature, of his or her own person, and of history.

Concerning this, Freire (1968b) says, "Because he admires the world and therefore objectifies it, because he grasps and comprehends reality and transforms it with his action—reflection, man is a being of praxis. Still there is more; man is praxis . . . his ontological vocation, which he ought to put into existence, is that of a subject which operates and transforms the world. By being forced to yield to concrete conditions that transform him into an object, man will be sacrificing his basic vocation. . . . Nobody is if he prevents others from being" (p. 18).

But because humanization for Freire is a process of dialectic and intersubjective relationship, it is in this process that the truly human can come to be plundered (as the product of labor is plundered in Marxist thought). Why? Because intersubjective mediation can be altered by prescription: A consciousness prescribes the human limits of the other.

And yet this plundering remains unpunished. It remains unpunished since there are men and women who cannot manage to say their piece because there are others who prevent them from being. The oppressor (the prohibitive consciousness) arrogates to himself the right to be the only humanity—humanization by what one has and not by what one is. Moreover, for this oppressor consciousness, it is not a question of crime, but of logical action, because oppressors are only in accordance with what they have, and if they were to start losing some of their possessions, they would start to lose some of their humanity.

Now, what happens to the victim? The prohibited, prescribed consciousness does not cry out in protest of the plundering but rather awaits its chance. Very often it keeps stored within itself the values of the prohibitive consciousness and hence only awaits the opportunity to be able to have in order to be. It is a *dual* consciousness.

It is also a *fatalist* consciousness: If other people reduce it to the status of thing, it seeks to adapt itself, drawing its identity from the function they have assigned to it. Within the relational sphere of this consciousness there exists a myth that was also prescribed for it and that is found strongly rooted there: The prohibited consciousness is clearly inferior to the owner of the hacienda or boss (who is seen as the symbol of culture, power, and order). Thus, in the final account, this consciousness is also *magical* because it cannot control its alienating experiences. Therefore, Freire, in the same manner as existential philosophers, upon deepening his reflection on human experience, conceives it as a project to be carried out, as words about to be spoken. Authentic existence is a painful tension between the struggle for personalization and the risk of alienation. Freire's concrete referential situation leads him to propose a demystifying education, one that reveals the trappings of the oppressor (not only in its specific forms at the educational level, but also at a social and preponderantly political level). Announcing his hope in the new man and woman, he denounces the plundering of their humanity by the oppressors. Thus, for Freire—the educator par excellence—education fulfils, within this process of annunciation-denunciation, a well-defined role. It has as its mission "cultural action for freedom and therefore an act of knowing and not of memorization" (Freire, 1972a, p. 13).

At this level, the anthropological concept of culture used by Freire is very important: For Freire, *culture* is the systematic acquisition of human experience. Knowing is equivalent to modifying. Freire identifies here with the personalist concept of culture. Let us, once again, examine Mounier's (1952) view on the matter: "Culture is not one sector, but a comprehensive function of the personal life. For a being who finds himself, and forms himself by a process of development, everything is culture, the management of a factory or the formation of a body no less than the conduct of a conversation or the cultivation of the soil. That is to say there is not *a* culture, in distinction from which every other activity is uncultured (a 'cultured man') but there are as many kinds of culture as of activity" (p. 118).

The realization by the person in the process of acquiring literacy of his cultural "making" is deeply transforming and dramatic. For that reason, the discussions of the existential situations designed by Freire, in his psychosocial method regarding the concepts of nature and culture, lead the person who is acquiring literacy to recognize his or her own human condition and furnish him or her with indispensable tools to begin on the critical existential path.

Consequently, Freire assumes the crucial theme of existentialism—the situation of contemporary men and women—and reinterprets this situation in light of the Latin American experience whence the pedagogy of the oppressed emerges.

PHENOMENOLOGY: ITS INFLUENCE IN PAULO FREIRE

> *Viewing dialogue as a process of openly negotiated meaning and value has a close kinship with a metatheory about how generalizable moral values can be identified and justified.*
>
> *(Burbules, 1993, p. 13).*

Phenomenology is, above all, a meditation on knowledge. As such, it puts consciousness face-to-face with the phenomena and appears, thus, as consciousness of the given. The most significant representative of this tendency and, to a great extent, its initiator, is Edmund Husserl[8] who, at the turn of the 20th century, published his *Logical Investigations*, thus generating a new philosophical direction.

As Julio de Santa Ana (1974) says so well: "The initiator of this tendency, the German philosopher Edmund Husserl indicated in his works that it is not possible to separate consciousness from the world of life. Man and nature are co-participants in the constant re-creation and reinterpretation of the world, one making itself felt more strongly on the other and viceversa. Consciousness goes towards the world: it tends to recognize it, dominate it, imagine it, and plan its future. In this manner, it progressively creates the instruments that allow consciousness to know the world, thereby extending the radius of human culture. Husserl sticking close to Brentano[9] on this point, then speaks of the intentionality of consciousness: consciousness thus tends to set out towards the world, towards things, towards the creating of new beings, towards the level of imaginations. Brentano understood intentionality as the specific characteristic of psychic phenomena inasmuch as they all refer to an immanent object. In such a fashion, representation is intentional insofar as it makes an object present; so is judgment, because it affirms or negates the object or one of its qualities; and, lastly, so is sentiment because it refers to beloved or despised objects" (p. 39).

Consciousness, if it does have an individual dimension in human beings, is a social product. It is constituted in such intimate interaction with objective reality that we might come to wonder: What is consciousness? But in order to avoid falling into overly aprioristic and not always useful definitions, let us define, in the first instance, the historical possibilities of consciousness according to Freire's original analyses.

Psychological (individual) consciousness carries out a movement toward things, toward objective reality, with the purpose of knowing them, while things, in turn, calling out to this psychological consciousness, challenges it. This is because things are not presented in their immediacy but are covered in a patina (what Karel Kosic calls the "pseudoconcrete quality").[10]

The essence of things—and let us not forget that phenomenology was defined initially as an eidetic science—is alternately manifested and shown in the phenomenon of those very things. This two-way movement of consciousness toward things and of things toward consciousness shapes one moment of the process of knowledge.

A short digression can allow us to avoid a wrong interpretation. Husserl, still overly influenced by Platonism, postulated a phenomenological reduction. If in the *Logical Investigations* (1970), it appeared as the simple suspension of the judgment of existence, in the *Cartesian Meditations* (1999) it seems like a real *doubt.* From this, such a reduction led Husserl toward a transcendental idealism, in contrast to his students Max Scheller[11] and Nicolai Hartmann[12] who, when considering the phenomenological reduction as simple abstention from taking any kind of a position with regard to the transcendental, believe they are not opposed to *realism.* It is important, then, to clear away this initial unknown. If there is in Freire a marked phenomenological influence, there in no way exists a reduction of the transcendental being to the purely intentional being of consciousness.

Let us now return to consider the perspective of the process of knowledge. The first movement or historical possibility of consciousness is denominated—according to what has already been said—as *intentionality*. Consciousness is always about something, about some object; it is always sensed projected toward the outside, toward the "other." This first possibility is ground-laying at the genetic level, since it cannot remain there paraphrasing Hegel,[13] taking appropriate license—even at risk of being left for lost in the world of objects.

The second historical possibility or movement is that consciousness transforms the "thing in itself" into an object of knowledge. We will denominate this second possibility as *objectivity*. In this moment, consciousness carries out an inventory of the objects surrounding it: It is descriptive. We would still be in the domain of the *doxa* or opinion and not in that of the *episteme*—that is, the level of "vulgar" understanding of reality without yet having arrived at the threshold of Science.

A third historical possibility that unfailingly presupposes the other two is *criticality*. Here, the consciousness scans the identified "thing in itself" in an effort to know its internal components. It is no longer only simple identification and recognition—the level of objectification—but rather tends toward discovering the laws of the development of the object. This moment is qualitatively superior to the previous ones.

Finally, *transcendentality* constitutes a fourth possibility. Concerning this, Freire (1972a) says: "Transcendence in this context signifies the capacity of human consciousness to surpass the limitations of the objective configuration. Without this 'transcendental intentionality' consciousness of what exists beyond limitations would be impossible. For example I am aware of how the table at which I write limits me—only because I can transcend its limits and focus my attention upon its limits" (p. 52).

This transcendentality in no way resembles vertical transcendentality, which directs its explanatory effort outside of the material and concrete universe, in search of an infinite beyond. This transcendentality, on the other hand, is eminently "finite," an unfailing property and characteristic trait of the human being. Their finiteness allows human beings to seek the tendential laws of the development of the phenomenon at the same time that the consciousness grasps the internal components of the object. That is, human beings grasp the laws of development, as phenomenon, just as much as they grasp the phenomenon's inherent contradictions, and also capture the material immediacy and pure essentiality in their tendential forms. If we were to express this metaphorically, we would say that the consciousness tends to capture the life of the object and its destiny.

Only in this last level of maximum qualitative consummation is consciousness able to operate on the phenomenon in order to transform it, given that, upon knowing its direction and tendential legality, it will establish a historically viable transformation and will not tend toward mutating the object (be it a historical process, a cultural situation, a philosophical relation, a method of teaching literacy, and so on).

To summarize, the first historical possibility, *intentionality*, marks genetically the effort of consciousness to express the moment of knowledge, going outside of itself (abstract); the second moment, or *objectivity*, converts the object into an object-of-knowledge; the third moment or historical possibility, *criticality*, discovers the internal components of the object-of-knowledge and expresses it in concepts, to arrive at the fourth moment or historical possibility, *transcendentality*, which captures the internal movement of the object-of-knowledge in its fundamental components and in its contradictions in such a way as to facilitate the projection of a "rational" action—praxis—that does not affect the object as such (it does not mutate it), whereas, in turn, it is a historically viable action.

Paulo Freire assumes these elements of phenomenology but relates them to the dialectics of the consciousness to the social structure. Concerning this relationship, he says: "As men act upon the world effectively, transforming it by their work, their consciousness is in turn historically and culturally conditioned. . . . According to the quality of this conditioning, men's consciousness attains various levels in the context of cultural historical reality" (Freire, 1972a, pp. 56–67).

Hence, the historical possibilities of consciousness invite Freire to reflect upon the degrees of possible consciousness, relating them to the social structure or historico-cultural context. César Jerez and Juan Hernández Pico (1971) have synthesized in a brilliant manner this essential relation of Freirean thought: "In Latin America Freire distinguishes three types of socio-cultural historical contexts; closed societies, societies in the process of transition, and open societies. A different type of consciousness corresponds to each one of them: semi-intransitive, or submerged consciousness; unaffectedly transitive, or emergent consciousness; and critically transitive, or committed consciousness. Moreover, there exists the massified society, which open societies, as much as those in transition are at risk of becoming, either through degeneration or through abortive growth. The irrational (or fanatic) consciousness corresponds to this last type of massified society, which Freire also calls a floating one" (p. 508).

Defining the characteristics of the semi-intransitive consciousness, Freire (1972a) says: "There is a mode of consciousness which corresponds to the concrete reality of such dependent societies. It is a consciousness historically conditioned by the social structure. The principal characteristic of this consciousness, as dependent as the society to whose structure it conforms, is its 'quasi-adherence' to objective reality. . . . [The] dominated consciousness does not have sufficient distance from reality to objectify it in order to know it in a critical way. We call this mode of consciousness 'semi-transitive' . . ." (p. 62).

The second level of possible consciousness has been denominated as *transitive naïve* consciousness that "is characterized, among other aspects, by simplicity in the interpretation of problems; by the tendency to judge that the better time was the past time; by the underestimation of the common man; by a strong inclination towards gregarianism, characteristic of massification; by impermeability to research, to which corresponds a heightened taste for fabulous explanations; by fragility in argumentation; by a strong emotional fear; by the practice not exactly of dialogue but rather of polemics; by magical explanations" (Freire, 1973d, p. 82).

The last phase of consciousness is represented by the *transitive-critical consciousness* that, being the immediate opposite of the previous one, obtains a structural perception of problems resulting from its (committed) critical insertion in the process of transformation (social change). Freire uses Goldmann's concept here, by which consciousness would attain its antithesis, which is the *maximum consciousness possible* (Goldman, discussed by Freire in 1972c, p. 84).

Freire describes the characteristic points of this consciousness in *La educación como práctica de la libertad* (Freire, 1976a), the main one being according to his conception—and returning again to the existential slope—the capacity for dialogue. This consciousness, on all its characteristic points, progresses toward political consciousness because only such a consciousness can make possible the so-called "untested feasibility," when consciousness is confronted with the extreme situation.

This consciousness is, according to Freire, a consciousness of totality, since only in this fashion can it come to be liberating: "Only the consciousness of totality is liberating. Without it, it is impossible to be able to act upon reality" (Freire, 1972c , p. 40). Incorporating the elements of phenomenology, Freire understands that consciousness is constituted as an intended totality which symbolizes-signifies temporally.

Hence, conscientization exceeds in amplitude the phenomenon of individual psychological consciousness: "It is phenomenon that goes beyond psychological consciousness (Freud's *uber-ich*), beyond the same individual consciousness and it touches fully upon historical and collective consciousness, that is, the so-called field of intersubjectivity" (Adames, 1971, p. 206).

Here, it now makes sense to refer to conscientization in Freire. Let us use, for this purpose, a short and concise text in which the author synthesizes the epistemological content of the concientization phenomenon: "If conscientization cannot be realized without the revelation of objective reality, as an object of knowledge for those subjects involved in the process, then this revelation—even when it may be a clearer perception of reality—is still not sufficient for an authentic conscientization. In the same way that the epistemological cycle does not end at the level of acquisition of extant knowledge, but continues through the stage of creation of new knowledge, neither can conscientization be stalled at the level of the revelation of reality. It is authentic when the practice of revealing reality constitutes a dynamic and dialectic unity with the practice of transforming reality" (Freire & Illich, 1975, p. 28). We will return to this point later. Mainly, though not solely, from the perspective of phenomenology, Paulo Freire constructed the levels of consciousness and action of contemporary human beings.

MARXIST THOUGHT: ITS INFLUENCE IN PAULO FREIRE

In place of the old bourgeois society, with its classes and class antagonisms, we shall have an association, in which the free development of each is the condition for the free development of all.

(Communist Manifesto, quoted by Maximilian Rubel [1973], Marx theoretician of anarchism, http://www.marxists.org/archive/rubel/1973/marx-anarchism.htm).

Paulo Freire's initial contact with dialectical materialism starts from the influence that Herbert Marcuse and Erich Fromm, from a "humanist" stance, albeit with the Marxist conceptual apparatus, had on his early works.[14]

It is not a coincidence, then, that both Marcuse and Fromm bring about, from their reading of the *Manuscripts*, an abridged version of "concrete humanism," as rediscovered in Marx. Marcuse is strongly felt in Freire with his analyses of negative reason in industrialized societies and the phenomenon of massification. Fromm's analyses of "thingification" and psychological freedom can be noticed in Freire, especially with his arguments on democracy as political context.

It is also possible to find in the initial work of Freire the influence of the Marx of the *Manuscripts*, especially in the analyses that discuss the educator and alienation in language. Let see how Freire himself connects certain themes of his thought with the analyses of historical materialism.

This can be done by comparing a comment of Freire's and one of Marx's. In *Extension o comunicación*, Freire (1973b) says: "If truly solipsism is in error by conceiving the lone existence of the Ego, and by pretending that its consciousness grasps everything, considering it absurd to think of a reality external to it, a critical and mechanicist objectivism, grossly materialistic, also is in error, for according to it, in the final analysis, reality would transform itself without the involvement of men, mere objects of the transformation" (p. 85).

He contrasts this with the third Thesis on Feuerbach, where Marx says: "The materialistic doctrine concerning the changing of circumstances and education forgets that circumstances are changed by men and that the educator himself must be educated."

Paulo Freire does not postulate a neutral science nor a neutral education. His analyses of the relationship between pedagogy and politics show, congruently and concurrently, autonomy and dependence in their development and practice.

Politics is mentioned as the concrete sphere of the realization of what is human, which, through its collective aspirations shaped in action, floods the sphere of what is individual and, in the same manner, is intertwined with the spheres of knowledge.

Education forms subjects for a specific society, for the assumption of specific values. For Freire, education is not a process of manipulation, but, at the same time, neither does it have the ingenuous aspiration of bringing to light an objective, technical, neutral and apolitical educational act. Freire's realism is absolute in this aspect: Education is not the lever for social change. It conditions and at the same time is conditioned by the society from which it emerges. It expresses and at the same time is expressed by the politics that it assumes. Every intentional act is, in a broad sense, a political act.

> Educational practice is part of the superstructure of any society. For that reason, educational practice, in spite of its fantastic importance in the sociohistorical processes of the transformation of societies, is not in itself the key to transformation, even if it is fundamental. Dialectically, education is not the key to transformation, but transformation is, in itself, educational. (Freire in Torres, 1998d, pp. 103–104)

Education has, as cultural action, only two possibilities: Either it assumes the role of domestication, that is, education that advocates the prohibiting consciousness, or it assumes that of liberator—education that shapes the prohibited consciousness.

Paulo Freire's political thought, set out in his earliest writings, is eminently socialist. Nevertheless, he was frequently criticized for not making explicit in a theoretical manner all the dimensions of a socialist education. Thus, Freire recognizes, when referring to the *Pedagogy of the Oppressed*, that:

> For instance, in relation to the fourth chapter in which I clearly set forth the political dimension of education (I do not think that anybody can criticize me for the fact that I spoke of neutral education), it is impossible that, upon making the critique of what appear to constitute the characteristics of a domesticating cultural action and the counter-position that upon criticizing, for example, manipulation, cultural invasion, etc., I would be agreeable in recognizing that I need more experiences with Marx. (Freire in Torres, 1978a, p. 57)

That is, Paulo Freire began to investigate and exercise an educational practice, united by a specific philosophical formation. In this cultural philosophical baggage specifically, the preponderant elements are, in the first instance, existentialism and phenomenology as well as the criteria of a Judeo-Christian anthropology that are situated in these beginnings and that continue to accompany the author on his intellectual pilgrimage—Chapters 7 and 8 will dwell on Freire's political anthropology of education.

Hegelian dialectic would form part of this initial conceptual nucleus. Prevailing for the most part in his basic work the *Pedagogy of the Oppressed*, Freire's Hegelian underpinnings were evident. Nevertheless, his constant interaction with reality and his educational experiences developed initially in Brazil, Chile, and Africa continuously tested Freire's thought, on par with the fact that such factors also forced him to increase his effort toward theoretical characterization, incorporating in a major way, within his whole philosophical context, the analysis of historical materialism.

Undoubtedly, his most important analysis is the characterization of social classes, not only as a descriptive category but already as an analytical category indispensable for social processes:

> The traditionalist churches alienate the oppressed social classes by encouraging them to view the world as evil. The modernizing churches alienate them in a different way: by defending the reforms that maintain the status quo. By reducing such expressions as *humanism* and *humanization* into abstract categories, the modern churches empty them of any real meaning. Such phrases become mere slogans whose only contribution is to serve the reactionary forces. (Freire, 1985, p. 136)

Returning to the strictly philosophical level, the most important concept, but also the one that acquires here the greatest complexity in Freire, is the concept of social alienation. The process of social alienation is linked with the consciousness-ideology dialectic. In order to avoid discussing Marxism in detail, despite the fact that when Freire wrote *Education as the Practice of Freedom* and *Pedagogy of the Oppressed* Marxism was the theoretical template dominant in the region, I refer the reader to Freire's own analysis in the fresh expression of oral interviews (Torres Novoa, 1978a). To summarize, by incorporating different theoretical concepts of historical and dialectical materialism, Paulo Freire analyzes the situation of contemporary human beings and how people constitute their consciousness and how they confront the perils of social alienation.

HEGELIAN PHILOSOPHY: ITS INFLUENCE IN PAULO FREIRE

> *And it is solely by risking life that freedom is obtained... The individual who has not staked his life may, no doubt, be recognized as a person; but he has not attained the truth of this recognition as an independent self-consciousness.*
>
> *(Hegel, 1967 p. 233)*

Hegel distinguishes four situations: In the first, the subject (understood as reason) is found to be affirming itself as the Universal Abstract (the situation of the Mind before leaving its own realm), but as it will only come to the full possession of itself through the objective world, it brings about a departure from its own realm, a flux toward the object (nature). This flux or exteriorization causes the Mind to negate itself as such, and it loses itself in the world of objects (a world defined as specific and concrete). This allows its prior situation to be modified into this second one, by which the negation of the Universal Abstract through the exteriorization of the Subject in Nature produces an estrangement of that Subject. It is here that is generated the moment of the consciousness of the subject that, outside of itself, recognizes others that are not the same as itself.

The third situation is the existential risk of the subject. Estrangement implies a most serious risk for the consciousness: alienation. Being lost in the world of objects, having become a thing: "The world of objects, originally a product of work and of the knowledge of man, becomes independent of it and comes to be governed by uncontrollable forces and laws in which man no longer recognizes himself. At the same time, thought becomes alien to reality and truth; it is converted into a powerless ideal preserved in thought, while the real world remains quietly outside the reach of its influence. Unless man manages to reunite the different parts of that world and place nature and society within the reach of his reason, he will forever be condemned to frustration. The task of philosophy in this period of his general disintegration is to demonstrate the principle capable of restoring the lost unity and totality.This alienation (*Entfremdüng*) is the opposite of its appropriation" (Marcuse, 1967, pp. 25–26).

The following situation shows consciousness making an effort toward reflux, returning toward itself, negating in turn this situation of exteriority and even "thingification." But now the subject that returns from the world of things (in principle, the world of concrete specifics) does not return to the abstraction of its initial affirmation, but as returns as Universal (which is a communicable attribute of the Subject) and concrete (Universal Concrete).

Thus, Hegelian dialectic is the rational construction of reality, by which the subject progressively assimilates its vital experience until it finds itself with its own self by determinate negation. Hegel foresaw that the Subject would only appropriate things for itself (basic property), but that it could arrive at the point of appropriating other subjects for itself, too (the struggle of opposed consciousnesses). When the conflict between two self-consciousnesses (the consciousness that had left itself and was for itself) that fought to appropriate the same good was established, the road to a solution was a pact in which one of the two consciousnesses submitted itself to the other so as not to die. There arose in this fashion an independent consciousness and a dependent consciousness (dependent on the former): in classical terms, the Master and the Slave (Torres, 1976a, 1976b).

Let us quote a dense paragraph of Hegel's, which will allow us to compare his dialectic with some elements of Freirean dialectic. In his *Phenomenology of the Mind*, Hegel (1931) says: "[The master] is thus not assured of self-existence as his truth; he finds that his truth is rather the unessential consciousness, and the fortuitous unessential action of that consciousness. The truth of the independent consciousness is accordingly the consciousness of the bondman. This doubtless appears in the first instance outside itself, and not as the truth of self-consciousness. But just as lordship showed its essential nature to be the reverse of what it wants to be, so, too, bondage will, when completed, pass into the opposite of what it immediately is: being a consciousness repressed within itself, it will enter into itself, and change round into real and true independence" (p. 237).

Let us contrast this with the central definition of the *Pedagogy of the Oppressed*: "The pedagogy of the oppressed, animated by authentic, humanist (not humanitarian) generosity, presents itself as a pedagogy of man" (Freire, 1973e, p. 53). Why can it alone attain this objective? Because early in his work Freire states: "This, then, is the great humanistic and historical task of the oppressed: to liberate themselves and their oppressors as well" (p. 39).

The historical process brings man and woman face-to-face with tasks and challenges that, starting from their own reality, lead them to carry out a mediating movement, which, when it takes on the riches of the instant, displays a winning, qualitative leap, conserving the best of the "human" past to fertilize the action of the present—where conscientization is not only knowledge or intersubjective recognition, but also option and compromise—and in this way to be projected toward a future of men and women in search of sharing the truth among the whole community without exception.

There will then be only one pedagogy, that of the oppressed, restorer of the humanity of both the oppressor and the oppressed. This double restoration, in the same liberating act, indicates the presence of the Hegelian supposition by which consciousness, in itself, is wanting of the consciousness of itself and for itself, while the latter only recognizes itself as such through the former, which in its relationship with nature gives it the possibility of being proprietor (of the good that the consciousness in itself toils over) and owner (of the slave, in itself, that toils in nature).

For this reason, just where the center of power of the Master would appear to be (property-possession) we find rooted his greatest weakness—that is, his immediate need for the slave (consciousness in itself). Meanwhile, this weakness is not completely overlooked by the slave, since servitude is self-consciousness in Hegel's way of thinking and this self-consciousness can start the road toward class consciousness. The muting between class consciousness and critical consciousness is the last step of conscientization.

The philosopher Ernani Maria Fiori, who wrote the prologue to Freire's *Pedagogy of the Oppressed* (1973e), affirms: "*Pedagogy of the Oppressed* is, then, liberator of both the oppressed and the oppressor. We would say in a Hegelian manner that the truth of the oppressor resides in the consciousness of the oppressed" (p. 11).

The *Pedagogy of the Oppressed* possesses two instances: In the first instance, the oppressed bring about a change of perception; they choose to leave the culture of domination. This first instance has, in turn, two complementary movements: (1) the oppressed reveal the world of oppression and (2) they establish a commitment by means of praxis.

In the second instance, once the myths created in the oppressing structure are expelled, Freire (1973e) suggests that "pedagogy of the oppressed ceases to belong to the oppressed and becomes a pedagogy of all men in the process of permanent liberation" (p. 32).

This second instance implies, with respect to Hegel, the passage from abstract reason (as oppressed consciousness) to liberating praxis (as negation of the oppressed consciousness), and finally, to the negation of the negation (or synthesis), the new reason or complex reason—as consciousness in the search for liberation in the context of a revolutionary project.

It remains for us to express the meaning of magical consciousness for Freire (1972c), who says, in this respect, that "this culture of silence, characteristic of our colonial past, a culture that continues stuck in conditions favorable to the possession of land in Latin America has constituted the peasant consciousness, historically and culturally, as a servile consciousness, in the expression of Hegel" (p. 82).

Hegelian dialectic, then, allows Freire (as a historical anticipation) to postulate the dialectic of the oppressed–oppressors. The anthropological dimensions of this dialectic prevail over the positivity of the determinate negation (Torres, 2009a, Chapter V).[15]

The end of the road for Hegel was Absolute Knowledge. On the other hand, Freire—speaking from another historical situation and with qualitatively different material—rejects the Hegelian ideological structure while keeping part of its dialectical method and establishes the critical path of a consciousness that becomes critical through the re-existentiation of his or her world.

After this long journey through the political philosophy of Freire, let us present a synthesis of Freire's philosophy.

1. Freire starts from the supposition that education is not changed by changing the social relations with educational institutions and that education does not provoke social change, either. Education is only modified in a revolutionary way once the relationships of social power are altered in an equally revolutionary way. Thus, the preferable way to carry out popular education is on the interstices of the educational system and has as its essential trait the task of constituting itself into educational work brought about with the popular sectors in the process of their organization.
2. Inasmuch as education has a defined class option and class horizon, and inasmuch as pedagogy has a name and is called "the pedagogy of the oppressed," then Freire's philosophy of education challenges the rule of capital and is truly libertarian; that is contestatary of the established banking educational praxis.
3. In its foundations, the Freirean proposal seeks to bring about a break in dualisms, such as subject–object, consciousness–reality, thought–being, and in effect, theory–practice, by looking to reestablish their dialectical unity. Thus, insofar as Freire's political philosphy of education is mostly an analysis on the consciousness–ideology relationship, it suggests that consciousness is not only a copy or reflection of reality.

That is not to say that consciousness is a temperamental construct of reality, either. This contributes greatly to understanding the role carried out by consciousness (subjective conditions) in the processes of social transformation.

4. In this way, the process of conscientization appears as one of the most important processes of demythification of the ideological practices of the dominant classes. On the one hand, characterizing these practices (e.g., authoritarianism within the school, the separation of manual work and intellectual work, and so forth) as banking education outlines a significant watershed in pedagogical terms. On the other hand, the practice of popular education situates itself as the point of rupture and generator of contradictions and imbalances in the educational system. The practice of popular education has a crucial importance in undermining the hierarchical ideological-scholastic mechanisms of social reproduction as instruments of the hegemony of the dominant sectors. Freire is very clear when he argues that: "Conscientization is never a kind of aspirin which we give or prescribe to the oppressed people. That is as if for example, I could sell twenty pills for the oppressed and twenty-five for the oppressors. The pills of conscientization and then they get better tomorrow. No, no, it is not a medicine. It is an exercise of understanding much more rigorously how society works. This is the task of knowing, education as a process of knowing" (Freire in Torres 1995e, p. 177).
5. Hence, in the first Freire the process that initiates conscientization is the passage from the consciousness of the necessity of class (or class instinct), where the dominated sectors are spontaneously found, to the level of "class consciousness," which is only arrived at by means of a concrete, political, educational action where the "organic-intellectual" of the subordinate classes and the political parties of the working class have a precise educational responsibility.

In essence, the political philosophy of Freire emerges as an educational philosophy and an anti-authoritarian educational practice that postulates a breakdown in the educator–pupil dichotomy by reestablishing democratic horizontality. Starting from the discussion of "generating themes," this breakdown gives rise to a confrontation of the dominated consciousness with its own existential reality. It revolves around the notion of oppression as an "ontological" characteristic of the Latin American social being—though this ontological characteristic cannot be restricted only to developing societies. *Pedagogy of the Oppressed* becomes another educational tool in the process of the political organization of the subordinate social sectors (Freire, 1977).

FOUR

Education as the Practice of Freedom

The most important weapon in the hands of oppressor is the mind of the oppressed.
(Steve Biko, cited in Gibson, 2011, p. 210).

Freirean discourse begins by establishing the central relationship of all philosophy, the relationship between thinking and being: "we understand that for a human, the world is an objective reality, independent of himself, possible to be known. Nevertheless, it is fundamental to begin with the idea that human is a being of relationships and not just of contacts. Not only is he in the world, he is with the world" (Freire, 1976a, p. 28). As understood through Freire, human beings represent "relational beings" living a plurality within their own singularity, and with their own share of criticism. This insertion in the world does not come to humans from immanence. On the contrary, because our ability to understand and our consciousness, we humans retain the potential for a higher or more profound existence: "His transcendence, to us, is also rooted in his finitude, in his consciousness of this finitude, of the incompleteness of his being whose plenitude is found in union with his Creator. A union that by its very essence, will never be one of domination or of domestication, but always one of liberty" (Freire, 1976a, p. 29).

This Freirean affirmation, with its deep theological meaning, is interwoven with a second, equally profound affirmation, that of the liberating value of a non-alienated religion: "Precisely because he is finite and indigent, human has, in his transcendence though love, the possibility of returning to his source which frees him" (Freire, 1976a, p. 29). Here, we encounter Freire's first anthropological option, in which humans transcend their finitude in union with their creator. It is a religious thought—in this case, via an anthropologically Christian base.[1]

But for Freire, humans are not outside of time, for they remain in all ways temporal. "In the history of his culture one of his first perceptions will be that of time—that of the dimensionality of time . . ." (Freire, 1976a, p. 30). Humans can only acquire their temporal category emerging from their time; that is why it is said that human beings are within time and also that they are outside of it, that they are "wet with it." It would appear that the discovery of the dimensionality of time and its subsequent objectification allows a human to begin to walk the path of liberation.

But are humans self-constituted by their own affirmation, or are they the fruit of an effort—the "patience of reason," and/or of a process? Humans live a daily drama—the permanent struggle for their humanization—and that is why the integration or communion with their context is crucial. "His integration to his context—the result of his being *with* it as well as *in* it, and not the simple adaptation, accommodation or adjustment, behaviors proper to the sphere of contacts and symptom of his dehumanization—implies that both his vision of himself and of the world cannot be made absolute and at the same time cause him to feel unadjusted or helpless. His integration establishes it" (Freire, 1976a, p. 31).

So then, what does Freire (1976a) mean by "integration"? In a footnote, he defines it: "Integration comes from the ability to adjust oneself to reality rather than transforming it, that is joined to the ability to choose, whose fundamental note is critical. To the extent that a human being loses the ability to choose and submits himself to foreign prescriptions which minimize him, his decisions are no longer his own because they come from alien orders and are no longer integral. He accommodates, he adjusts" (p. 31).

In other words, the integration with reality is not a process that lasts only one unit of time, one moment. For humans, integration is a gradual process of becoming that constitutes a determining factor of their consciousness, one they keep attaining in this process.

From this personal experience of the human being, the struggle for humanization, Freire (1976a) yields to the immediate product, to the story put into motion: "to the extent that he creates, recreates and decides the historical eras take shape . . . [a]nd it will make him better each time he appropriates one of life's fundamental themes by integrating himself with its spirit and recognizes his concrete tasks" (p. 33).

In this process that is at once ontological and historical, Freire (1976a) highlights one of modern human's greatest tragedies, that "dominated by the power of myths and driven by organized publicity, ideological or not, he increasingly and unconsciously renounces his ability to decide. He is being expelled from the decision-making orbit." But an "ordinary human being does not grasp the essential tasks of his time, they are presented to him by an elite which interpellates them and delivers them to him in the form of recipes, prescriptions to be followed" (p. 33).

This is one of the first of Freire's "social" insinuations—the danger of massification, or another that for him is just as nefarious, that of alienation. As a provisional cure for these maladies, Freire suggests the need for a permanently critical attitude. According to Freire, following Rumanian philosopher Zevedei Barbu, all humans must become integrated with their time, they must grasp these developmental tasks and perform them, and they increasingly have to exercise their intellectual functions and develop their intellectual probity in order to become less dependent on the purely instinctive and emotional.

Freire (1976a) begins to reflect about his own situation, that of his contemporary Brazil in the 1950s and 1960s, saying in a metaphorical way: "In this shock between a disintegrating yesterday that desires to be permanent and a consubstantiating tomorrow that characterizes the passing of an annunciatory time, it is possible to attest to the highly dramatic tone of the changing of the guard of those who promote the society" (p. 36).

Freire then puts forth his thick description of Brazil and its historical trajectory as a society. Cultural alienation marks the nature of the colonial society. A society that rather than becoming a reflexive society develops a cultural atmosphere involving the same elite who assume an alienated and alienating task, distanced from its people and superimposed on, rather than rooted in, its reality.[2]

What is the role of the Brazilian people, faced with this particular historical-cultural process? Are they immersed in the process or are they dialogically unconnected to this elite that only cares about importing economic, politico-cultural models and making sure its mandates are obeyed by this reified people? It is an imagistic society, one that does not know itself, a "closed society."

But times change and the solidified forms of society fall apart and begin to spread the seed of interests other than those of this society of images. New themes arise; the society begins to transform itself into a society "in transit toward. . . ." Old themes are redefined; there is a great dynamism in the whole process, but its course is not totally determined. In other words, Brazil may be on its way toward an open society or it may run the risk of becoming a mass society, detaching itself from the critical spirit.

With the passing of history, the meaning of education in theory and practice has also changed; its meaning rebounds in the impulse that it gives to people to become part of this voyage, seeking understanding of their own identities and societal development. Completing his thoughts about the society that is starting to age, Freire outlines on different occasions the fundamental characteristics of the "closed society." This sketch serves to locate us, as pedagogues, at our starting point at the beginning of the voyage.

As measurable aspects of a "closed society," we find that the center of decision about its economy is controlled by an external market; it is basically an exporter of prime materials inasmuch as its growth comes "from outside." This paradigm reflects on both the economy and the culture, which together are alienated and alienating, making the search for meaning and identity even more cumbersome. It is a society without People's power and People's freedom and antidialogical, which makes vertical social mobility difficult. It has a precarious urban life, a high rate of illiteracy, and a ruling elite that governs and retains power from a superimposed rather than an integrated position.

This sociological vision of Freire's seems to reflect the central characteristics of a colonized society, a dependent capitalistic society. It is this colonial situation in its theoretical conceptualization that helps Freire determine the historical roots of alienation, its sociohistorical enclave.

In terms of the mechanisms that provoke the destruction of the closed Brazilian society, Freire concludes that it destroyed itself and surmises that the rupture of the powers that maintained its equilibrium were an important factor in this destruction, especially the economic alterations that arose around the turn of the 20th century.

Following this widescreen view of society, the sociohistorical background in which his pedagogical experiments begin, Freire begins to reflect meticulously about human behavior and the kind of response Brazilians give as they confront this process marked by its profound contradictions. And because this is eminently dialectical, he never allows us a glimpse of the final horizon as he goes from one new horizon to the other. Freire verifies two antagonistic types of attitudes: on the one hand, flatly rejecting progress while intending to return to the past, and on the other, accepting this particular transit and its emerging tasks.

Freire insists that humans and institutions both assume one of the two attitudinal positions but that, given the characteristics of the transit itself, there are also intermediate categories. He outlines an instrumental dichotomy that tries to be the beginning of a truly structural analysis.[3]

But the historical process crushes humans' expectations because not everyone is prepared to deal with it in all its magnitude. Contradictions determine two very different forms of dealing with this commitment to reality: (1) Radicalization, Freire (1976a) argues, "implies the rootedness of people who choose this option. It is positive because it is preponderantly critical. Critical and loving, humble and communicative. People who take the radical option, do not deny others the right to choose. Nor do they impose their choices, preferring to dialogue about them. They are convinced they are right but they respect others' rights to believe that they too know the truth; they try to convince and convert, but they do not oppress their opponents; they are duty-bound, through love, to respond with violence to those who attempt to keep them silent." And (2) sectarianism: "[which] has a preponderantly emotional and acritical matrix, is arrogant, anti-dialogical and therefore anti-communicative"(pp. 41–42).

The radical will always be a progressive and the sectarian a reactionary, whether of the right or the left; a "born" sectarian—a leftist sectarian—is the product of an incomplete understanding of the vital process that transmutes the energy of the struggle for justice into dogma.

This is the first indication that Freire was beginning to focus on violence and domination, which would become the crux of his pedagogical work. He believes that all relations of domination, exploitation, and oppression are violent per se. They represent a lack of love, but also an obstacle to love. Now we introduce a qualitatively different aspect in this drama (in the Greek sense) of humanization. The will to power of the bourgeoisie determines how exploitative relations are engendered, and thus signifies a universe of violence. Yet Freire has emphasized countless times—and this is one of the key tenets of *Pedagogy of the Oppressed*—that you are nobody if you prohibit another person from being somebody.

As the immediate result of this relationship between the oppressors and the oppressed, we find that both are dehumanized, not only through excess (the former) or absence of power (the latter), but also because each depends on the alienated relationship with the other to continue being what they are. This is the central problem of the Hegelian dialectic of the Master and the Slave.

Hegel reflects about humans who are positioned to know by their practical historical experience, that is, their world. Their consciousness is defined by this self-conscious and objective world, with the property of recognizing this self-consciousness as conscious of things and among things, thus returning from its exteriorization. But the relationship is not always between an individual and a thing, as we frequently find ourselves in individual-to-individual relationships as well. The only way that either individual can have a true consciousness of themselves is through consciousness of the other individual. In this struggle of opposing consciousness, each individual has to definitively deny the other to be able to achieve their own consciousness as distinct, as him/herself. Nevertheless, this relationship is not a gift but, rather, a *confrontation* (to come to recognize oneself as a distinct other), and that is where the *conflict* arises, in the sense of the philosophical negativity.

Returning to the analysis, as far as the conflict is concerned, there can be no resolution in favor of one of the contenders because that would destroy the very structure of the negativity and make it impossible for the winner to recompose his or her self-consciousness. For this to happen, one of the two consciousnesses must surrender: If the Slave stops struggling so as not to die, his dependence on the Master becomes total, and he thus ceases to be independent. In relating directly to nature and mediating it for his Master, the Slave discovers himself as the Master's immediate necessity. Without his Slave, the Master would possess neither nature nor his slave. It is an alienating relationship that extends to a second alienation, that of the Slave who, in his relationship of appropriating nature, is robbed (by the Master) of the object of his labor. This is the alienation of labor that Marx revisits. When Freire refers to the oppressor–oppressed dialectic, he attempts to express the basic Master–Slave relation of Hegel as a last resort, standing firm in the double Master–Slave/Slave–Master alienation and the alienation of the work of the Slave and, through him or her, in the Master.[4]

The radical considers action but from a reflective position; the sectarian, on the other hand, leans toward activism, or a kind of action without the control of reflection. Freire makes an interesting typology of the two. The radical rejects activism and always submits his action to reflection. Not the sectarian. The radical takes a subjective stance toward the historical process, has a critical attitude and understands its inherent contradictions, and thereby advances steadily toward a more diaphanous, vital, and liberating horizon. On the other hand, the sectarian assumes a "proprietary" position vis-à-vis history, reduces the people to a domestic and malleable mass, and intends to impose his convictions rather than dialoguing about them. Finally, there is the nuance of his provenance; whereas the rightist sectarian would like to detain history, the leftist sectarian wants to anticipate it.

While the radical makes himself at home in the climate of hope that prevails in Brazilian society, because it is ready to overcome the alienation that restricted it as a closed society, the sectarian adapts himself to the climate of violence and reproduces it.

The Brazil Freire considers is ruled by sectarians, especially those on the right. The radicals are confined to some Christian groups (with which Freire himself allied), in certain sectors of the organic left, and in different base organizations (Cândido, 1996; De Kadt, 1970).[5] In all this, the people continue to be immersed but not stagnant, clamoring to participate in the process. Freire makes it clear that participation does not imply a mere raising of consciousness—to agree with obtaining some knowledge and be amazed by new facts and chatter on about these aimlessly—but more pointedly becoming fundamentally aware. He defines this phenomenon as the development of consciousness-raising by moving from self-consciousness per se to being mediated by Hegel's consciousness of Self.

The ruling elite, on the other hand, seeing the dangers that lie in wait for their privileges and social status, gather together in groups and associations; crisis theorists (intellectuals at the service of the wealthy classes) appear; aid-giving and intervention institutions are created, which attempt to ward off requests for the people's participation and denounce foreign ideas as "exotic;" classifying any attempt at participation as subversive of the statutory order.

For the first time the people are referred to in terms of their historical process: "Since the defenders of this kind of 'democracy' claim that it is necessary to preserve the people from what they call 'exotic ideas' which amount to anything that might contribute to the people's active presence in their historical process" (Freire, 1976a, p. 48).

So, are the people present and operative historical subjects? Freire catalogs the historical moment as a highly emotional climate that provokes irrationalism and leads to the augmentation of sectarian positions. In his thesis doctoral (2001, p. 32) Freire confronted the naïve consciousness with the critical consciusness as two historical possibilities in the development of Brazilian society. As defended in his thesis doctoral, Freire focuses on the antinomy that he considers fundamental in his time: the democratic inexperience of Brazil given its colonial past, and the emergence of the people, the *pueblo*, in the political life given the process of urbanization and industrialization that the country was experimenting (2001, p. 51).

The superation of this fundamental antinomy for Freire cannot be achieved unless a democratic education for development can be obtained: "an education for development and for democracy among ourselves, has to be an education through dialogue. An education for the participation, that will develop in the Brasilian man his criticity" (2001, p. 51). Thus the great political-educational challenge for Freire was how to develop the critical consciousness of the people, the *pueblo*.

In the debates in the nascent Theology of Liberation a key controversy was about which theoretical category will anchor this new theology defined by the preferential option for the poor. Many defended the concept of *pueblo* or people with its biblical connotations (the people of Israel) and their liberation. Yet many criticized this category as amorphous, and suggested instead the category of class as an analytical category, and class struggle as a different political strategy. A most prominent intellectual in the movement, Dussel (1985) in his historical analyses concluded that the concept of *pueblo* in the end was the concept adopted by the majority of the fractions in the movement.

To categorize the *people* or *pueblo* in terms of political theory is difficult because *pueblo* seems not to represent a concept that can be rigorously inscribed within the analytical traditions beyond populism and is an ideologically manipulable term. For Paulo Freire at this stage of his theoretical development, this category represents the popular sectors in general (as opposed to the elites). The problem with this terminology is not only that it lacks terminological rigor but could be used as an emblem: the theory of the "people" as the political subject of the revolution. At this moment, Freire is positing the construction of a "fundamental democracy" as the epicenter and immediate objective of all efforts.

As far as he is concerned, this fundamental democratization was impossible to construct unless it was based on responsibility. "That is exactly why responsibility is an existential fact" Education arises to confront the foundational responsibility of the process; once again, we shift from the society to the specifically educational to find that "[education] must come to the aid of the people who are already emerging in the urban centers and attempting to emerge in the countryside as well so that they can be critically inserted in the process" (1976a, pp. 51–52).

This rite of passage is absolutely indispensable for the humanization of the Brazilian people and "cannot be accomplished by deception, fear, or force but only through education, which, being cultural action, would need to be courageous, offering the people the possibility to reflect about themselves, their times, about their responsibilities, about their role in the new culture of this transitional era" (Freire, 1976a, p. 51). Referring to the role of education in this milieu, Freire (1976a) writes: "An education which facilitates reflection about its own power to reflect and which has its instrumentation in the development of this power, in making its potentialities explicit, will witness the birth of its ability to have options. An education that takes into consideration the various degrees of the power of understanding what the Brazilian people are capable of is a fundamentally important factor in their humanization. This explains the concern we have always had in analyzing these degrees of understanding reality and testing their historical and cultural validity" (pp. 51–52).

This quote shows that for Freire the process of humanization lacks structures favorable to attaining reflection (and criticism); therefore, education seems to be the most appropriate instrument to achieve the passage from naïve consciousness to critical consciousness in people's consciousness so that they can be *critically* inserted in the process.

This concept of liberal democracy would be abandoned by Freire soon after his participation in the Instituto de Capacitación e Investigación en la Reforma Agraria (ICRA) [Training and Research Institute of Agrarian Reform] (Gajardo, 1972), given its ambiguous and unspecific character and its resumption with different intensity and connotations in the 1980s, particularly after a longer exposure to the conversation on education and democracy in industrially advanced democracies. What's more, the initial references to the concept of the people are made explicit, beginning with *Pedagogy of the Oppressed* making a phenomenology of the bourgeoisie as the oppressor class and the working class as the oppressed class (Freire in Torres, 1978a, pp. 51–77).

Fausto Franco (1973) has this to say on the subject: "[Freire] has gone about making a study of the oppressed that transcends the isolated actions of individual people and falls back on the oppressive situation. The oppressed individual becomes 'the oppressed class—dependent and marginal societies,' and the oppressor becomes 'the oppressive class—metropolitan and dominant societies' " (p. 142).

Above all, Freire (1976a) is the pedagogue of *consciousness*, and he dwells on its development from his earliest writings onward. In this respect, he says that his fellow Brazilians "from their initial position of 'intransitive consciousness,' characteristic of the 'inversion' they were undergoing, had begun to emerge into 'naïve transitivity" (p. 52).

Intransitive consciousness represents a people's or a community's lack of historical bearings; one might say it is the reluctance of people to commit to their existence. Freire (1976a) defines it this way: "What we mean by 'intransitive consciousness' is the limit of its sphere of understanding, its impermeability to the challenges that come from outside the vegetative orbit. In this sense, and only in this one, intransitivity represents almost a lack of commitment of human to his existence. It is difficult to discern things, the objectives and external challenges become confused, and human reaches for magic because he or she cannot capture the authentic cause and effect" (p. 54).

In this regard, what does the *transitivity of consciousness* mean? "Insofar as it amplifies human's power to understand and respond to the suggestions and questions that originate externally and add to his ability to dialogue, not only with other men but with his world, his consciousness is 'transitive.' His interests and concerns are prolonged to other spheres, not just to the simple sphere of his life" (Freire, 1976a, p. 53). But this process is still unfinished: "Thus transitive consciousness is, in this first stage, preponderantly ingenuous" (p. 54).

Before delineating the characteristics of this first stage of transitive consciousness, I would like to call attention to another genuinely theological definition that Freire (1976a) expresses: "That is why existence is a dynamic concept, it implies an eternal dialogue between human and human, between human and world; between human and his Creator" (p. 54). Freire seems to have borrowed from the first two chapters of the Book of Genesis to express his feeling of totality (of the dialogue with totality), of theology, of his own relational experience, of his "living the experience of immanence tremendously" in the quotidian, starting with the "transcendence of faith" that signifies his Christianity.

The elements that would express naïve transitive consciousness would be simplicity in the interpretation of problems through the underestimation of the common human, through a strong inclination to gregariousness that is characteristic of the masses, through being impermeable to investigation through the practice of polemics rather than dialogue, because it seeks magical explanations for facts.

In this regard, it seems that Freire is proposing a *critical transitive consciousness* that would overcome the pseudo–*prise de conscience* as a product of pedagogical work on socioeconomic transformations. However, there is a qualitative change in his concept[6] that leads him to postulate the idea of political consciousness,[7] as a process of dialectical and intersubjective recognition that motivates praxis. Julio Barreiro supplies a very useful clue when he writes how "illiteracy is a phenomenological explication that reflects the structure of a society at a given historical moment" (see his Introduction to the Spanish-language edition of *Educación como práctica de la libertad,* p. 12). Barreiro is suggesting that the *prise de conscience*, concomitant with the process of literacy learning, produces effects not only in the individual consciousness (Freud's *uber-ich*) but, what is more, in the collective dimension of the empirical-cultural process—in other words, at the level of class consciousness. It follows that the consciousness-raising process is part and parcel of popular education strategy in that it reveals oppressive reality to groups of oppressed literacy learners at the same time that it establishes a commitment to the practical transformation of that reality. This ingressive praxis can only be concretized as political consciousness, due to the resultant dimension of political class struggle and consciousness.

Critical transitive consciousness, which could be accessed by dialogical education, would be the negation of the naïve transitive and implies, in Freire's (1976a) early work, a return to the "true mother of democracy" (p. 55).

The process of conscientization is also a humanizing process. Freire demonstrates that, in the meeting of democracy and critical transitivity, the latter is characteristic of permeable, restless, interrogative forms of life. Freire (1970d) explains: "I think that through the problematic relation between people and the world it is possible for them to return to creating and being. This natural process through which conscientization appeared in the evolutionary process precisely at the moment which Teilhard de Chardin calls 'hominization.' When conscientization appears, there is reflection, there is intentionality directed toward the world. People become different, essentially different from other animals. Human not only knows, but he knows that he knows" (in Torres, 1978a, p. 39). This process is what Freire refers as the archeology of consciousness in many of his interviews (Torres, 1978a, 1980b, 1994a, 1994b).

Faced with the latent danger of the massification of Brazil within an industrial society, Freire first confirms the importance of pedagogical-educative-critical work to advance toward the dominant critical transitive consciousness. In any case, the risk is always latent, as naïve transitive consciousness can evolve toward critical transitivity or toward the involution of intransitivity, aggravated by mythical stances regarding the masses. But irrationality can also arise in the fanatical consciousness nourished by magic, often reflected in the mythical.

What is the meaning of myth—in other words, the mythical consciousness—for Paulo Freire? We have already mentioned that he points out the risk run by people who are dominated by the power of myths. To analyze the theme correctly, it is fundamental to establish the following distinction: It would appear that the social sciences harbor two dissimilar concepts about "myths"; the first defines the mythical as the type of thinking that expresses reality from the slope of fiction, as the pseudoconcrete representation of reality so that we would find the mythical diametrically opposed to the rational, when it comes to understanding the origin of the organic totality of things.

However, confronting this position there is a more "culturalistic" stance that understands the mythical as a primitive phenomenon of people (rather than a phenomenon of primitive people) that is, moreover, typically human and has every right to coexist with the "logos" of science wherever human's encounter with reality is considered in its entirety, or the meeting of human and God.

Therefore, Freire understands "mythology" as a determined form of thinking and of expression, always valid as a means of developing concepts about the world, and a durable way of thinking and talking about images, allegories and symbols.[8]

The implications of any concept about myth reside in the concept that we have about human consciousness. The first concept will tend to negate the mythical from a "rational" perspective and will demand a better understanding of the world, which leaves mythical intransitivity behind so it can advance toward a more "realistic" and "rational" consciousness. The second concept will understand that the mythical is part of the process of human knowledge and therefore it is impossible to separate "the mythical" from human's Gnostic sense, even at the risk of disturbing the "scientific" in a myth that slips under the threshold of scientific certitude.[9]

Thus, it is important to understand that the process of knowing has to express humanity in its totality, both from rational and reflective sources as well as the "mythic" wellspring of understanding the world. Both, united at the crossroads of sense and intuition, collaborate with that substantial human event, objective praxis. It is also important to understand that the "rational"—even though it is opposed to the "mythical" in Freirean thinking—has nothing whatsoever to do with the "rationalist" thought of the 19th century.

This leads to another aspect: What is Paulo Freire's underlying concept of History? One of the many criticisms heard about Freire is that his thinking is ahistorical. Freire begins by defining concrete tasks that, to the extent that they are grasped and assumed by people in their praxis, could constitute the same history. Yet, these tasks are not understood among the humble people of Brazil where Freire initiated his pedagogical experiments. Rather, it is the elite that interprets and hands them down in the form of recipes for society and its anonymous masses.

So who engenders these historical tasks? Who proposes the fundamental concrete themes, the spirit of the age? Who, if not the humble masses, the people who, by their objective actions, generate the era's tasks? Freire is accused of not making the historical subject explicit. He is also blamed for positing "history as subject," as an absolute spirit that, in its immanent development, converges all phenomena en route to its own existence. The underlying hypothesis of this critique suggests that perhaps it is Freire's Hegelian philosophical influence that leads to his ambiguity. It is even claimed that the basis of his thinking is found in a theological concept called "the theology of the signs of the times," which, in a strange symbiosis of eclectic philosophies, would constitute the cause of Freire's "ahistoricism."

According to this theology, certain everyday happenings are raised before the people as the historical manifestation of Christ and, by certain signs, challenges and concrete tasks are proposed; when such tasks are recognized by the people as the "epiphany" of God, they have no choice but to assume and accomplish them. This concept runs the risk of dichotomizing human history at the same time that it dichotomizes what Christian theology calls the "History of Human Salvation."[10]

I believe that both hypotheses are far from the reality of Freirean thinking. Even if, in his first written works, it appeared from the way he dealt with his (preponderantly philosophical) themes that his thinking would not assume the concrete historical determinants of reality, the writing that followed (particularly *Pedagogy of the Oppressed*) evince the historical rather than the "historicist" sense of Freirean thinking (Barreiro, 1975; Freire, 1969, 1974c).

This historical sense is exposed, paying tribute to the classical humanist tradition and to the juncture of Freire's thinking and historic materialism, in very general terms—not history the way men think it is, or want it to be, but basically, as the daily struggle for humanization, the struggle for the construction and redefinition of the "factum," in the Greek sense of drama.[11]

In reviewing the historical sense that underlies Freire's writing, we also begin to understand that if it is not the common people who give birth to this original process of reconverting to the basic democratic process, it is certainly not the elites.

The entire history of humanity has shown us that those who hold power (whether estates, strata, elites, or social classes) do not willingly renounce their privileges, not even if they "modernize," recognizing the people's participation as a demand worthy of those who have come to maturity, rather than the exact opposite.

This problem of history is connected to the problem of democracy. In Freire's first writings, the meaning of democracy seems to have to do with the socialization of power at all levels, but with the people's participation as the basis of a just society.

Let us admit as a working hypothesis that Freire doubted the process that was advancing the government of João Goulart. As Sanchez (1975) writes, "Freire's efforts for a consciousness-raising literacy represent a serious uncertainty. If, for the populists, the primary objective was suffrage, since under Brazilian law non-literates were not allowed to vote, the secondary result was the beginning of a progressive separation. We can foresee how this attempt would have developed had it not been mediated by what came to pass in 1964. Only two possibilities occur to us: either the consciousness-raising effort would have been compromised by its being linked to the populist power play, depriving it of any deep-seated critical posture, or else it would have had to settle for a marginal position because it went against the grain of its own sponsors" (pp. 9–10).

Nevertheless, it is worth mentioning that the *prise de conscience* has to do, in the final analysis, with becoming conscious of forms of reality (what Freire calls "tasks") that escape the objective praxis of the people. In other words, we are conscious of something that is developed without being made an object. To think about *non-objectification* could lead Freire up a dead end street, according to some mistaken readers (Torres, 1978c),[12] because then the only way of achieving critical transitivity would be to rationalize the process, reflecting about the practice itself.

The risk run by interpretations like Argentine anthropologist and professor of philosophy of the University of Buenos Aires Rodolfo Kusch is that they fail to appreciate the high value given to the daily construction of reality by oppressed people who, despite being bound by dominating strictures and the high level of repression (overt and covert) to which they are submitted, are able to convert their objective praxis into a deep unity born from below, from the roots, in search of participation. This engenders a historical praxis that is qualitatively different from that of the masses—one that demonstrates that you do not always have to be "conscious" to achieve real goals, although you should perceive the struggle's final horizon on a conscious level.

We encounter another important theme in Freire when, referring to popular education, he argues that popular education truly enables the people to think about themselves, to think about their era and responsibilities, and about their role in the new culture of this age of transition. But to whom is his definition of the meaning of the educative delivered? Who is his interlocutor? Is it the government of João Goulart? Possibly, but this is doubtful. Is it addressed to the Christians? This is also possible, but it gives the impression of being directed at a somewhat broader public. It seems to be directed at teachers in particular, and at intellectuals in general. It is clearly *not* directed at "the people," because, in that era, they lacked the organic and reflective qualities that Freire solicits. Yet Freire in 1972 expressed clearly his desires to be able to write and teach in a language that will facilitate communication to the people: "I am not Hegel, or Marx, or Merlau-Ponty or Sartre. And I have to make an option. What is my option? Sartre continues to write for intellectuals. I would like to write less exclusively for intellectuals. Hence I have to make an option in relation to my language" (quoted in Torres, 1978a, p. 56).

In conceptualizing the meaning of education, Freire believes that it enables the people to think about themselves. But this invitation to reflective activity, like all dialogical relations, goes together with constant active listening and attention to the "wisdom of the people," to the words of the oppressed and marginalized sectors. When these people are heard, they not only construct their own educational program in the process of becoming literate, but they also begin to emerge from an oppressed mindset toward an awareness of their oppression, thereby initiating the process Freire called "*conscientização.*"

But this educational and cultural process is ultimately bound by the historico-social conditioning of the society in which it is developed, and that is why Freire, understanding the global process of change as one that he calls "a process of fundamental democratization," tries to get at the reasons why the "forming of a democratic mentality is made impossible." There is little doubt that, in 1960s Brazil, "democratic mentality" was a substantial leap forward, and we might imagine how the subjective conditions for an early outline of the objective transformation of reality were being generated.

In the proverbial spirit of the Latin American Left at the time, Freire was aware that no socioeconomic formation can simply renounce its traditions as "voluntary acts." In other words, it can only modify the complex of institutionalized mechanisms with the passage of time, a revolutionary transformation directed according to the revolutionary theory of conflict and the social dialectic, by the historic subject of such change (the working class and the complex alliances around it) driven by the political subject of the transformation: the revolutionary political party.

Nevertheless, this was not the situation in Brazil where, like anywhere else, the past was still weighing on the present. Freire thought that the constitution of a democratic mentality (as the basic ground for the construction of a more daring project) was impeded by the problem of the articulation of power and, especially, by the tradition of slave labor.

In conclusion, we can say that for Paulo Freire, education is a process that permanently accompanies changes in the socioeconomic structure. By its specific nature, education establishes a place within politics that sustains the dialectic of social transformation. Nevertheless, Freire in his earlier writings sees education as part of an ideological superstructure. As a basic agent of social reproduction, education can operate within limits as a decisive factor in the processes of social change, together with the mutation of the structures and the conflictive dialectic of the society. To educate is fundamentally to hear and dialogue with the people about their problems in a transformative dialogue of interacting subjects. Such transformation has immediate social projections for the process of *conscientização*. In this vein, Paulo Freire explores the paths of pedagogy as a poet seeking the ineffable, rather than as a caretaker of musty monuments.

Freire's thinking about education is definitive: We are educated by an era, there is no proto-pedagogy, but one that is continually conditioned by history. The pedagogy Freire suggests possesses a radical shape rather than a discursive one. He does not describe it in a textbook written in the tranquility of his study, but rather by recapitulating his lengthy practical experience with the background of the historically stratified Brazilian society: a real educational laboratory for the psychosocial method of adult literacy teaching.

FIVE

The Sociological Imagination

The ideological mark of the Fourth Epoch—that which sets it off from the Modern Age—is that the ideas of freedom and of reason have become moot; increased rationality may not be assumed to make for increased freedom.

(Wright Mills, 2008, p. 194)

The underlying thesis of Freire's historical analyses is that the roots of Brazilian democratic inexperience are found in the type of predatory colonization that Brazil suffered—the use of slave labor and the brutal utilization of power on the part of the dominant elite, which engendered the "muteness" of the Brazilian people and their seeming incapacity to speak for themselves.

Therefore, "the democratic inexperience [is] rooted in truly cultural complexes" (Freire, 1976a, p. 60). Moreover, joining the postcolonial tradition, Freire presents the exploitation of slave labor as a fundamental characteristic of the kind of societal analysis he undertakes: "Slave labor from which arose a series of obstacles and, simultaneously, the impossibility of forming a democratic mentality, a permeable consciousness, experiences of participation and of self-governance" (p. 67).

This exploitation made the creation of "community life" impossible because of the demographic dispersion that characterized the vast feudal landholdings of the great estates that, together with the growth of urban nuclei and because of the unlawful use of power, gave rise to a marked individualism. The balance of the analysis is that: "Without a doubt, it is the exacerbation of power that has characterized our formation from the beginning. It was the strength of this power around which an almost masochistic lust to be all-powerful continued to grow. Submission was part and parcel of this exacerbated sense of power. From this submission was born a consequent adjustment; accommodation rather than integration. Accommodation requires a minimal dose of critique. Integration, on the contrary, demands a maximum of reason and consciousness" (Freire, 1976a, p. 69).

Thus, the Brazilian people found themselves castrated from the start when it came to saying their "word." "Marginalized and devoid of civil rights, the common human found himself irredeemably alienated from any experience of self-government or dialogue: made constantly submissive, 'protected,' the only way to react was by a clamorous outcry—the voice of those who are mute when faced with the growth of communities and never have the option of finding an authentic voice. This voice must be won by the people with the growth of new historical conditions that will provide the first attempts at dialogue" (Freire, 1976a, p. 71).

Ultimately, Freire does not explain how the crisis of 1930 and the fall of the international stock market and consequent transfer of monetary focus from livestock to industrial interests stimulated the rise of an urban bourgeoisie and proposals for a free market economy, as a way to generate a workforce that would also act as internal market consumers, thereby beginning the "Europeanization" of Brazil. This process was made possible by the abolition of slavery in 1888. Brazil was the last Latin American nation to abolish slavery, perhaps the last in the Western world. This emancipation was done without giving the freed slaves full citizenship, since most of them couldn't read or write, and literacy was a precondition for voting and election to public office.

Democracy appeared, then, to be a kind of politics that would bring with it a great change in consciousness. However, as Freire (1976a) points out, "Since it did not require the 'decomposition' of the Brazilian society, allowing the established powers to participate, it had exactly the opposite result: the alienation of the people through 'public welfare.' In a general way, it can be said that, with few exceptions, the common people were either marginalized from all these processes or participated in them as a clamorous mob without a discernible voice" (p. 77).

In broad strokes, Freire offers a socioeconomic-historical focus and a political theory analysis. Gradually, slave labor emerges as the historical-cultural element that will have the most profound effect on the educational analysis of contemporary Brazil. As a central explicative element, we find that the feudal mode of production accentuated "intransitive" characteristics and that the submissive situation of the so-called "popular classes" was a lever for their further exploitation. Here, Freire's definition of (the oligarchy's) exacerbated use of power in terms of the domination of the common human and his consciousness is very suggestive.

When Freire proposes that the Brazilian people were submissive when confronting power, there is no doubt about the objectives of his reflection. He is interested in the objective process of colonization rather than in verifying the internal differences between colonized sectors or between the politics of colonization and what kind of results another type of politics might have brought to Brazil. His immediate conclusion is that the causes that gave rise to *democratic inexperience* should be sought out in the colonization process itself. It follows that the roots of the country's cultural backwardness originate from its very history and, thus, the possibility of elaborating a new Brazilian pedagogy conforms perfectly with the analysis of this concrete process and the detection of the cause of those cultural complexities that block the way to freedom (Torres, 1981b).

Liberalism generates the individual's education as a function of the dominant power system. This makes it to some degree an adaptive rather than a critical education. But it appears, according to Freire's writing at the end of the 1950s, that Brazil was not able to reach even this adaptive phase of educational development. The truth is that the popular masses received no education at all.

In *Pedagogy of the Oppressed,* Paulo Freire (1973e) writes: "The educator faces those seeking education as her/his necessary antinomy. (S)he recognizes the reason for her/his existence in the absolute ignorance of the latter. Those who seek education are themselves alienated like the slave in Hegel's dialectic; they recognize in their ignorance the reason for the educator's existence. What they 'get' even less than the slave in the aforementioned dialectic is that they are also the educator's educators" (p. 73).

This "banking" education sanctions certain individual values in the context of its system: Teachers must scrupulously comply with the legal standards established by rules, sticking to their schedules and maintaining discipline, among other things. To ensure their pension, teachers demand the same of their pupils—punctuality, discipline, and obedience to the rules as well as satisfying the requirements for entering and exiting the grade level (Freire, Illich, & Furter, 1974).

In short, to counterpose to this a paradigm wherein which teachers and students are capable of dialoguing and problematizing together, and where teachers have a guileless faith in the people they teach, is absurd[1] —as absurd as proposing that the student grasp the world's challenges that unite consciousness, reflection, and practice in a single process. Liberal education[2] in its defense of private property, in its self-definition as a natural and ahistoric liberty, in its judicial and formal pulchritude, will always be "banking" education, education for domestication, as long as it sustains a bourgeois ideology.[3]

In synthesis, it appears that the Brazilian people are advancing (confirming their historical praxis) but without being able to objectively reflect about that praxis. Paulo Freire's pedagogical stance basically intends to integrate the individual to the people, rather than creating a "political individual" in the practical and spiritual sense.

The historical experience of democracy would thus be expressed in the "people" category, as is the case in Brazil. For Freire, moreover, this would be a necessary antecedent to the category of "political individual" and one that would represent the cultural ground for political, economic, and social self-determination.

In conclusion, the common people are, for Paulo Freire, the prime movers and shakers of the process of liberation, but they still have to be "deconstructed" and "'reconstructed" by becoming sufficiently "conscientized" to discover the mechanisms of their domination by the forces of antidialogical and domesticating cultural action. This is not a process of deconstruction and reconstruction from the outside—either through the consumption of a revolutionary theory, or the presence of a revolutionary party, or the process of counter-hegemonic culture.

All those elements may help the process of revolutionary leadership, but the seeds of change, and the process of interrogating its own kaleidoscope of domination, exploitation, and oppression, rests in the hands, and we must add, in the consciousness (the possible consciousness) of the common people (Torres, 1981b).

Pedagogy of the Oppressed attains fulfillment as a transformer of consciousnesses and of structures in the process of cultural revolution. It is a pedagogy that proposes "to pass from being of the oppressed to being the pedagogy of all people in the process of permanent liberation" (Freire, 1973e, p. 52).

SIX

Education for Social Change

> *We should not call the people to school to receive instructions, postulations, recipes, threats, reprimands and punishments, but rather to participate in the collective construction of knowledge, which goes beyond the knowledge of the past experience and takes into account the necessities of the people and turns that knowlege into an* instrument of struggle, *making possible the people's transformation into subjects of their own history.*
>
> *(Municipal Secretariat of Education, 1992, emphasis in original, cited by O'Cadiz and Torres, 1994, p. 210)*

In *Educación como la práctica de la libertad* (Education as the Practice of Freedom), which as I have already indicated is essentially a rewriting of his 1959 doctoral dissertation (2001), Freire (1976a) summarizes his fundamental preoccupation with the Brazilian historical past. He writes: "In the analyses of the preceding chapters, we have been trying to find a response to the conditions of the Brazilian transition in the pedagogical field, a response in which I have taken into consideration the problems of economic development, of the people's participation in this development and of the critical insertion of the Brazilian people in the process of 'fundamental democratization' that characterized us and cannot overlook the signs of our democratic experience, our historic and cultural roots, in contradiction to the new position that the process demands of the Brazilian people" (p. 80).

Freire (1976a) immediately attempts to describe the contribution of Brazilian educators to the process: This would have to be "about an education that attempts to pass from naïve to critical transitivity, broadening and deepening the ability to understand the challenges of the time, giving the Brazilian people the wherewithal to resist the emotional force of the transition itself. To arm it against the power of the irrationality of those who were easily caught in the position of transitive ingenuousness" (p. 80).

He says that to succeed in developing, a "change of mentality" is necessary, one that is not concerned with reforming only the technical and economic aspects. Evaluating the process wherein the psychosocial method was born, he mentions that, on one side, the people start to emerge, although they can still be easily trapped by irrationalism and, on the other, an antipopular pole comes into being, that is to say, the oligarchy and the elite who hold steadfast to their positions and try at all costs to maintain them.

Oscillating between the two, but with a great desire to rise and obtain privileges was the middle class, which saw in the people's coming to consciousness a threat to its peace and therefore assumed a reactionary attitude toward the process.

Freire believes that it is very important to analyze the relationship between education and society. It is his opinion that education, "even if it cannot be seen ingenuously as something miraculous that can transform Brazilian society, possesses an *instrumental force* that cannot be denied" (Freire, 1976a, p. 82).

What follows is a list of the most striking aspects, the most basic objectives that an "education for development" should attempt to achieve:

1. "to provide students with the necessary instruments to resist the deracinating powers of an industrial civilization . . ." (Freire, 1976a, p. 84). Here Freire's reflection pauses, apparently to examine the meaning of work, of the social organization of work, and the risks that exist in an industrial society.
2. "an education that makes it possible for people to fearlessly discuss their problems . . ." (p. 85).
3. "education that is situated in dialogue . . ." (p. 85). He emphasizes the constant revision and the constant critical analysis of his discoveries.
4. ". . . that makes it susceptible to a kind of rebelliousness . . ." (p. 85). He appears to reiterate individuals' efforts to affirm their ethics in the face of all this, a bit of the feeling of the importance of freedom that was born of the Gospel which we would locate as the source of this reflection. This popular rebelliousness, usually very naïve and emotional, must be transformed into social "engineering. . . ."
5. An education that ". . . is identified with scientific methods and processes" (p. 85).
6. Education should orient people in their lives. It should ". . . help people reflect about their ontological vocation as subjects" (Freire, 1973e, p. 52).
7. Freedom, democracy, and critical participation are key ideas that initially constituted the core of Freire's pedagogy. Thus, he rejects the school for a more flexible circle (the culture circle), and likewise the role of teacher as "factotum" in favor of an animator or coordinator of the pedagogical experiences inside the circle. Freire also rejects prescribed curricula for a program created in and with the people. As a result, the essential dimension of all this pedagogical process is dialogue.

"In this way Freire outlines the basic premises of what he will later call a 'Political Pedagogy', conceived as a revelatory process, by means of the action and reflection in a situation of oppression, and as the acquisition of a conscious and creative ability [honed by] historical reality. This pedagogy based on dialogue and the unity of action and reflection is a response to the brainwashing ideology by which the dominant classes manipulate the consciousness of the oppressed, forcing them to internalize their values and inculcating a feeling of inferiority and impotence that ultimately favors the isolation and artificiality of the [political] positions they choose" (Oliveira & Dominice, 1975, pp. 13–15).

Because of this, Freire modifies certain organizational details of his pedagogical layout, especially those relating to politics. From 1970 onward, in his role as education consultant for the World Council of Churches, he abandoned the idea of base education groups, relatively isolated from their context, and began to think of a form of pedagogical militancy connected organically to revolutionary movements and political parties.

Thus, the theme of rebellion becomes an important aspect of the analysis: "We understand rebellion as a symptom of ascension, as an introduction to plenitude. For this very reason, our sympathy can never be rooted in its preponderantly passionate manifestations. On the contrary, our sympathy adds up to a profound sense of responsibility that always leads us to fight for the immediate promotion of critical candor, of the rebellion in insertion" (Freire, 1976a, p. 87).

Advancing this analysis, he sets forth the dimensions of the problem he had to undertake in his pedagogical work: "Thus, our great challenge, within the new Brazilian way of life, was not just to overcome the alarming rate of illiteracy. For just overcoming illiteracy, purely mechanical illiteracy, would not lead to the rebellion of the people. The problem for us transcended the conquest of illiteracy and had more to do with the need to conquer our democratic inexperience as well. Or to attempt the two things at once" (Freire, 1976a, p. 90). In other words, the leitmotif of the democratic mentality that moved within the dynamic of social change will be the *critique.*

Evaluating the education of his time, Freire (1976a) says: "There is nothing in our education that develops in our students a taste for study, for substantiation, for revising the 'discoveries' that would develop transitive critical consciousness. On the contrary, their tenuous relationship to reality intensifies our students' ingenuous consciousness" (p. 90).

He synthesizes everything said until now in a paragraph in which he refers to his culture: "We are increasingly convinced that our fondness for hollow words, rhetoric, the emphasis on elegantly worded speeches has its root in our democratic inexperience. All this oratorical filigree, almost always lacking any substantive depth, reveals a mental attitude in which the permeability that characterizes critical consciousness is totally absent. This is precisely because critique is the fundamental note of the democratic mentality" (Freire, 1976a, p. 91).

It returns permanently to the verbiage-laden, deflective, and ponderous pedagogical culture. Freire (1973e) writes in *Pedagogy of the Oppressed* that "The more we analyze the dominant educator-*educatee* relationships at any level in today's school (or outside it), the more we are convinced that such relations present a special and determinant character; one which presents relations of a fundamentally narrative, discursive and disquisitive nature . . . that refer to reality as something spiritless, static, divided and well-behaved which, in default, speaks or writes about something completely alien to the existential experience of the *educatees.* Actually, it becomes the supreme uneasiness of this kind of education, its unmanageable anguish" (p. 71). When Freire (2001), in his doctoral dissertation defended in 1959 and published post-humorously, cited Fernando de Acevedo arguing the *intransitive consciousness* of the vegetative communities was "bounded and turned in upon itself" (p. 108), he was suggesting the path upward through the techniques of reduction and codification. He implied the reduction of the existential elements, conscious or unconscious, of such a community and the thematic and dialectic codification of such elements so that, when presented anew to the group by a coordinator, they would provoke the unfolding of such a consciousness. His evaluation enters a tangle of culturally verifiable ideological processes, which were tethered to a group of clearly delimited prejudices.

Thus, the *critique,* as it was initially understood, resulted solely from the pedagogical work, supported by propitious historical conditions. This critique pointed out that a person could understand his or her position inside its context. Gradually, Freire went about radicalizing this option until conscientization came to be as much about commitment as recognition.

With respect to these initial arrangements of Freire's, a group of questions arises that need to be explained—that is, the notion of the transitivity (or not) of the consciousness—so that we can then approach the difference between "ingenuously" and "critically" transitive consciousnesses.

It would seem that all consciousness is transitive because history passes through it and because it has the capacity to be reflective and reflexive—to think of itself as consciousness in respect to history and in respect to itself. Thus, an intransitive consciousness could not exist because it would negate the very foundation of a conscious being.

Now it remains to determine in what way one is "conscious." Freire establishes two forms: the *ingenuous*—grasping reality without visualizing the causes that engender it—is ingenuous transitivity, which he refers to as *magic, mythical,* or *fanatic consciousness.* The other form is the *critical*—which grasps not only the challenges of history, but also understands itself as being in a state of transit, thereby questioning its very reality.

Thus, the central problem for Freire will be to determine what kind of consciousness the people express. He says that the people of Brazil, before it became a republic,[1] had an ingenuous transitive consciousness and were therefore easy prey for irrationalism.[2] Soon an advance toward a greater criticality was verified.

When Freire refers to the industrial society and to the necessity of an education for development, it appears to us that there is a qualitative leap in his reflection. His earliest thinking was directed at the humble Brazilian peasants who were at the beginning of their transformation, and in his later work we observe the focus on people "imprisoned" by the industrial society. The question would be whether this coincides with a historically similar leap of Brazilian society, or if Freire is here incorporating a distinctly Eurocentric *problematique* that does not encompass the historical experience.

When Freire made his position on work and alienation in an industrial society explicit, he was beginning to read Marx and to get in touch with the idea of a Critical Theory of society. In *Education as the Practice of Freedom* (1967/1976b, p. 90n14), he mentions Erich Fromm's book *Marx and His Concept of Man*, in which Fromm considers the philosophical economic manuscripts of 1844, fruits of the first investigations undertaken by Karl Marx, with the intention of beginning a study of the objective world of economics from a philosophical perspective.

Marx, motivated by his preoccupation with the miserable existence of the English working class, attempts to demonstrate how these people—whom Hegel had identified as "historical beings" because of their mediating relationship with nature through human toil, and who were trying to construct their social reality as an immanent expression of the idea they externalized— expressed exactly the opposite: that the fruits of their labor, rather than belonging to them and, as such, reconstituted in their search for totality, were snatched from them by the mechanism of bourgeois "private property," which also alienated them from their ability to work (their raison d'être), thereby converting them into a "labor force" that could be bought and sold like merchandise in the market. As merchandise, they produced and reproduced the system of commodity production, the social relationships of production, and certainly the capitalist mode of production.

So, following the dialectics that Marx and Freire embraced, the negation of the negation of humans again in possession of themselves and the fruits of their labor was hindered by the private appropriation of goods, which left them "exteriorized," lost in the world of things, distracted, alienated.

Erich Fromm utilized the concepts of alienation and distraction as synonyms, as did Freire in his attempt to describe the atmosphere of deracination born of assembly-line piecework, the typical social organization of labor in the industrial society. These concepts had a stricter connotation in historical materialism, which I do not intend to examine in depth here. However, the alienation of labor in the opulent society that Freire initially points out does not represent the strict Marxist conceptualization of alienated labor (especially the young Marx of the Manuscripts).

In Freire's initial work, the passage where he refers to the importance of an attitude of rebellion reflects his Christian thinking that the personal experience of human freedom be taken to its greatest profundity, to its ontological radicalism, to being permanently both *of* and *in* the world and with this spirit that emanates from heavenly bliss. The profound humanism that floods it, this "subjective" humanism, is rooted in Freire's understanding of freedom.

In this early period, Freire underscores the complexity of his intellectual evolution, linking key tenets of liberalism with his first readings of Marxism and his belief in the emerging Theology of Liberation. For him, freedom is humans' richest dimension and the one that relates them to God. Those who can live this dialectic of immanence and transcendence assume the limits of their finitude, as the framework of their infinitude, and lead their lives in rebellion against it as the most authentic way of being human beings.

SEVEN

Education, Conscientization, and Liberation

> *The French "prise de conscience," to take consciousness of, is a normal way of being a human being. Conscientization is something which goes beyond the "prise de conscience"; it is something which implies to analyze. It is a kind of reading the world, almost rigorously. It is the way of reading how society works. It is the way to understand better the problem of interests, the question of power. Conscientizing implies a deepened reading of reality. What I mean by a deepened and critical reading of reality is some kind of reading or understanding of reality which is starting and respecting. The common sense goes beyond the common sense, Conscientization implies that we begin to establish relationships between facts.*
>
> *(Freire, quoted in Torres, 1995e, p. 177)*

Paulo Freire (1976a) confirms a fact that has deep relevance for educational praxis: "The urban populations' appetite for education surprises us, a fact that is associated directly with the transitivity of their consciousness [while] the rural populations' lack of appetite is linked to the intransitivity of their consciousness" (p. 97).

He again refers to the problem of participation, claiming that the nonparticipation and noninterference in the processes "must be supplanted by critical participation, which is a form of wisdom. Only thus will it be possible to transform themselves into people capable of opting and deciding by means of critical participation" (Freire, p. 98).

To achieve this participation, he conceived of two ideas that became basic institutions of *popular education*: the "culture circle" and the "culture center." Beginning with this project, Freire schematizes the necessarily antagonistic elements that begin to arise between the old education and the new education:

BEFORE	NOW
a. School	a. Culture circle
b. Teacher	b. Debate coordinator
c. Discursive class	c. Dialogue
d. Students	d. Group participants
e. Alienated subjects and programs	e. Units of learning (compact, reduced, and codified programs)

For Freire, the redefinition of terms is not a semantic caprice but, rather, a way to remove meanings from words used in education whose consonance has been vitiated by discursive pedagogy (Freire, Gadotti, & Torres, 2005; Mafra, Torres, & Gadotti, 2008).

At various occasions, he has made his ideas about the significance of *alphabetization*[1] explicit. Let us examine what he says in *Education as the Practice for Freedom* (1967/1976b): "We were thinking about a method of alphabetizing that was itself an act of creation capable of unshackling other creative acts, of a way of alphabetizing where people, not being its objects, would be able to develop impatience, vivacity, invention and recovery—all characteristic states of study" (p. 100). In this way, then, given that it is set up as a political pedagogy, "to alphabetize" would be synonymous with "to conscientize."

Freire (1976a) goes on to synthesize the fundamental premises of putting his categorization of knowledge into action: "We begin with people's normal position, which we discussed in this book's first chapter, which is not just *to be in* the world but also *to be of* it, to bond permanently with it by means of relations that arise from the creation and recreation or the enrichment of what they make of the natural world, represented in cultural reality. Through these relations with reality and in reality, people attach themselves to the world in specific ways—as subject to object—from which comes knowledge expressed through the language" (p. 101).

From what he says, it can be deduced that one has only to be a person to participate in the world of culture and, therefore, there is no such thing as absolute ignorance or absolute wisdom. But Freire (1976a), pedagogue of consciousness, feels it necessary to describe the forms of people's conscious being, which are, in the final analysis, a reflection of their social being, thus:

Critical consciousness "is the representation of things and facts as they appear in empirical existence, in their causal and circumstantial correlations" notable for "its integration with reality" (Freire, pp. 101—102).

Ingenuous (or naïve) consciousness: "(on the other hand) believes itself superior to the facts, dominating them from outside and therefore thinks itself free to interpret them however it wishes." It is notable for "what it superimposes on reality" (p. 102).

Magical consciousness: "on the other hand, does not consider itself superior to the facts, dominating them from the outside, nor 'does it think itself free to interpret them however it wishes.' People simply believe them, granting them a greater power which they fear because it dominates them from outside and they docilely submit to it. This leads to fanaticism" (p. 102).

Fanatical consciousness: "whose pathology of ingenuousness leads to the irrational" and its hallmarks are " [to settle for] what is adequate, to accommodate, to adjust, and to adapt" (p. 102).

Having defined consciousness in all its dimensions, Freire shows us his "educational program" at the beginning of his pedagogical experience. He also explains: "What we should do in a society in transition like [that of Brazil in the 1960s], in a large-scale process of fundamental democratization in which the people are emerging, is to try to create an education that is capable of collaborating with them in the indispensable reflexive organization of their thinking. An education that puts at their disposal the means with which they are able to overcome the magical or ingenuous understanding of their reality and acquire a predominantly critical one. At the time, this meant to collaborate with the people so that they would be able to assume positions ever more in keeping with the dynamic climate of the transition, positions integrated with the fundamental democratization and, therefore, contrary to their democratic inexperience. Thus, we were attempting to create an education that seemed necessary to us, in keeping with the conditions of our reality. If it integrated to our time and to our space and helped people reflect about their ontological vocation as subjects, it would really have to be instrumental" (Freire, p. 103).

On the one hand, a democratic education has to be instrumental in keeping the understanding of the conditions of the society while transforming it in the perspective of development. On the other hand, this instrumentality cannot and should not deny the fundamental role of education, which is to help people reflect about their ontological vocation as subjects!

To be sure, all education (relating means to ends) must assume an active method (the systematic reflection about means), and of course some techniques (to implement the method). Freire requests that we make a place for an active method that contributes to shaping critical beings through group debate about challenging existential situations. To achieve these objectives, he proposes: (1) an active, dialogical method with a critical spirit; (2) a codification of the educational program; and (3) the use of techniques such as reduction and codification.[2]

Reflecting on the famous literacy training experience of Freire in the City of Angicos, in Rio Grande do Norte in 1963, an experience that needs to be analyzed and celebrated 50 years after the Freirean literacy training program—see Chapter 10—Freire argues that the imprint, perhaps a better word is the *lynchpin*, of the new program of alphabetization is given by the anthropological concept of culture. That is, the distinction between two worlds—that of nature and that of culture—attempting to show people's active role in and with their reality and the sense of mediation that nature has in relationships and communication among people.

Freire (1976a) gives us a definition of what he understands as the anthropological concept of culture, displaying its humanistic dimension: "Culture as a systematic acquisition of human experience, a critical and creative incorporation rather than a juxtaposition of 'given' information or prescriptions" (p. 105).

To introduce the concept of culture in both its gnosiological and anthropological dimensions, Freire reduces the concept to its broadest outlines in 11 to 15 "codified" existential "situations" that challenged the groups of literacy[3] and developed their self-awareness by means of a praxis of decoding.

Freire (1976a) writes: "Once they recognized, after the first 'situation,' the two worlds—that of nature and that of culture and the role people played in them—other 'situations' followed in which their understanding of the 'cultural' domain was clarified and broadened" (p. 107).

After these discussions about culture, where conclusions deal with the dimensions of culture as a systematic acquisition of human experience, the debate was oriented toward the "democratization of culture."

One of Freire's (1976a) most explicit definitions of the role of an adult educator comes from this stage: "The role of the educator is basically to dialogue with the unlettered person about concrete situations, simply offering him or her the instruments with which to become 'alphabetized' " (p. 108).

Let us get back now to the discussion of consciousness. Freire understands it is possible that the *consciousness of affirmation* is an intransitive consciousness, while the consciousness of negation is transitive (in its double relation with myth and magic, and its risk of fanatical consciousness); and the consciousness of self-improvement is the critical transitive consciousness. This logical mechanics rest on the dialectic method, relating to the Hegelian idea of an unfolding consciousness.

If it is true that the negation of one consciousness by another, from the perspective of Hegel's philosophy, does not imply its elimination but, rather, its conservation, its maintenance, its *Aufhegen*, then it is also true that the negation of the negation ends up determining only one type of attitude in respect to the aforementioned processes and that "knowing" has an eminent practical sense: being able to operate with respect to the natural world and to the cultural world while experiencing this "drama" through humanization.

Although Freire knows that a "complex consciousness" exists, following Teilhard de Chardin's line of reasoning, he strives to construct this Latin American totality of consciousness in all its many meanings of being and thinking.

However, the Freirean concept of culture is very important in that the systematization of human experience includes both the ideas that accompany a particular historical epoch (civilization) and the cultural artifacts of which people avail themselves to transform the world. Each epoch also possesses its distinctive style of "emotionality" since the way feelings are held also changes from epoch to epoch. Thus, we understand that what Freire calls cultural tasks has little to do with literary or intellectual work. They are essentially practical tasks that spring from the way common people live and construct their daily lives.

This brings the theme of conscientization and its political impediments into sharper relief. Doubtlessly, as we advance in the consciousness of our reality, not only do we discover the causalities of things (rationality), but our feelings toward that reality also start to change. We change along with our mindset. If the problem is a lack of participation, to be aware of it does not just remain on an ideological plane; it also transforms into an existential expectation.

Insofar as conscientization means just that, it is made of "praxis"; in other words what Hegel said and what Marxist thinking critically recast and what we must always remember is this: People can understand their reality because they engender it and can transform it because reality is an eminently social product (the obvious example would be Karl Marx's *Theses on Feuerbach*).

Freire beliefs that in opposition to the impetus of conscientization, the liberal scientific framework would reiterate the need for objectivity and for education to remain apolitical. So it is inevitable that each of our actions carries a political nuance because we live in a society and interact in it with other beings like ourselves. Everyday practice has political meaning. Thus, to negate politics from an apolitical perspective is tantamount to affirming the spontaneous individual who is free and able to act with originality in the natural world and who owes nothing to anyone. This is, ultimately, the thesis of the possessive individualism.

Even those who claim to be apolitical maintain a clear political posture. Moreover, with respect to objectivity, the spirit of Freirean thinking suggests that objectivity is ultimately an effort to express and understand reality correctly. That is to say, it is an effort that should not be reduced solely to an attitude of intellectual honesty (ethics), but should be based even more on the rigorous use of instruments to capture this reality (methodology, techniques, ontology, epistemology, gnoseology, and so forth).

The question of neutrality and objectivity of science were central questions for Freire in the development of his theories. In an interview he gave in 1972 in Santiago de Chile, he spoke at length about neutrality (or lack thereof) of science and addressed also the question of objectivity that for Freire cannot be dissociated from subjectivity. The following paragraphs that I quote at length shows Freire's criticisms. His starting point is to argue that scientific neutrality doesn't exist, nor the impartiality of scientist, and above all that there are multiple epistemologies at play in trying to understand reality and truth.

> It seems to me that the so-called "neutrality" of science does not exist. Neither does the impartiality of scientists. Neither one exists nor, for that matter, does any human action stripped of its intentions and objectives, its ways of seeking. There is no such thing as an a-historical, a-political human being. This doesn't mean, however, that we should confuse the non-neutrality of science with the lack of systematic, serious, profound and scientific rigor, in the search for the truth of what you want to know. They are two completely different things. For example, the fact that I am not neutral when investigating does not mean that I must mystify the reality I want to know, particularly because, if I do that, I would be jettisoning my critical ability as well. After all, the critical investigator wants to know the truth about the reality and not to adjust the reality

to his truth. However, the critical person cannot contest the myth of the neutrality of science by refusing to recognize the virtual truth of the reality he or she is attempting to know. On the contrary, the more committed I am, the more I aspire to the objective truth. (Torres, 1978a, p. 71)

Next, Freire goes on criticizing non-participative research and strongly defending participatory research as central component of his *Pedagogy of the Oppressed* (Torres, 1984, 1992c). In doing so, he is also affirming a dialectical epistemology as his method:

In the third chapter of *Pedagogy of the Oppressed*, where I propose a method of participative research as a hypothesis, I attempt to denounce nonparticipative investigation. If I want to get to know the rural workers' reality, I have to make this research along with the rural workers, not about them or against them. On the other hand, the way a social scientist conducts herself or himself is very different from the behavior of a natural scientist. People who analyze nature are not analyzing something static. This is the same problem that comes up in physics: that the very presence of the researcher modifies the experiment. Now, when we bring this to the human level, what happens to objectivity? In the first place, I would ask if objectivity can exist without subjectivity. In the dialectical perception of reality, the two do not comprise a duality. All subjectivity is objectivity and vice versa. There is a dialectical unity between the two. Nevertheless, an immense amount of work and many ideological difficulties go into the formation of a group of social scientists. I would still say that not all the social scientists that defend the neutral stance do so from acuity or self-interest. They do it without knowing, because they are ideologically convinced of their own neutrality. But I don't believe that someone can remain neutral, especially when it comes to the *raison d'être* of her scientific work, of his investigation. I consider scientists who don't care about what is done with the results of their work immoral. (Torres, 1978a, pp. 72–73)

Despite what seems to be a paradox, a critique of objectivity but a defense of an objective truth, Freire's original epistemological perspective, and his views of objective and subjectivity, method, scientific rigor, ethics and the politicity of education have been defended and debated throughout his life (Gerhardt, 1983, 1993). Freire's narrative is straightforward and indeed an indictment of positivism as a dominant paradigm of research. His work, particularly in the fifties to the seventies, is a challenge to scientific work and pedagogy that is not participative. Already in the sixties and seventies, in the middle of the Cold War, and with the dominance of grand narratives, Freire was arguing for understanding of and respecting different ways of knowing. He called for an understanding as well that there are fundamental and unavoidable political questions that we need to address in our educational praxis, teaching and research:

> I always say that it's necessary to ask: "Who's going to know as a result of this research? Whom will this knowledge serve? With whom do I know? Against whom do I know? How do I know? What do I know? Why do I know? So we discover that these questions clarify an epistemology. You cannot think of doing research without thinking of this epistemology. There is a theory of knowledge implicit in all analysis, in each investigation. But there are many epistemologies, not just one: just as there are different kinds of knowing. (Torres, 1978a, p. 72)

In terms of opposition, as a kind of bête noire par excellence, both conscientization and participation are vigorously combated through various means by elites who are opposed to the advance of the popular processes and of the working class. Recognition and understanding of how this paradigm, one based on systematically unequal relationships, manifests in temporal and practical terms, through both micro and macro modes of analysis, is essential to cultivating viable projects for liberation, in particular those in the Freirean sense that involve education as a vehicle for emancipation.

Therefore, Julio Barreiro, in examining popular education as a contributing instrument of social participation in the liberation process, or as an instrument of mobilization in its dependent-development social context (Torres, 2009a), intends to clarify the different interpretations attributed to the consciousness-raising process that is the basis of Freirean pedagogy:[4]

1. ". . . conscientization as discovery of the dimension of a person and as commitment to the consequences;"
2. ". . . conscientization as conquest of critical transitive consciousness along a progressive scale of related discoveries;"
3. ". . . conscientization as passage of oppressed consciousness toward the consciousness of oppression;"
4. ". . . conscientization as emergence of oppressed existence toward the consciousness of the oppressed." (Barreiro, 1974, p. 98)

These different interpretations of the consciousness-raising process are synthesized in the idea of popular education as a tactical and strategic instrument of formation and organization of the oppressed sectors, following and in service of processes of popular struggle.

In summary, Freire understands the consciousness-raising process as one where education is converted into an instrument of liberation by the oppressed classes. Education and conscientization remain critical contributions to revolutionary social change, as a means to help expose and rupture the domesticating practices of banking education, through which the unequal relationships are cultivated and maintained, thereby subverting and ultimately undoing the privileges of the hegemonic elites (Freire et al., 1974).

EIGHT

Political Anthropology of Education

[T]he day that the forces of power and domination which govern science and technology are able to discover a way to kill intentionality and the active character of consciousness which makes consciousness perceptible to itself, we will no longer be able to speak of liberation. But precisely because it is not possible to kill or blot out the creative, re-creative and receptive force of consciousness, what do those in command do? They mystify reality because, as there is no reality other than the reality of consciousness, when the reality of consciousness is mystified the consciousness of reality is mystified as well. And by mystifying the consciousness of reality, the process of the transformation of reality is obstructed.

(Freire, quoted in Torres, 2009b, p. 4)

Consciousness and history are the two concepts that seem to polarize the subjective and the objective dimensions in the social sciences. The term *consciousness* intuitively reminds us of Hegel's self-consciousness and, in the Marxist tradition, to class consciousness; it is as if intimate or private consciousness lost its "status" and became the matrix of social transformation and reception, having been inundated by history. The concept of history in turn starts to lose the meaning of disconnected and anecdotal facts, chronological historical descriptions of the past or vignettes, and changes into turbulent historical processes with immediate social results.

Freire's thinking calls attention to the dialectic of a consciousness that becomes historical. With his educational experiments, Freire burst onto the historical scene advancing a political anthropology that reflects on human beings to such an extent that the "human" ceases to be studied in sections but rather as a global synthesis where anthropology is intimately united with pedagogy, politics, philosophy, and even theology. Freire thinks as a humanist, reflecting on the human problematic from a synthetic perspective. Within this global synthesis, political anthropology is one of the main axes from which to articulate the whole theoretical edifice, since it not only provides the vision of the human as a historical being, raising his or her consciousness of reality through praxis, but also fecundates pedagogical reasoning by supplying its sustaining bases and fundamental lines of action.

As we have discussed in Chapter 3, the underlying philosophy of Freirean thinking is shaped by four different philosophical traditions in a far-reaching amalgam or synthesis, reuniting the confluence of existential thought (people as beings-in-construction), phenomenological thought (people constructing their consciousness through intentionality), Marxist thought (people living in the drama of the economic conditioning of the infrastructure and the ideological conditioning of the superstructure), and the Hegelian dialectic (people as self-consciousness departing from shared experience until they lift themselves up to science, and through the movement of dialectical becoming, that which is *in-itself* starts to be *in* and *for itself*). In the first Freire, and in the balance of this confluence, the Hegelian dialectic has the greatest weight; moreover, it is a historical avatar of the "pedagogy of the oppressed" (Torres, 2009a).

Our central thesis is that Freirean anthropology, nourished by the Hegelian dialectic and the other currents already mentioned, is, above all, a response to the relationship of consciousness (human beings as social beings) and history (human beings as historical beings).

Thus, Freire, seeking to define human beings in intimate dialogue with Hegel and Marx, agrees with the former that people are conscious of themselves (and seeks the phenomenological explanation of this fact), but they are also conscious of the other. He introduces the dimension of interpersonal relations (alterity) here, reconsidering the basis of the "personalist" current of Emmanuel Mounier, to finally agree with Marx that people represent the workforce while disagreeing with the notion that this is the only attribute that defines them as common beings. For Freire, self-consciousness, alterity, and the ability to work are all defining characteristics but as Raymond Morrow and I (2002) have explained in comparing Freire with Habermas, even in the first Freire he believed that communication is a fundamental attribute in becoming human.[1]

THE MEANING OF ANTHROPOLOGY IN FREIREAN THINKING

> *Learning to read is a political act. In a literate society being able to read is a necessary step toward making decisions and sharing power. A nonliterate person may be very powerful within a non-literate subculture, but within the dominant culture a nonreader is marginal.*
>
> *(Brown, 1978, p. 5)*

The pedagogical, anthropological, and political compose the conceptual nucleus from which Freirean reflection departs.

People are "relational beings" (existence) whose being "with others" (opening) is constituted conjointly with the world. As social beings and historical beings, they are both existence and opening. What, then, is the intersubjective mediation of the aforementioned existence as opening? In other words, how do people relate directly to the world? For Freire (1973e), it is through education that people begin to govern the world, to conceptualize the world, to find their direction in the world: "education must help people to reflect on their ontological vocation as subjects" (p. 52).

Education could be a mediator between people and the world, but such education must not be neutral, dispassionate, and apolitical. Education must assume all human conditions (including alienations) as well as the breadth of human potential (people as a project), and therefore converge toward the political insofar as this is the force that allows human destiny to be structured by all people. Politics, as understood by traditional contract theory of politics, is for Freire the rational direction of all human action, is the meeting place par excellence of all collective expectations—all efforts at sustaining or effectively transforming reality are synthesized in it. It is truly the "art of the possible." Thus, educational mediation and its orienting tasks are inevitably pulled toward the wellspring of politics. So it is not by chance that all Freire's pedagogical efforts in adult education are synthesized in a concept that expresses these three dimensions equally: *conscientization.*

Conscientization is not only the development of the individual's *prise de conscience* of empirico-cultural causality. It is also the result of educative work. Alphabetization and conscientization are two components of the same process, one in which education is politicized and politics educates. Freire (1974b) writes about this: "Just as the gnosiological cycle does not end with the stage of acquiring existing knowledge but is prolonged through the creation of a new knowledge, conscientization cannot cease at the stage of the unmasking of reality. Its authenticity occurs when the practice of the unmasking of reality constitutes a dynamic and dialectical unity with the practice of the transformation of reality" (p.165).

Conscientization does not operate as a phenomenon of the individual's psychological consciousness. Instead, its dimension is collective—according to Freire (1974a): "Thus, conscientization implies that one transcends the spontaneous sphere of the apprehension of reality to arrive at a critical sphere in which reality is a knowable object and in which the person assumes an epistemological position. . . . For the same reason, conscientization is a historical commitment. It is also historical consciousness and, as an insertion in history, implies that people take the role of subjects and make and remake the world. It demands that people create their existence with the material that life offers them . . ." (p. 30).

In Freirean thinking, conscientization is the conceptual synthesis of people's action-reflection: a synthesis of anthropology, pedagogy, and politics. Freire's pedagogy is not a neutral pedagogy. It is a pedagogy with an active political content, a pedagogy of the oppressed. Similarly, politics is the orientation of this praxis with the goal of generating forms of popular organization to accompany the gestation of a critical consciousness for social transformation.

Before analyzing Freire's anthropological dimension in greater detail, I must offer an initial caveat: Freire does not consider education as the lever for social change. To argue to the contrary would be to completely ignore the anthropological content of Freirean discourse. An anthropological basis—and Freire is completely lucid about this—allows one to focus on the entire human *problematique*, to accurately gauge the possibilities of an educative praxis and its human experiences, and, above all, to recognize the utopian aspect that must enliven all educational projects. Freirean anthropology is fecundated by utopia.[2]

FREIRE'S POLITICAL ANTHROPOLOGY

> *"I ask you to ensure that humanity is served by wealth and not ruled by it."*
> *(Pope Francis message read at the opening ceremony of the annual meeting in Davos, Switzerland by Cardinal Peter Turkson, president of the Pontifical Council for Peace and Justice, January 21, 2014.)*

For Freire, anthropology is thinking about the totality of the people's historical existence and their world. Social and historical being are unified, although they remain categorically discernible and separate. Let us therefore examine what Freire considers human characteristics.

First characteristic: People as "relational beings" are situated and dated. This has two consequences: Temporal-spatial position of human beings, their location, historically determines the concept of humanity that people are trying to recuperate. Without any doubt, humanity is historically observed and what, in one historical occasion, is humanizing can become dehumanizing in another. For example, when the "human" was intimately associated with Christianity in the late Middle Ages and to be a human meant being Christian, the cultural forms of the Inquisition were justified, as much in their orientation as in their methods, because they facilitated the construction of what was "human" in the perspective of the era. These days, our humanist criteria make the coercive and inhuman activities of the Inquisition repulsive because they are colored by our search for humanization through confrontation and acceptance of different positions about religious freedom and the freedom of worship, and the meaning of modern atheism and secularized civilizations.

In sum, from the Freirean perspective, the first consequence of this being "situated and dated" is that the actual work of humanization passes through the oppressor–oppressed dichotomy and its dissolution. Freire has repeated endlessly how we cannot be, if we prohibit others from being.

The second consequence of this affirmation is that, to be able to live as a self-actualizing being requires, on the one hand, that we recognize people's lives as works-in-progress. People are continually "becoming;" they are works in progress (this is a prime example of the existentialist vein in Freire). Human beings are "projects." On the other hand, one has to accept that this "project," as a *social being*, is only capable of being described by *conscious beings*. Animals cannot grasp their historical tasks for the simple reason that they have none, at least as we perceive the historical conditioning in the constitution of consciousness. They live adapted to and immersed in their world, relating to it by means of instinct. People, however, only become perceivable social beings when their existence is consequential, when they are conscious of themselves and their history, when, through consciousness, they manage to capture the historical determinants of their human activities.

Second characteristic: People are confronted by the challenges of a given era and, in responding to them, become historical. The paradox here is that people are historical beings par excellence. In a very real and concrete way, some people, as conscious beings, become involved with epochal work, whereas others are just as likely not to, and history passes them by without receiving their contribution. Of course, this takes into account the often highly subjective nature of history, not only in terms of what is included in the record, but also what is excluded. According to Freire, people limit or mutilate their historicity when it remains driven by myths, when they live a life immerse in the massification of signs and symbols they cannot understand, or (in one of the most dramatic examples of our contemporary situation) when their consciousnesses remain "magic" or "semi-intransitive." That is to say, when they refuse to understand the challenges of their age or live under a negative cultural burden, that provokes a false take on reality or what the Marxist tradition has termed "false consciousness." People who remain submerged, unconsciously immersed in their reality, can also lack the language to identify or explain it.

The first case, a life driven by the simplified myths of the masses, need not correspond, in the strictest sense of the word, to a determinate social class. If we look for its correlative on the sociological level, we would have to say that the human of the technological era are victims of the consumerism of the consumer society. It may be said that people live mystified or "mass-produced" lives. When they fail as the protagonists of the social construction of reality without an iota of intention manifest in their actions, it can also be said that those who manipulate ideas or intend to be the interpretative consciousness of their generation (the intellectuals) can also lead manipulated lives. Although they develop theories and live in the environments of science or humanities in which they often feel called upon to analyze phenomena related to a mass-produced world, they do not always perceive that they are more than suitable instruments for revitalizing and reproducing the whole system of alienation.

As for the second case, those who live with a magic or semi-intransitive consciousness are typical of those from dependent societies, according to Freire's analysis. That is to say, in terms of consciousness, the correlative would probably be a peasant or a marginalized inhabitant of one of the thousands of shantytowns, *favelas*, and lost cities that proliferate in Latin America and many other parts of the world.

The drama of this situation is rooted in different conditions that render it highly complex and problematic. Very often, these are beings without options in the capitalist social formation, many of whom have stopped being part of the workforce of the underemployed, which is technically referred to as "the industrial army of reserves" (or "marginal masses"); instead they become part of a population without any integrative attribute other than their marginality. So, their way of integrating into the system is to subsist on its margins. The marginalized slum-dweller and the landless or tenant-farming peasant have some characteristics in common. For instance, they feel identified as people when they present their identity cards, the piece of paper that many of them cannot read because of their illiteracy. In most ways they exist anonymously, like the virtual army of service-sector workers in the core nations who toil away "unseen" in hotels, airports, restaurants, and other establishments, often in hazardous conditions and for scarce remuneration. It is hard to believe the look of satisfaction on their faces when a literate person, reading their identity card, or a nominal check that they have received, or a letter sent to them, pronounces their names! Suddenly, they are men and women even though, until that moment, they have lived in painful anonymity, in a culture of silence.

The culture of silence has absorbed them in silence; they cannot pronounce "the word." Freire has always indicated that literacy training should help individuals to read the world and to read the word (Freire, Gadotti, Saúl, & Torres, 2005; Freire & Torres, 1994). Speaking of the Latin American world, a peasant's "vocabulary universe" is very restricted in Spanish or Portuguese. The original native idiom still resists being obliterated in many places—especially in Central America, Mexico, Peru, and Bolivia. Hence we are confronted with oppressed or displaced indigenous cultures, long since subjugated by Western cultural forms—androcentric, male-centric, and Eurocentric.

The indigenous cultures have provoked a profound conceptual eruption in the Latin American cultural synthesis. There are few definitions of the people as evocative as the Quechua expression that defines them as "the earth that walks." However, the rural populace lives, for the most part, in unsanitary conditions, undernourished, and with little access to the civil minimums—their schooling, under the best conditions, does not exceed the early grades of primary school and their life expectancy is certainly much lower than that of the overall population.

In the cultural struggle, Latin American indigenous cultures have long been displaced, though recently there has been a strong re-affirmation of indigenous cultures, particularly through the work of the Zapatistas in Chiapas, Mexico, or the different indigenous social movements in Bolivia, Ecuador, and Peru; these remind the larger society of their intense human values, including very high coefficients of solidarity and community-mindedness among the native Latin Americans, fused in their decision to struggle for their rights after being suppressed for centuries by the colonizers and ladino societies.

From the perspective Freire outlines, the semi-manipulated citizen, the comfortable bourgeois, the disoriented intellectual, the illiterate peasant, and the exploited manual laborer who is blind to his fate are all incapable of realizing the challenges of the age. They are inserted in history but they neither live it nor share it in any significant way.

Third characteristic: Possible options or tasks are multiple without being prescribed, like animal instinct, and are presented like a kaleidoscope of possibilities in the landscape of choice. People, because they are historical beings, are both obliged and invited to exercise their critical faculties. Freire would say that semi-intransitive consciousness, were it not for an unforeseen objective or subjective condition, remains generally incapable of reaching the sphere of criticality. However, a second, more evolved kind of consciousness can come to achieve this criticality—this is called ingenuous transitive consciousness. But even this cannot capture the depths of reality because it is given to fanciful explanations and cannot grasp empirico-cultural causality, both because of its simplicity in interpreting problems and because it lives buried in the past.

Magical explanations still survive in this consciousness. However, in spite of not possessing total critical capacity, it can at least recognize the options and judge them precisely.

Fourth characteristic: This critical activity only makes sense in the execution of daily and permanent transformation through praxis within its own sociocultural context. A human is a being of praxis. Here, Freire breaks radically with idealist thinking. People do not create the world through ideas, but rather by means of their historical and practical activities, transforming nature and, by implication, themselves. Without doubt, ideas are valuable cultural artefacts whose development accompanies people's cultural awakening, but these only partly modify it.

People can modify, alter, and transform their physical and ecological surroundings, but they cannot fully re-create them because they are to some degree independent of them. However, they can and must re-create their sociocultural world because it is the product of their own historical and cultural activity. Since people are complex beings of action-reflection-action, they can participate, both consciously and historically, in the re-creation of their sociocultural world. This re-creation makes up part of the enormous work of humanization.

Fifth characteristic: This transformative action has a transcendent meaning, expressing at the same time the possibility of self-escape and also the possibility of relating (relinking) with the creator. We have already cited Freire (1976a) when he writes: "Our transcendence is based, as well, on the roots of our finitude and on the degree to which we are conscious of this finitude, on what incomplete beings we are and how our plenitude is found in the union with our creator" (p. 38).

Freire connects his political anthropology to the Judeo-Christian tradition. On different occasions, he has identified himself as a Christian, and even one formed by theology. To a great degree, this explains why his political anthropology has so many points of contact with what Freire calls prophecy (defined as annunciation-denunciation). Perhaps this is due to the convergent aspects of prophecy and politics, since the prophets were men politically obsessed with the struggle for justice in the pagan-theocratic societies of their age. Men like Nathan, Elias, Isaiah, Jerome, and Ezekiel are faithful witnesses of this political role. Thus, Concatti (1975) writes: "To be faithful to God's exigencies, which demand that justice be realized 'here and now,' they will be hated and assassinated by the powerful men of their time. Prophesy, justice and martyrdom form a tragic equation that is repeated throughout the Bible and that Jesus can only confirm, taking it to its fullest expression" (p. 13).

Sixth characteristic: People are "communicative beings;" therefore, they need one another to set up a dialogue, and therefore they have the right to pronounce their word. This characteristic is fundamental. Freire understands that the people's right to pronounce their word comes from a profound internal reality; people are the word because, by naming things, their consciousness is related to the world. A human and the world are mutually constituted.

For Freire, alphabetization always concludes with conscientization because, in his so-called psychosocial method of adult literacy,[3] people place their own reality as the object to be admired. Generative words arise from generative themes that come from the people themselves. They recognize words that they always hear because they are *their* words. People learn to admire their words and themselves. And, in this dialectic of admiration, they discover one another.

These six characteristics of Freirean anthropology can now be reckoned in the conceptual triad that I outlined in our initial thesis: self-consciousness, alterity, and labor force.

By defining people as "self-conscious," Freire introduces the developments of phenomenology, which is a meditation about knowledge. In phenomenology, consciousness is constituted as an intentional totality that symbolizes (signifies) temporality.

People, when they are conscious of themselves, manifest intentionality and feel themselves projecting outward toward others. This projection comes to be a totality. Beings discover themselves limited by other subjectivities (infinitude), but discover themselves as well in the notion of its possibility (finitude). This discovery takes place in the background of a process of symbolization that implies a certain structure between the symbolizing subject and the symbolized object, and, finally, this process of consciousness manifests as temporal movement. The consciousness of self is instantaneous, but is actualized permanently because it is always traversed by the experience of time: Today is actualized by yesterday, while it prepares tomorrow.

Alteration or alterity, in its dualistic or person-divinity dimension, refreshes the discoveries of Mounier's "personalism." The person reflects conceptually how she is as a being and how she is in the world. People tend to transform nature according to their own needs. As a subject, a person is conscious of himself and of the world he knows and transforms. But in this process of transformation of the world, people discover two things: On the one hand, they are not alone because they interact permanently with one another, with others, with other consciousnesses (this is one of Hegel's central premises), and, what is more, that from this activity a new reality arises that was not totally perceived before. Its transformative activity creates a distinctly human domain, the world of culture.

It is worth noting that the concrete reality of human activity does not present a specter of solidarity but, rather, one of conflict and antagonisms. The work of appropriating the natural world and its transformation signifies confrontations and dominating relationships of some humans over others. Consciousness bifurcates into dominated consciousness and dominant consciousness. The former lives its relationship with nature and with the other as an alienating relationship. The product of its work, when it is perceived as such, does not remain in people's hands. Rather, it is diluted in a process whose control escapes them and from which they receive minimal benefits. In spite of this, the other, dominant consciousness remains similarly unfulfilled. It is alienated as well because it can only transform the world through the dominated consciousness and also, according to Freire, because it is dehumanized by not allowing the other to be. It loses its human commitment to the historical consciousness of its reality.

"Personalization" comes from becoming conscious of people's rights and duties in a solidary and efficient way: assuming historical consciousness. If people finally recognize an explicit faith by forming a nonalienating concept of God, then they can establish a "personalizing" relationship.

Ultimately, people who are conscious of self, who appropriate nature and the sociocultural world, who live the oppressor–oppressed antagonism, are also a workforce. They find themselves in a productive process—dependent on a salary or some form of payment for their efforts, establishing relations of production and relations of power, subordinating to a routine, and ultimately producing surplus value. Work makes up part of the essence of humans. Marx (1972) said, in the *Economic Philosophical Manuscripts of 1844*: "Thanks to the production practice of an objective world and the manufacture of inorganic nature, people can experience themselves as conscious generic beings. . . . " Precisely in the manufacturing of the objective world is where they begin since they get to experience themselves as generic beings. And he said, with respect to alienating work—an opinion with which Freire coincides—that "in snatching from people the objects of their production, alienating work also snatches their generic lives, their true generic objectivity, and transforms the advantage that people possess over animals into the disadvantage of having their inorganic body—nature—stolen from them" (p. 108).

Gradually, Marx (1972) begins to concentrate his reflections on people as a workforce—not only but principally—until he arrives at the first chapter of the first volume of *Das Kapital,* where he defines them as commodity. Freire elevates the character of the workforce in his analyses about their alienation, but he includes them within a vaster philosophical schematic, together with self-consciousness and alterity.[4]

In conclusion, we may say that Freire elevates consciousness and ideology as people's social being, and history as the category that defines their historical being; that is to say, people construct themselves as social and historical beings. In fundamental terms, their sociability comes from consciousness of the reality of their historicity—from daily praxis about this reality, praxis that culminates in reflection and action, and that, issuing from people as historical beings, gradually makes history.

NINE

The Methodology of Thematic Investigation

> *The question for me is that, inside of practice, we have a hidden theory. The point for me is how to unveil the practice in order to get into the hands of the unknown theory, the not-yet-perceived theory, and how to discover in the practice the not-yet-knowledge, which is a theoretical task. The more I think critically, the more possibilities I have, first, to understand the raison d'étre for the very practice and, secondly, to become able to have a better practice next time. To think that theoretical practice is something which can be mastered just inside of classrooms or laboratories, to lose any kind of contact with reality, is a fantastic mistake.*
>
> *(Freire, quoted in Torres, 1995c, p. 180)*

This chapter will offer insights about the understanding and use of methodology for social sciences in Latin America in the sixties, and some of the debates that may have impacted Freire's methodological work. Freire's method was originally referred to as the psychosocial method of adult literacy. Although I do have serious differences with those who believe that Freire "invented" a new method of literacy training, I do believe that some of Freire's original insights made important theoretical and methodological contributions to literacy training and participative oriented methodologies, and had an important impact on the epistemological approaches to literacy training and social sciences in general.

The "psychosocial method of adult literacy" follows the dialectical method of research. This method assumes an intimate unity of theory, experimentation, implementation, or praxis and the new knowledge resulting from praxis. It follows that the whole philosophy of problem-posing literacy, when taken to the realm of adult literacy, shows an indissoluble unity between *investigation and education*, resulting in a double product—*alphabetization-conscientization*—making the differentiation between both stages difficult.

Approaching the basic theoretical underpinnings of the methodology of thematic investigation requires that we reflect on the classic methodological frameworks, particularly those that were current at the time when Freire was designing his method; this way, we can demonstrate the specificity of thematic investigation and its internal structure. Needless to say, this reflection on methodologies of social research is sketchy and purposeful—suggestive, if you will—rather than analytical and exhaustive (Torres, 1992c).

METHODOLOGIES FOR SOCIAL INVESTIGATION

> *The normal-scientific tradition that emerges from a scientific revolution is not only incompatible but often actually incommensurable with that which has gone before.*
>
> *(Kuhn,1962, p. 103)*

The Spanish sociologist Manuel Castells, residing in Santiago de Chile in the 1960s, offered a systematic appraisal of research methodology. The investigation process is, according to Manuel Castells (1968), the basic interlinking of three operations (theory, hypothesis, experimentation), each one of which is related, in a specific way, to the real-concrete: (1) *the demarcation of a particular theoretical system* or set (with respect to the *problematique* to be investigated), even though included in a general theoretical framework within a set of basic theoretical propositions (that is to say, not that the researcher *assumes* any particular system that may be useful for the research, but that the researcher selects a number of appropriate theoretical presuppositions from a theoretical framework of his or her choice); (2) certain *specific hypotheses* are then identified; and (3) the hypotheses are later put to *experiment* (falsifiability), in order to systematize the knowledge of the real-historical process in which the concrete totality is developed and to which it conforms.

Thus, the scheme of the process of scientific investigation, as a "particular discipline" of the social sciences (e.g., research methodology), can be synthesized in three moments: *theory*, *specific hypothesis*, and *experimentation*. The method of thematic investigation begins with its formalization at two levels: first, understanding how this abstract and mechanical *process of investigation* lacks meaning if the historico-structural context where the investigation takes shape is not explicit, and second, seeking the connection of the underlying meaning to the logical hypotheses with historical and existential process (represented in the language) and the real practice that contains these forms of the process of investigation.

In the creation of the modern social sciences in Latin America in the sixties, one could detect in the usual scientific practice of the social sciences four great paradigms or logics that are employed in the quest for knowledge:[1] (1) empiricism; (2) formalism; (3) voluntarism, and (4) dialectics.

The *empiricist methodology* understands that the truths of things are immanent in the outlined scientific object and that science tends to register and confirm this "telos" as credible, abstracting its significant lines; in this way, the mission of science is reduced to registering the *factual,* that which is meaningful to the investigator's eyes, and to communicating it clearly. Science thus consists of a good capacity for observation and registering, and especially, *good language.*[2]

Nagel distinguishes four fundamental types of causal explanation in the empiricist layout, as follows (Ayer, 1963):

1. *Deductive:* The object of the explanation is the logical consequence of the causal premises;
2. *Probabilistic:* The probability that one fact will occur is conditioned by the probability that another will occur;
3. *Teleological:* A fact is explained in terms of its pertinence to the process or structure that conditions it in immanent form;
4. *Genetic:* One cause-object explanation followed by another, and so on, ad infinitum.

In terms of influential contemporaries, the most important methodologists who might have impacted Freire in his early essays include Johan Galtung (1966), Paul Lazarsfeld (1968), and Boudon & Lazarsfeld (1974).

The methodology called *formalist* is the "scientific practice in which the production of knowledge takes place completely within the theoretical discourse, without any interaction between the subject and the object of knowledge by means of the operation of the proof" (Castells, 1968, p. 67).

This model renounces *experiment* as a functional part of the building of *theory,* in such a way that the whole truth has already been contained inside the theoretical discourse, whose internal logic justifies per se the validity of the propositions without passing through empirical verification (the "phagocyte" theory of empirical analysis includes Talcott Parsons and the entire structural-functionalist current). The theoretical suppositions underlying this model hold that science is a formalized image of the probable (as well as in terms of mathematical logic) rather than a practical activity of reality transformation.

The methodology known as voluntarist could also be called "relativist" or "abstract historical." It originates from the perspective of Max Weber (1973), and adopts a radically different posture from the previous two. It affirms how, because no repeatable or measurable laws exist to be reiterated within the historical process, the logical consequence is the negation of the legality of scientific practice and its reduction to the context of purely social practice. While Castells identifies Weber as voluntarist or relativist, this is obviously a matter for discussion. The distinguished Italian political scientist Norberto Bobbio in his studies in the history of philosophy disagrees. He identifies Weber as the last of the classics, and defines Weber's theories and methodologies as part of the realistic tradition in political theory (Bobbio, 1985, p. 261).

Weber theoretically distinguishes the rationality of the ultimate ends and the rationality of the means. This allows him to define rational social action adequate to the ends and *social action* adequate to the means. The labor of science is to orient individuals in the labyrinth of decisions that permit them to adjust their conduct to the rational action. What, then, will be the methodological path? The answer is the elaboration of *ideal types.*

The *ideal type* will be an outline of reality that can be observed in determined situations (for instance, the rational legal, charismatic, and traditional types of domination). Called *ideal type* (or historical summary), it serves as a means of comparison with reality and, in this way, a kind of *descriptive synthesis* can be carried out. However, the *ideal type* itself is undiscoverable in reality; it is just a good heuristic instrument to investigate reality.

The methodology we call "dialectical" originates as a product of the Hegelian dialectic that, sifted through and modified by Marx, becomes historico-structural analysis. Galvano Della Volpe (1963) briefly synthesizes the substance of this method: "which is located in the very terrain of experience as well as in the terrain of historical-material or social instances (opening, or first movement of the distinguished circle: from the concrete to the abstract) . . . that consequently formulates abstractions to the ends, from an objective comprehension of the problems, whose character of synthesis—abstraction's inseparable synonym, concept or category—is also inseparable from analysis. While, with such abstractions, it is a matter of revalorizing the meaning of historical antecedents in their conceptual nexus with consequent ones, present and problematic historical characteristics to be resolved" (p. 134). This dialectic method has been defined countless times as the *concrete-abstract-concrete circle.*

As the methodology of thematic investigation is developed in the "interior" of the dialectic method, it is worthwhile to attempt to formalize the dialectic's epistemological suppositions a bit more.

DIALECTICAL EPISTEMOLOGY AND ITS IMPORTANCE IN THEMATIC INVESTIGATION

> *Freire clearly stated that education is not a reflection of the relationships between classes but, rather, a product of the dialectical relationship between culture and the social means of production. In Freirean theory, subjectivity is not reduced to a reflection of objectivity, but consist of a complex product of human praxis about this materiality.*
>
> *(Adriana Puiggrós, quoted in Torres and Noguera, 2008, p. 169)*

As Enrique Dussel mentions, the dialectic is a *meta-hodos*, or radical, introductory path to those who use it. There are, however, multiple dialectics not just one model. Aristotle, Descartes, Kant, Fichte, Schelling, Hegel, Marx, Heidegger, Sartre, Zubiri, and Lévinas are among the many significant philosophers or thinkers who have sustained distinct "dialectics." However, as Dussel (1972) states:

> all the dialectics begin with a *factum* (a fact), from a limit *ex quo* (outside) the point of departure. From this *factum*, the dialectic will depart in one direction or another, according to its sense of being (meaning determines direction) and for which the *ad quen* (arrival point), the "to where" of the dialectical movement, will be very different. (p. 10)

I am not so much interested in giving an account of the diversity of dialectical thoughts as I am in showing the philosophical direction that corresponds to the underpinnings of the dialectic of the thematic investigation.

Thus, the value of the dialectic in thematic investigation, as João Bosco Pinto (1970) mentions, is that "the dialectic presupposes the unity of the process of knowledge and of concrete reality, the subject and object of knowledge are not two distinct entities which enter into relationship by means of a third identity, sensation, which is also different from the first two but, rather, two aspects of one and the same reality in unity and dialectic contradiction. It is not about a subject outside the object of knowledge but about a real, concrete person who, in the course of and as a function of his or her existence, makes of the universe—of which he or she is an integral part—the object of his or her thinking and who transforms this objective reality into a devised reality. As part of this human activity, they converge into one time and are united by thinking that directs people's action and is stimulated by it, and the outside world, within which and as a function of which people act, either to adapt themselves to the world or to transform it" (p. 3).

Thinking directs the praxis and is, in turn, conditioned by praxis. The production of knowledge is contained in this mutual conditioning. Freire has said countless times that consciousness and world are mutually constituted. This knowledge of objective reality is verified by the concept which simultaneously encapsulates a description and analysis of the real, but as part of the real, is itself transformed in a proverbial tension between subject and object that Freire addresses in his epistemological discourse. In the dialectic methodology there is the synthesis between thought and the outside world because, being a characteristic of subjectivity, it induces and exposes objectivity categorically (as determinate historical abstraction). This same concept results in the dialectical surmounting of the subject–object dichotomy.

We again adopt the reasoning of Bosco Pinto (1970) when he argues "Therefore the point of departure of the methodology of thematic investigation is objective reality, not understood as something separate either from the investigator who approaches it to understand it, or from the group member who finds herself inside that same reality, but as a dialectical unit in which reality serves as a mediating element that permits a horizontal, dialogical social relationship in which both subjects discover themselves united and in opposition to the objective reality" (p. 4).

The dialectical surmounting of empiricism is rooted in the *factum* from which it departs. Here the object-of-knowledge confronts the subject-of knowledge who may begin to recognize (in the critical transitive consciousness) the challenges and tasks of the outside world in such a way that the scientific attitude will never proceed to register and communicate data but, rather, will attempt to orchestrate the means to respond to the challenges and prolong its action toward the "untested feasibility" in Freirean terminology (Bohorquez, 2008).

In this way, it will overcome *formalism* by systematically declining to hypostatize the theory to the detriment of objectivity and by understanding that all concepts are the expression of the subjective–objective dialectics. Thus, there exist laws of causality that are intrinsic to the nature of the investigated object (for instance, the existential referents of the alphabetized community) that must be captured by subjectivity (to guide the practice of social transformation).

Finally, it will overcome *voluntarism* because, if it really intends to obtain a descriptive synthesis—in the phase of thematic investigation, for example, this synthesis should be "projective"—that is, to project certain basic elements of the social structure or community under analysis to avoid reducing the action in the pedagogical stage and in the postliteracy tasks to mere activism or pure social practice without scientific direction which, for Freire, would be action without reflection. It is this way because the critical transitive consciousness or political consciousness is never marked by historical relativism but, rather, is marked by the value of the community's empirical-cultural praxis, which is constituted in subjectivity that is transformed by and, in turn, transforms this sociocultural world. This consciousness operates on objective, reiterated, measurable, and quantifiable laws from the objective world (thence, the value of the team of specialists, or interdisciplinary team, to engender the "circle of investigation").

SOCIO-ANTHROPOLOGICAL REFERENTS OF THEMATIC INVESTIGATION (SYNTHESIS)

Life is what happens while you are busy making other plans.
(John Lennon)

We have already analyzed the socio-anthropological or politico-anthropological referents of problem-posing literacy. These include:

1. People as *relational beings* are situated and dated.
2. People confront the challenges of their era and, in responding to them, become history, or historicize themselves. People are culture-makers.

3. The options or tasks display a plurality that, not being proscribed, like animal instinct, are presented to the subject as an array of possibilities (in a field of options).
4. As beings of praxis, their critical activities attain meaning in the execution of the daily and permanent transformation of their culture by praxis.
5. This transformational action has a transcendental meaning expressed both by the possibility of getting out of oneself and also by the possibility of relating (relinking) to one's creator.
6. People are *beings of communication* and, as such, require others with whom to establish dialogues—that is, to have the right to pronounce their word.[3]

THEMATIC INVESTIGATION AND THE THEORY OF PRAXIS

Power is an educational system that divides us into subjects and subjected. Nevertheless, it's an educational system that forms us all, from the so-called ruling class all the way down to the poorest of us. That's why everybody wants the same things and everyone acts in the same way.

(Pier Paolo Passolini, last interview, a few hours before he was assassinated, quoted in Hirschman, 2010, p. 236)

Thematic investigation implies overcoming the reflection–action or knowledge–practice antimonies, preferring to be research for action rather than a purely empirical method. It is a model of participatory action research (Torres, 1992c). Freire (1970c) says: "While the codified representation is the cognizable object that mediates knowing subjects, decodification—breaking down a code into its cognizable elements—is the operation by which the knowing subjects perceive relationships among the elements of the codification and among facts presented by the real situation, relationships that were not perceived before" (p. 15).

This implies the first gnoseological moment of the pedagogy of the oppressed, or rather, the pedagogy of the revelation of reality. Being represented as the matrix of oppression, it implies the beginning of recognition of the mechanisms of domination (in educational terms, these would be the specific mechanisms of the domination of consciousnesses or mechanisms of alienation) by the oppressed classes.

But, as Freire (1975) also states: "If conscientization cannot be produced without the revelation of the objective reality, as an object of knowledge for those subjects implicated in the process, then this revelation—even when it is a clear perception of the reality—is nevertheless insufficient as an authentic conscientization. In the same way that the epistemological cycle does not terminate in the degree of acquisition of the already existing knowledge but, rather, continues through the phase of creation of new knowledge, neither can conscientization be detained in the degree of revelation of reality. *It is authentic when the practice of revealing reality constitutes a dynamic and dialectic unity with the practice of transforming reality*" (p. 28, emphasis added).

In conclusion, we will say that the theory of praxis, in thematic investigation, has a profound incidence in the two basic gnoseological moments of problem-posing literacy: the *praxis of revelation* of reality and the *praxis of transformation* of this reality—moments that are unified in the act of consciousness-raising literacy or conscientization (Furter & Fiori, 1975).

METHODS OF PROBLEM-POSING LITERACY STAGES

The objective of thematic investigation is to find the generative themes or expressions of the people's word so that an educational program can be carried out, developing a consciousness-raising cultural action.

The whole trajectory of thematic investigation[4] (investigation-education) can be stated in three stages as follows. These are chronologically and analytically distinguishable, but closely linked because it is a dialectical process: (1) *the eminently investigative stage or phase*; (2) *the eminently pragmatic stage or phase,* and (3) *the eminently pedagogical stage or phase.*

THE BASIC TECHNIQUES

Like all methodologies, thematic investigation possesses certain specific techniques, among which the most important are the processes of *reduction, coding,* and *decoding.*

1. *Reduction:* The process of finding a generative theme, as we have already seen, has the goal of elaborating themes; later, in a specific pedagogical order, these are returned to the alphabetizing community, where they were discovered as "problem-posing."

   The group of specialists[5] analyzes what has been observed and gathered, with the participation of the people and each shapes the units of learning from a specialist's perspective, taking the substantive aspects into account. There are three criteria necessary for the selection of a generative word: (1) syllabic richness; (2) phonetic difficulty, and (3) practical existential content, intimately referential to the social, political, cultural and economic themes of a specific alphabetizing community.

The technical process of reducing into units of learning that will then allow the selection of generative words assumes two "moments" in the circle of investigation.[6]

a. *A moment of internal critique,* where the *thematic investigation* team submits the group of epochal themes[7] that have been collected to a disciplined, scientific critique until it succeeds in detecting the functional and linguistic value of the themes "captured" in the existential-referential context of the investigative area.
b. *A moment of external critique* is one in which the first results with volunteers from the future group of alphabetizing people are compared. These people, in their double role as *key informants and representatives of the popular classes,* sift through the information selected, in succeeding meetings of the investigation circle, until the central axes of a pedagogical program are defined. Substantively, this is the objective presentation to the people of the elements of the dominated consciousness (the ideological visions) of the central themes: *human-nature-culture.* They will confront these through a *dialogical and dialectic* process within the central categories of a liberated consciousness, beginning with an analysis undertaken from the categories of economics and sociology.

2. *Codifying*: This is the graphic representation of each one of the strategic existential situations, reduced into learning units. The codification can be:

   a. *Simple*:
      - *Visual channel:* picture, graphic
      - *Sensible channel:* socio-drama, psychodrama, short film, slides, audiovisuals
      - *Aural channel:* narratives, popular music, popular poetry, readings, conversations

   b. *Composite:* simultaneity of channels

3. *Decodifying:* This is a discussion of the existential codification. It can happen inside the circle of investigation, in the moment of *exterior critique*, where the first descriptive stage is intent on integrating with a second, more analytical stage to finally arrive at a projective synthesis of whatever meaningful themes are detected. This should also lead to a *culture circle*[8] as the expression and result of the dialogical work between the coordinator and the people who are learning to alphabetize.

PAULO FREIRE'S PRACTICAL SUGGESTIONS

Before underlining some practical suggestions from the course of Freirean work, we want to propose to the reader a synthetic scheme of the steps of problem-posing literacy (thematic investigation):

STAGES

1st moment:	*Eminently Investigative* Defining and understanding the working area Existential codification and decodification Circle of investigation Verification of results
2nd moment:	*Eminently Programmatic* THEMATIC TREATMENT (focus of each discipline) Circle of investigation Thematic reduction Thematic codification Manufacture of didactic materials
3rd moment:	*Eminently Pedagogical* PUBLICIZING THE PROGRAM (to the people) Thematic decodification (initiating decodifying dialogues): *1st sphere:* Decodification of the strategic existential situations *2nd sphere:* Presentation of the generative theme *3rd sphere:* Picture with the generative word in small letters
4th moment:	Picture with the generative word in small letters and separated into syllables
5th moment:	Picture with the first syllabic family
6th moment:	Picture with the second syllabic family
7th moment:	Discovery card
8th moment:	Picture with the vowels of the word
9th moment:	The alphabetizers listen, verbally construct, and write new words
10th moment:	Dialogical, dialectic, and intersubjective decodification. The stage of alphabetization gives way to the stage of postalphabetization.

Having outlined this general introductory scheme to the entire method, we will now delimit, in an introductory and synthetic form, diverse practical suggestions from Freire; he had been cultivating these in the course of his pedagogical practice for a better and more effective application or implementation of the psychosocial method of adult education:

1. To be a coordinator, the person must possess two qualities: On one hand, he must *avoid directing* the group toward its objectives (either because he possesses a personal charisma of leadership or simply because he is accustomed to imposing his point of view on the group dynamic), but, on the other hand, he must go slowly, increasingly challenging and *problematizing* the alphabetizing group.

   The coordinator's task is to be the craftsman of the union of individual experiences (especially in the initial phases), until the group comes to a moment of qualitative advancement, when he changes from being the *coordinator* to being the *moderator* of the debates, which are a product of the culture circle's own dynamic.
2. Along with the coordinator (who must always be the same person), another member of the thematic investigation team should attend the meetings (as a *witness* or *nonparticipant observer*). Her task will be to record the entire *production* of the culture circle (if the group has decided not to tape the sessions), and what is significant in terms of *structured observation* as defined by the investigative team itself. Typical observations include expressions, sayings, idioms, and all kinds of interesting linguistics traits that may work toward educative ends, and the behavior, attitude, and participation of the alphabetizing group.
3. The types of questions that the coordinator poses to the group must always be set forth in communal rather than individual terms. For example, when Freire speaks of the vertical and horizontal reading of the *discovery card* (a term minted by Professor Aurenice Cardoso, Freire's assistant in the Brazilian National Plan of Adult Literacy), he says that "the educator will always ask the people who are alphabetizing 'Do you think that *we* (never do you think that *you*) can create something with these pieces of words?' " (Freire, 1970c, p. 54).
4. Popular education groups must *never* begin the work of *alphabetization-conscientization* without previously and exhaustively reflecting about the possible paths to develop, when they intend to reach the limit of *untested feasibility* (not between being and not-being, but between being and being more) (Streck, Redin & Zitkoski, 2012, pages 216–217; 412–415).

   This does not mean that the investigation team has "recipes" or a "political program" for the people who are alphabetizing. Such a perspective would be what Freire insists on calling "cultural invasion" or the manipulation of consciousnesses. The suggestion is valid in this sense: It is advisable not to elaborate a pedagogical process with the radicality that the method possesses if the horizon of possible options has not been anticipated. It cannot be used as a method of domestification because of the flagrant contradiction to the method's spirit and dialogical structures. When individuals penetrate the dynamism of the transit of their critical consciousness, there is no better antidote for conscientization than frustrated expectations (false expectations, we daresay) of the alphabetizers and the investigative team, provoked by this lack of evaluative praxis.

5. A very important suggestion here results from the practice of popular education. Grassroots groups that implement the method should be in relationship with political segments of greater breadth, such as social movements, community organizations, political parties, and so on in order to guarantee the continuity and especially a certain political "coverage" in moments of repression of the alphabetizers-alphabetizing and the alphabetizing-alphabetizers.[9]
6. Finally, Freire makes some fragmentary suggestions for the postliteracy stage. He insists that, once the stage of basic reading and writing is finished, and the group members are initiated in the operations of basic mathematics, it would be advisable to propose a real challenge for the group: to make a textbook for future groups, and perhaps books that come from the "quill pens" of newly literate people rather than intellectuals.

This will generate a review of the difficulties of the road just traveled by the group, and perhaps highlight possible paths to solutions. It will also awaken the people's creativity: Meaningful drawings could be made by the recently "alphabetized" group, and these may even replace certain slides about specific generative words that hitherto were used as didactic material.

Reading between the lines, some of Paulo Freire's suggestions seem to us to indicate that he believes the specifically "political" discussion about the basic and immediate recovery of community organizations in the popular sectors needs to be deepened and hastened in order to contribute to their liberation. It is important that such discussions incorporate certain social science concepts that permit an increment of theoretical discussion about the "complex consciousnesses" in search of their permanent liberation.

Finally, it is worthwhile to mention how some popular education groups have successfully utilized health education programs in attempting to counter critical community problems, such as groundwater pollution and basic sanitation (garbage, sewage, harmful animals, rodents), as well as starting workshops for nursing mothers and/or social prophylaxis. Also in this sense, the incorporation of food conservation techniques or projects to achieve balanced and nutritive diets has proven effective at the postliteracy stage.

Nevertheless, today there is an open path for new creative experiences, because valid formulas for different times and places do not exist. Only imagination and tenacity combined with the utopian spirit that Freire insists on can make the practice of popular education a practice of revelation and transformation of reality. This is the only way that Marx's (1975) deep "utopic" meaning will be of value: "Each one of human's attitudes about human and about nature have to be a resolute manifestation of his individual and actual life, a manifestation that corresponds to the object of his will. People who experience love without its being returned, in other words, without their love provoking the love of the object of their affection, those for whom the manifestation of their lives as lovers is unrequited will feel that their love is impotent, a source of disgrace" (p. 160).

TEN

The Paulo Freire System

THE ANGICOS EXPERIENCE: SHORT CHRONOLOGY

Requiem for Paulo Neves Freire
With you
we knew that the pilgrimage of this world
only has meaning in struggle.
With you, a teacher who sheltered himself beneath the mango tree,
practicing words and world
there
on the back patio of your childhood home in Recife,
we came to understand the anguish and hopes of all teachers.
(Carlos A. Torres)

Que un individuo quiera despertar en otro individuo recuerdos que no pertenecieron más que a un tercero, es una paradoja evidente. Ejecutar con despreocupación esa paradoja, es la inocente voluntad de toda biografía.
(José Luis Borges)

We should recall that it was 50 years ago, in the small and impoverished municipality of Angicos, 178 kilometers from Natal, in Rio Grande do Norte, northeast Brazil, that the first systematic experiences of Freire's literacy training took place. Freire, together with a group of utopian, left-leaning Catholic students at the outset of the Theology of Liberation movement, transformed literacy training, making it possible for 300 rural workers to learn to read and write in 40 hours, working at night, after long days of tedious and demanding agricultural work completed under the extenuating sun of northeast Brazil.

Let us briefly recall what was happening in the region at the time. Freire was already known by educators and policymakers, having presented the theoretical foundations of his adult literacy system at the Second National Conference of Adult Education in Rio de Janeiro, July 9–16, 1958. The following year, he applied for the position of the chair of History and Philosophy of Education at the School of Fine Arts in Pernambuco, with the dissertation that is listed in the bibliography

(Freire, 2001). However, because the radicality of his positions the dissertation was not accepted (Gerhardt, 1993). Instead, he was appointed director of the faculty of extension.[1]

These were times of enormous political activism. The foundations of the Popular Culture Movement (Movimento de Cultura Popular, or MCP) were created in Recife under the administration of newly elected mayor Miguel Arraes. The MCP fused culture with political struggle, aiming to increase people's consciousness and promoting literacy through cultural circles. Education and culture were understood as tools of liberation. On March 21, 1961, the Movimento de Educação de Base (MEB) Grassroots Education Movement was formed through an initiative of the Catholic Church. This was a partnership between the federal government and the National Conference of Bishops of Brazil (NCBB) to contribute to the process of adult literacy and help develop communities.

In April 1961, the National Union of Students (UNE) created the Centro Popular de Cultura or Center of Popular Culture (CPC), paving the way for the politicization of social issues. They wanted to create and disseminate popular revolutionary art with engaged artists in order to challenge people's alienation and naïve consciousness.

In 1961 President João Goulart was inaugurated after a military coup. On April 13, he signed the Acordo Brasil-Estados Unidos sobre o Nordeste-Brazil-USA Agreement on the Northeast. On September 18, 1962, anthropologist Darcy Ribeiro, one of the most influential Brazilian intellectuals of the 20th century, took office at the Ministry of Education. Ribeiro knew Freire and considered him a most insightful pedagogue, recommending him to a number of colleagues and political pundits.

In September 1962, Calazans Fernandes, secretary of education of the state of Rio Grande do Norte and coordinator of the Serviço Cooperativo de Educação do Rio Grande do Norte (SECERN) [Office of Cooperative Education of Rio Grande do Norte], and Maria José Monteiro, a former student of Paulo Freire's, meet with Freire at the University of Recife to discuss the Angicos Literacy Project.

Freire, fearing that resources from the Alliance for Progress could interfere with his work, insisted on having complete autonomy to hire coordinators and teachers, as well as freedom from political-academic and ideological interference. In December 1962, Marcos Guerra, a law student and president of the National Union of Students, formed a team of teachers (facilitators) for the Angicos Literacy Project. Thus, the project became a partnership between SECERN and the Serviço de Extensão Cultural da Universidade do Recife (SEC/UR) [Cultural Extension Service of the University of Recife] while being directed by Paulo Freire. The work began with a survey of the number of illiterates in Angicos and a study of people's specific vocabulary (words and generative themes) using the methodology described in Chapter 9.

December 3, 1962, marked the signing of the agreement among the Ministry of Education, Superintendência do Desenvolvimento do Nordeste (SUDENE) [Superintendence for the Development of the Northeast], the state of Rio Grande do Norte, and the U.S. Agency for International Development (USAID) within the guidelines set forth by the Alliance for Progress.[2]

The project was officially launched on January 18, and 380 residents became the inaugural class of the Angicos Literacy Program. A few days later, on January 24, 1963, the first class of the program took place, entitled "The Anthropological Concept of Culture." This marked the start of the "Forty Hours of Angicos." During February and March 1963, classes for students took place at the same time as the meetings that were held for the training of coordinators in the cultural circles.

On April 2, 1963, the 40th, and final, hour of the program was taught by President João Goulart. The session was attended by several governors in the northeast, as well as by representatives of the Alliance for Progress. Aluísio Alves, Paulo Freire, and former illiterate Antonio Ferreira shared their experiences in this class. The oldest student, Maria Hermínia, gave the president a letter written by participants in the course. This was the first graduating class of Angicos.

General Humberto de Alencar Castelo Branco, commander of the Military Region in Recife and who later became the first military president after the coup d'etat of April 1, 1964, attended the meeting and told Calazans Fernandes, "Young man, you're fattening rattlesnakes in this area" (Fernandes & Terra, 1994, p. 18).

The experiment ended in April 1963, and the results of the evaluation of the Angicos Literacy Project were released: Three hundred participants were considered literate, with a 70% success rate on the Literacy Test and 87% success rate on the Test of Politicization (Lyra, 1996). In May 1963, the city of Angicos had its first labor strike. Landowners call the experience of Paulo Freire a "communist plague" (Fernandes & Terra, 1994, p. 126).

On June 2, 1963, the *New York Times* published a report on the experience of Angicos, spurring greater international attention. Reporters from well-established publications such as *Time* magazine, *Herald Tribune*, *Sunday Times*, *Associated Press*, and *Le Monde* also traveled to Angicos to cover the project.

Just over a month later, on July 16, 1963, Ministerial Ordinance #195 established the Committee of Popular Culture within the Office of the Ministry of Education in order "to deploy, nationwide, new educational systems eminently popular, to cover areas not yet reached by the benefits of education." Paulo Freire was appointed chairman of the committee. His first task was to survey the national number of illiterates to support the future National Literacy Program. The number of illiterates between 15 to 45 years of age totaled 20,442,000—out of a total population of 79,599,340.

In October 1963, an envoy of U.S. ambassadors visited Governor Aluísio Alves in Natal to prepare for the visit of President John F. Kennedy to Angicos, scheduled for December 1963. However, President Kennedy never made the trip. He was assassinated on November 22, 1963.

IT ALL STARTED IN ANGICOS: THE PAULO FREIRE SYSTEM

A thing of beauty is a joy forever.
(John Keats, "Endymion")

The main thesis of this chapter is that Freire's original experience in Angicos anticipated a grand design for the social transformation of educational systems. It brought together two key concepts that formed the basis of his educational system: *popular culture* as a counter-hegemonic project, and *popular education*—more particularly, what was later called *citizen schools* or *public popular education* (O'Cadiz & Torres, 1994; O'Cadiz, Torres, & Wong, 1998; Torres, 1998a, 1998b).

Any traditional definition of a system will agree that it constitutes "a set of detailed methods, procedures and routines created to carry out a specific activity, perform a duty, or solve a problem" (BusinessDictionary.com, 2013). I use the term *Paulo Freire System* to show that Freire's original attempts were more than simply a pedagogical challenge to the banking education system that was so pervasive in Brazil and Latin America at the time.[3] In challenging the hegemony of banking education, along with its narrative, theoretical foundations, epistemology, and methodology, Freire and his team sought to create a new system that could replace the old one. They viewed banking education as not only obsolete in terms of the modernization of systems but also as oppressive in gnoseological, epistemological, and political terms.

One could also use the term *Paulo Freire Model*, implying the design of organizational structures to enact a transformation of a given system. All models provide a narrative or coherence for a new architecture—in this case, a new architecture of knowledge—as well as capturing mechanisms to implement this new social and organizational venture.

What I would like to argue in this chapter is that the original experiences of Freire in the city of Angicos in Rio Grande do Norte, or the previous experiments on literacy training that also took place in the northeast, were attempts to construct this new educational system, or what I have called—for the lack of another term—the *Paulo Freire System*. An important early experience was the one carried out in João Pessoa, Paraíba, in January 1962 when Freire and his team from the University of Recife advised the Campanha de Educação Popular (CEPLAR), Campaign for Popular Education of Paraíba created by college students and professionals trained to work in adult literacy programs (Scocuglia, 1999).

The experience and spirit of the 1960s implied a most dramatic radicalization of the tensions between those who actually create culture in their everyday lives, the common people, and intellectuals who analyze these processes, making proposals for cultural action (Fávero, 1983; Rodriguez Brandão, 2013; Torres, 2007, 2009a).

I have already documented that Freire's original insights related to the work of Vieira Pinto and the intellectuals connected with ISEB, assuming that the process of social transformation of consciousness implies moving from a given level to a higher level of cognitive complexity (from naïve consciousness to transitive consciousness to critical consciousness). Yet eventually, Freire left this theoretical framework behind to get closer to George Lukacs's model of class consciousness or Gramsci's war of position in the struggle for hegemony (Scocuglia, 1999; Torres, 2009a). Freire, however, invoking in his writings of the 1960s, class consciousness and class analysis never entirely bought the prescriptive and linear deterministic analysis of some variants of Marxist socialism, emphasizing instead the "inédito viavel" or "untested feasibility" as an option (Bohorquez, 2008).

The idea of a Paulo Freire System was already present in the work of Freire and his team at the University of Recife in the early 1960s.[4] The earlier written productions of this group and the titles of their work are evidence of this. Consider, for instance, the fourth volume of the *Revista de Cultura* of the University of Recife, published in April–June 1963. Here are the titles: *Conscientização e alfabetização: Uma nova visão do processo* (*Conscientization and Literacy: A New Vision of the Process*), written by Paulo Freire (pp. 5–22); *Fundamentação teórica do Sistema Paulo Freire de Educação* (*Theoretical Foundations of the Paulo Freire System of Education*), written by Jarbas Maciel (1983) (pp. 25–58); *Educação de adultos e unificação da cultura* (*Adult Education and the Unification of Culture*), written by Jomard Muniz de Britto (1983) (pp. 61–69); and *Conscientização e alfabetização: Uma visão prática do Sistema Paulo Freire* (*Conscientization and Literacy: A Practical Vision of the Paulo Freire System*), written by Aurenice Cardoso (1983, pp. 71–79[5]).

As Carlos Rodrigues Brandão (2013) so cleverly observes, there is a difference in the way Freire and his group treated the terms *culture* and *education*: Paulo Freire subordinated a proposal for education to a process of democratization of culture. Thus "culture is the key concept in all of his writing. This is the cultural moment of the first texts of Paulo Freire post-Angicos" (p. 25).

The Paulo Freire System had several phases, including a first phase for children's literacy, a second phase of adult literacy (exemplified in the Angicos experience and later in the Commission for Popular Culture over which Freire was invited to preside), and a third phase of accelerated elementary education, initially implemented as a pilot program in the CEPLAR activities in Paraíba, mentioned above.

The fourth phase of the Paulo Freire system, intimately connected with the previous one, marked the origins of the Popular University in Latin America. It was the Service of Cultural Extension of the University of Recife that aimed to provide different levels of education, including popular education (adult education), elementary, secondary, preuniversity and university levels. The idea was to work with groups in the urban areas of Recife (Maciel, 1983).

The fifth phase of the system emerged in the work of the Institute of Human Sciences (*Instituto de Ciências do Homem*) at the University of Recife (Maciel, 1983). The sixth phase would have been the creation of a Center for International Studies (*Centro de Estudos Internacionais* [CEI]) as an effort to link the Brazilian experience with Third World experiences.

This was the overall design of the Paulo Freire System, which was to be implemented as phases of a service of cultural extension in a northeast university, with the hope of extending the system to the rest of the country. It was not a service "for the people" but "with the people," a concept that pervades the whole *oeuvre* of Paulo Freire and what Rodrigues Brandão (2013) has properly called "the recreation of cultura from the people" (p. 35).

Rodrigues Brandão (2013) centers his analysis on the epistemological foundations of the Paulo Freire System, along the same lines that I have described in this book, as Freire's concept of cultural development or the concept of the developmental subject that I will discuss below:

1. The ontological equality of all human beings.
2. The limited accessibility to knowledge and culture.
3. The limited communicability of knowledge and culture.

RE-CREATING THE PUBLIC SPHERE: REMEMBERING AND CELEBRATING ANGICOS

> *Truly, only the oppressed are able to conceive of a future totally distinct from their present, insofar as they arrive at a consciousness of a dominated class. The oppressors, as the dominating class, cannot conceive of the future unless it is the preservation of their present as oppressors. In this way, whereas the future of the oppressed consists in the revolutionary transformation of society, without which their liberation will not be verified, the oppressor's future consists in the simple modernization of society, which permits the continuation of its class supremacy.*
>
> (Freire, 1972c, p. 32)

This section will address what Freire learned from the Angicos experience: how he consolidated his pedagogical model through a social science based on a critical hermeneutics, and how his thinking evolved into a theory of social and cultural reproduction, looking particularly to the role of education. It will also examine how Freire then moved into a critical social psychology, focusing on domination and the developmental pedagogical subject, and how he, inspired by the profound political and pedagogical experience of Angicos and his political pedagogical practice, understood praxis as collective learning.

In the conclusion of this chapter, I will discuss the twin obsessions of Freire, already present in the Angicos experience, which stayed with him throughout his life: the relationship of democracy, citizenship, and education; and education as a postcolonial ethical act of social transformation. I would like to emphasize that the Paulo Freire System, as conceived in the Angicos experience and its aftermath, was a much larger and more comprehensive system than originally considered, even by his critics.

We should remember and celebrate the Angicos experience for what it signified as the first milestone of Freire's political pedagogical journey. It should be remembered not only as an experience of successful literacy training, but also as an attempt to expand the notion of the "public" and public education, enhancing the public sphere. As distinguished political theorist Nancy Frazer (2005) has persuasively argued:

> The concept of the public sphere was developed not simply to understand empirical communication flows but to contribute a normative political theory of democracy. In that theory, a public sphere is conceived as a space for the communicative generation of public opinion, in ways that are supposed to assure (at least some degree of) moral-political validity. Thus, it matters who participates and on what terms. In addition, a public sphere is supposed to be a vehicle for mobilizing public opinion as a political force. It should empower the citizenry vis-à-vis private powers and permit it to exercise influence over the state. Thus, a public-sphere is supposed to correlate with a sovereign power, to which its communications are ultimately addressed.

Angicos needs to be celebrated because it constituted a landmark in the process of the social transformation of Brazil, creating a public sphere moving from an unfettered capitalism in a social formation marked by distinct feudal forms of domination to a process of national and popular transformation. Angicos was also timely in the context of the social transformations of Latin America in the 1950s and 1960s. But the experience of Angicos and its possible aftermath was thwarted by the coup d'etat of the Brazilian military dictatorship that inaugurated the new authoritarianism of Latin America, particularly in the Southern Cone (Collier, 1979; O'Donnell & McGuire, 1988). The conclusion of this experiment of literacy training catapulted Freire to national fame, and as discussed above, the president of Brazil, João Goulart, made Freire the president of the National Commission of Popular Culture, in charge of developing a fast-paced and massive literacy training program in Brazil. Because in that time those who couldn't read and write could not vote, Freire's experiments were a true exercise in citizenship building, and as such, were an experience of creating and re-creating the public sphere in Brazil. If only for this, Freire should be remembered and studied, although there are many more reasons to remember and study him. His contributions made an enormous difference in the lives of people all over the world. Not surprisingly, the Brazilian government of the socialist democratic Workers' Party passed a congressional law in 2012 making Freire the patron of Brazilian education (Law Nº 12.612, April 13, 2012).

The next sections will delve into the epistemological and theoretical implications of the Paulo Freire System, starting from its beginning in Angicos.

EDUCATION AS CRITICAL HERMENEUTICS: AN EPISTEMOLOGY OF SUSPICION

De toda palabra ociosa darás cuenta a Dios.[6]

(Written on the door of a church in Viscaya, the Basque Country, Spain)

Freire shares with Paul Ricoeur a hermeneutics of suspicion. Their models of critical hermeneutics evolved from the tradition of textual interpretation that originated in methodological questions regarding the Bible, "a problematic that also becomes central for the study of cultural documents. Critical hermeneutics is differentiated by its orientation towards a 'hermeneutics of suspicion' or what in social theory has often been called the ideology critique of cultural criticism" (Morrow & Torres, 2002, p. 43).

Freire's intellectual life could be characterized as a form of eclecticism within a project of radical modernism. Reflecting upon the influences of his writings, he told us that:

> I remember, for example, how much I was helped by reading Frantz Fanon. . . . I was writing *Pedagogy of the Oppressed* . . . when I read Fanon, I had to rewrite the book in order to begin to quote Fanon. . . . I had different cases like this, which I felt conditioned, "influenced" without knowing. Fanon was one. Albert Memmi, who wrote a fantastic book, *The Colonizer and the Colonized*, was the second. The third who "influenced" me without knowing it was the famous Russian psychologist Lev Vygotsky . . . when I read him the first time, I became frightened and happy because of the things I was reading. The other influence is Gramsci. . . . When I meet some books, I remake my practice theoretically. I become better able to understand the theory inside of my action. (Horton & Freire, 1990, p. 36)

Freire's Critical Theory of Society, on parallel with the Frankfurt School, is based on a philosophy of science or a meta-theory that attempts to mediate between the polarization of subjectivism and positivism (or idealism and materialism) that has long plagued the Marxist tradition and social theory more generally. Freire works within the broader meta-theoretical tradition of critical hermeneutics that attempts to ground social inquiry in the understanding of agents (hence, its hermeneutic or interpretive dimension), while also taking into account the social structural context of action. Yet, one of the key elements of Freire and many others who work closer to the phenomenological tradition is to assume that every social exchange involves a moment, a relationship of domination. This is the reason that an epistemology of suspicion based on the belief that all social exchanges involve social domination is the trademark of pedagogy of the oppressed.

From this vantage point, Freire assumes a theory of social and cultural reproduction (Morrow & Torres, 1995, 2002). Freire does not presume that cultural reproduction is a static and deterministic process through which a society replicates itself from generation to generation. Rather, his theory of cultural and social reproduction is guided by an understanding of historical specificity and effectively deals with the dialectic of agency and structure.

Because the key elements of the Angicos experience are based on the dialectical unity between developmental subjects and processes of domination, Freire works from a Critical Social Psychology. Just now, some scholars, particularly Deborah Britzman, are beginning to look seriously at the intersections between *Pedagogy of the Oppressed* and psychoanalysis (Britzman, n.d.). This problematic of domination vis-à-vis the developmental subject was anticipated in Marx's theories of alienation and praxis, as well as in the work of the Frankfurt School, especially the studies on authoritarian personality. Freire added a substantial contribution to theories of a dialogical and developmental subject, positing that developmental models are suggestive of universal human possibilities whose realization is impeded by relations of social domination. Unequivocally, Freire (1985) states that:

> The pursuit of full humanity, however, cannot be carried out in isolation or individualism, but only in fellowship and solidarity; therefore it cannot unfold in the antagonistic relations between oppressor and oppressed. No one can be authentically human while he prevents other from being so. Attempting to be more human, individualistic, leads to having more, egoistically: a form of dehumanization. Not that it is not fundamental to have in order to be human. Precisely because it is necessary, some men's having must not be allowed to constitute an obstacle to other's having, must not consolidate the power of the former to crush the latter. (pp. 73–74)

Freire's theory of domination and emancipatory practices focuses on domination exemplified in the culture of silence. For him, education cannot be the lever of social transformation; instead, it plays a fundamental role as a cultural action for freedom. His solution is *conscientização*. Because the culture of silence is produced by antidialogical action—that is, distorted communication—it produces relations of domination that deceive subjects. Hence, Freire's extraordinary insight that a relation of dialogue—as a form of learning—may contribute to the possibility of emancipatory consciousness, which is grounded in the capacity for self-reflection that defines reason. We need not only language, narratives, and discourse (all central elements in the pedagogical process), but also—and very importantly—the capacity of social movements, communities, NGOs, and popular political administrations to be agents of cultural action for freedom.

For Freire, conscientization unleashes an ethical discourse through which agents develop a capacity for social criticism. Here, Freire shares Habermas's idea that particular ethical reflections are not completely situated and local, but are rooted in the human potential for ethical dialogue with universal dimensions as part of a discourse or communicative ethics (Morrow & Torres, 2002). Thus, and not surprisingly, Erich Fromm, after meeting Freire, declared, "This kind of educational practice is a kind of historical-cultural political psychoanalysis" (quoted in Freire, 1994, p. 55).

As we have said in another place: "Thus Freire's epistemological stance has at least two major implications. On the one hand, Critical Pedagogy emerging from Freire's contribution is concerned with how emancipatory education can validate learners' own culture and discourse while at the same time challenging their common sense, to identify the salutory nucleus, the 'good sense' that Gramsci, in his philosophical imagination, signals as the beginning of counterhegemony (Torres, 1992a). On the other hand, Freire's recognition of the tensions between objectivity and subjectivity, between theory and practice—as autonomous and legitimate spheres of human endeavor—lead him (departing from Dewey) to recognize that these dichotomies and tensions cannot be overcome. Nor can they be captured in their entire complexity through mainstream methodologies. Long live the creative imagination!" (O'Cadiz & Torres, 1994, p. 221).

In the next section, I will examine how this meta-theoretical tradition of critical hermeneutics, based on a theory of social and cultural reproduction, challenges the processes of domination that subjects confront in their developmental processes (challenging "false consciousness"). Freire's theoretical framework and the way it was implemented in Angicos constitute a central threshold in the tradition of popular education in Latin America.

PAULO FREIRE AND POPULAR EDUCATION

> *The mode of production of material life conditions the social, political and intellectual life process in general. It is not the consciousness of men that determines their being, but, on the contrary, their social being that determines their consciousness.*
>
> *(Marx, Preface to* Contribution to the Critique of Political Economy*)*

Popular education was born from radical models of education, many of which were linked to Paulo Freire's experiences in Brazil in the 1960s. Characteristics common to popular education have been discussed by various scholars, and synthesized in other places (Gadotti & Torres, 1992, 1993, 1994; Torres, 1990). Popular education rose from a political and social understanding of the conditions endured by the poor, as evidenced by their most visible problems, including malnutrition, unemployment, and illness, with the intention of shedding light upon these conditions at both the individual and collective scale of consciousness. Basing educative practices upon individual and collective experience, popular education took previously acquired knowledge about people very seriously, and worked in groups more than on an individual basis. These projects used an education that was intimately related to concrete abilities that could be taught to the poor (such as reading, writing, and arithmetic) but as a mutual process of teaching and learning (Gadotti, 2012).

Popular education sought to inspire a sense of pride, dignity, and confidence in participants, so that they might become autonomous both politically and socially. These projects could be integrated by governments into the process of rural development, as was done in Colombia and the Dominican Republic (Torres, 1995a, 1995b); as done by Freire himself, from 1989 until 1991, when he was secretary of education for the Workers' Party within the municipality of São Paulo (O'Cadiz, Torres, & Wong, 1998); and as done by popular education collectives in Nicaragua (Arnove, 1994). These popular education programs could span all ages of students, from children to adults.

For Freire, the main educational problems are not methodological or pedagogical, but instead political. Educational programs inspired by Freire's model had earned a strong historical presence within the field of adult and literacy education, by trying to constitute themselves within political-pedagogical mechanisms of collaboration with socially subordinated sectors. Popular education is a pedagogy for social change, defined by educational activity that formed a "cultural action" whose central objective was conscientization.

In its most radical form, conscientization resided within the development of critical consciousness, as knowledge revealed during this process of class-oriented social transformation, appearing as part of the "subjective conditions" of this process. In strictly educational terms, popular education was intended to be a non-authoritarian pedagogy. Its educational program could be realized as easily in a classroom as in a "culture circle," transmitting ideas and knowledge along a path of sharing provided by knowledge of previous knowledge, as known to those being educated (Freire, 1998a). One of the last books Freire wrote, *Pedagogy of Hope* (2004), offered an appraisal of the conditions implemented by his earlier work *Pedagogy of the Oppressed* (1968/1970).

Since its beginnings this liberatory pedagogy provided a model that was diametrically opposed to the predominant neoliberal agenda within Latin American education, paradoxically constituting an accumulation of the most conservative and capitalistic positions in the entire world, and a flagrant contradiction of the liberal tradition and the spirit of public, obligatory, and free education that predominated the history of education in the 19th and early 20th centuries (Torres, 1996d, 2009a, 2011a, 2011b).

Freire and many of those who endorse his political and pedagogical agenda have been linked to dissent and contentious politics, particularly the ways in which social movements throughout the world use education to pursue their political goals challenging neoliberalism. There is extensive research on the counter-hegemonic practices of new social movements, through the disciplinary lenses of political science (Rocco, 1990, 1997, 1999, 2002, 2010; Rocco & García Selgas, 2006; Tarrow, 2005), the political sociology of education (Torres, 1981b, 1989, 1991, 1995a, 1995b, 2009a, 2009b, 2011; Teodoro & Torres, 2007), and sociology and learning theory (Mayo, 2005; Morrow & Torres, 1995).

However, one area that is as yet relatively unexplored is the role of education in creating, facilitating, or renewing the political interaction between social movements and the state. Morrow and Torres (1995) have theorized regarding this question, and Paulo Freire put forth one well-researched example (O'Cadiz, Torres, & Wong, 1998) in the manner in which he created ties between the secretary of education in São Paulo and literacy initiatives within regional social movements. These insights notwithstanding, the extensive role that education has played in setting and pushing the political agendas of social movements has not been researched or theorized to nearly the degree that its pervasiveness warrants.

Freire's concepts and theories are still a source of inspiration for some of the most innovative counter-hegemonic processes in the world, including the Occupy Wall Street movements, the social movement of the *indignados* in Spain, and other experiences of social struggle in the creation of a global or transnational public sphere (Bryne, 2012).

While popular education and participatory research emerge as practical tools for research and social transformation, Freire also gave us a legacy of formidable insights dealing with some of the key dilemmas of contemporary education.

Freire's educational goals provide a shift in perspective. His critical hermeneutics produced an epistemological transformation that has had a major impact in literacy training specifically, and for pedagogy more generally. Here is the tension that he tries to overcome, a tension that has also been the concern of Habermas: how to resolve the contradictions between the pursuit of individual interest, and the need to provide for social cohesion in the polity. This tension is further aggravated by the tensions between agency and structure. Social transformation in Freire is articulated through the need to empower human agency while simultaneously transforming structures. His critique of banking education is also a critique of the politics of culture, outlining the seeds of a cultural action of freedom. Pedagogy of the oppressed emerges not as a new pedagogical theory but as a new revolutionary narrative, leading to conscientization as a social process and to social transformation as the ultimate goal. Hence, the appropriate title of Julio Barreiro, Julio de Santa Ana, R. Cetrulo, and V. Gilbert's book *Consciousness and Revolution* (1974), which impacted a great deal of the debates in the 1960s, particularly in the Christian quarters linked to Theology of Liberation (Morrow & Torres, 2002; Torres, 1992a).

In generating this process of social transformation, the focus on identities is one of Freire's early contributions to pedagogy. The Freirean model examines in Freire's *ouvre* a multitude of identities, including class, race, ethnicity, gender, sexuality, ability, and religious identities.

The epistemology of curiosity that Freire and other phenomenologists such as Ricoueur endorse is based not only on self-evaluation and self-reflection but also on the need to confront oppression of any kind anywhere. Linking popular education with popular culture allows Freire to identify the link between individual transformation and community traditions.

FREIRE'S DILEMMAS: EDUCATION, CITIZENSHIP, AND ETHICS

> *[El] escepticismo es un lujo de minoría. . . . Al resto le serviremos la felicidad bien cocinada y la humanidad engullirá gozosamente la divina bazofia.*[7]
>
> *(Roberto Arlt, Los Siete Locos)*

Freire addressed a serious dilemma of democracy, the constitution of a democratic citizenship. He expounded many of his ideas about the question of diversity and border crossing in education in the 1960s. Freire taught us that domination, aggression, and violence are intrinsic parts of human and social life. He argued that few human encounters are exempt from one type of oppression or another. By virtue of race, ethnicity, class, and gender, people tend to be either victims or perpetrators of oppression. Thus, for Freire, sexism, racism, and class exploitation are the most salient forms of domination. Yet exploitation and domination exist on other grounds as well, including religious beliefs, sexuality, political affiliation, national origin, age, size, and physical and intellectual disabilities, to name just a few.

Starting from a psychology of oppression influenced by psychotherapists such as Freud, Jung, Adler, Fanon, and Fromm, Freire developed the pedagogy of the oppressed. With the spirit of the Enlightenment, he believed in education as a means to improve the human condition, confronting the effects of a psychology and sociology of oppression, contributing ultimately to what Freire considered the ontological vocation of the human beings: humanization. In the Introduction to his highly acclaimed *Pedagogy of the Oppressed*, Freire (1973e) states, "From these pages I hope my trust in the people is clear, my faith in men and women, and my faith in the creation of a world in which it will be easier to love" (p. 19).

Freire was known as a philosopher and a theoretician of education in the critical perspective—an intellectual who never separated theory from practice. In *Politics and Education* (1998b), he forcefully states that "Authoritarianism is like necrophilia, while a coherent democratic project is biophilia" (p. 56). It is from this epistemological standpoint that Freire's contribution resonates as the basic foundation for transformative social justice learning. The notion of democracy entails the notion of a democratic citizenship in which agents are active participants in the democratic process, able to choose their representatives as well as to monitor their performance. These are not only political but also pedagogical practices because the construction of the democratic citizen implies the construction of a pedagogic subject. Individuals are not, by nature, ready to participate in politics. They have to be educated in democratic politics in a number of ways, including normative grounding, ethical behavior, knowledge of the democratic process, and technical performance. The construction of the pedagogical subject is a central conceptual problem, a dilemma of democracy. To put it simply: Democracy implies a process of participation where all are considered equal. However, education involves a process whereby the "immature" are brought to identify with the principles and life-forms of the "mature" members of society (Torres, 1998a).

Thus, the process of construction of the democratic pedagogical subject is a process of cultural nurturing, involving cultivating principles of pedagogic and democratic socialization in subjects who are neither *tabula rasa* in cognitive or ethical terms, nor fully equipped for the exercise of their democratic rights and obligations. Yet, in the construction of modern polities, the constitution of a pedagogical democratic subject is predicated on grounds that are, paradoxically, a precondition but also the result of previous experiences and policies of national solidarity (including citizenship, competence building and collaboration) (O'Cadiz & Torres, 1994; O'Cadiz, Torres, & Wong, 1998; Torres, 1997). A second major contribution of Freire is his thesis advanced in *Pedagogy of the Oppressed*, and reiterated in countless other writings, that the pedagogical subjects of the educational process are not homogeneous citizens but culturally diverse individuals. From his notion of cultural diversity, he identified the notion of crossing borders in education, suggesting that there is an ethical imperative to cross borders if we attempt to educate for empowerment and not for oppression.

Thus, Freire created specific contexts for emancipatory learning. Freire's thesis of critical literacies, which argues that critical consciousness depends crucially on forms of literacy that facilitate a structural perspective for understanding social reality, is well represented in his mantra of "reading the word and reading the world"—a dialogical understanding of the pedagogical practices required for acquiring critical communicative competence, and illustrated in Freire's account of the methodology of thematic investigation. Therefore, it may be possible to generalize Freire's political and pedagogical principles to formal and nonformal settings, challenging models of banking education based on the important distinction between reflexive and nonreflexive learning. From these principles, I identify the intimate interrelations of reflexive learning, the formation of critical citizenship, and the potential revitalization of democratic public spheres in diverse settings.

CONCLUSION: EDUCATION AS POSTCOLONIAL ETHICS

The real freedom is freedom from fear.
(Aung San Suu Kyi, Burmese Nobel prize recipient)

Freire is first and foremost a postcolonial thinker, and his focus on otherness is one of his central contributions. Combining a complex synthesis of existentialism, phenomenology, neo-Marxism, and the Latin American tradition of liberatory ethics, Freire (1993) understood otherness as personhood interaction mediated by love. He tells us:

> My love for reading and writing is directed toward a certain utopia. This involves a certain course, a certain type of people. It is a love that has to do with the creation of a society that is less perverse, less discriminatory, less racist, less *machista* than the society that we now have. This love seeks to create a more open society, a society that serves the interest of the always unprotected and devalued subordinate classes, and not only the interest of the rich, the fortunate, the so-called "well-born." (p. 140)

Clearly, Freire is in tune with Edward Said, who has asserted that "the responsibility of intellectuals is to 'speak the truth to power' " and to criticize "on the basis of universal principles: that all human beings are entitled to expect decent standards of behavior concerning freedom and justice" (quoted in Morrow & Torres, 2002, p. 171).

The Paulo Freire System was an attempt to reinvent the models of public education in Brazil and Latin America. The Angicos experience was one of the first and most famous steps in the attempt to formulate a system or a model, and one that cannot be simply reduced to literacy training. On the contrary, the model designed by Freire and his collaborators was simultaneously a model of bringing together political education with citizenship building at the school level, starting with the literacy training experience, and as a way to include those who had been pushed out or who couldn't attend the system. But it was also as a model to include the winds of transformation of the time—what some people may have considered simply a modernization of the educational system—by linking popular education with popular culture. [8]

This system or model was supposed to start at the kindergarden level (or, as in Angicos, with an effective and highly political model of literacy training) and would connect with all levels of education reaching the university, no longer a bastion of the middle classes or elites, but a new model of engagement in higher education with the presence of the social movements—hence, the presence of the MEB, the NAE, and other social movements. This new postcolonial approach, which was highly focused on dealing with diversity at all levels (gender, class, race/ethnicity, regions), was premonitory of many of the criticisms to the modernist project, and dovetailed very nicely with the traditions that inspired Freire and a whole generation of pedagogues of liberation—that is, the philosophy of liberation, theology of education, theories of dependency, and popular education as citizenship building.

Any analysis of the key actors of the Angicos experience prefiguring the Freirean system should include an array of characters and groups. It should include Freire and his group of researchers and collaborators associated with the faculty of extension of the University of Recife. Collaborating with Freire and his groups were social movements of diverse types, including trade unions, students' movements, and religious movements connected with the Catholic Church. As it happened, during Freire's administration as secretary of education of São Paulo, 26 years after the Angicos experience, the goal was to have the social movements—themselves learning sites—tactically inside but strategically outside of the state (English & Mayo, 2012).

There was also a formidable connection between democratic administrations (e.g., Arraes) at the municipal and state level, the federal government (also in connection with state governments as indicated in the work of the SUDENE), and international organizations, in this case, the presence of USAID providing the funding that was central to the articulation of the whole experience. USAID was fully involved in counteracting the radical trends of the Cuban Revolution by promoting the developmentalist project of the Alliance for the Progress. The agency tried to take advantage of showcasing the experience with a visit from President Kennedy; however, he was assassinated in 1963 before he could make the trip. The Brazilian coup d'etat of March 31, 1964, and the inauguration of the new authoritarianism in Latin America, brought this radical educational experience to an abrupt end.

I must conclude this chapter with two observations. The first is that, for critical theorists like Freire, research cannot be separated from political struggle; hence, scholarship and activism are inevitably part and parcel of our life journey. Paulo Freire argued that politics and education cannot be easily separated. The same applies to scholarship and political struggle, which cannot be easily dissociated, not even for purely didactic purposes. We conduct research and teaching to change the world, not simply to observe as detached scientists what happens around us or to manipulate knowledge as social alchemy or as social engineering. Critical scholars do not share with technocrats the illusion that manipulating knowledge, using technocratic means and the stern application of instrumental rationality, will solve most if not all the problems of education.

The second observation is that Freire's postcolonial positions were based on his consideration of education as an ethics of love. Enrique Dussel (1997) discussed the concept of emancipation as part of a non-Eurocentric liberation ethics, looking as the "other" as oppressed, where the "majority of the humanity finds itself sunk into 'poverty,' unhappiness, suffering, domination, and/or exclusion" (p.

285). It is in this context that Dussel turns to Freire's concept of conscientization as a description of the processes within which liberation ethics unfolds not only in the consciousness of the oppressed but also in those who have shared experiences with the dominated and/or excluded.

In the late '80s, I was interviewing Freire and I asked him what he would like his legacy to be. He answered that when he died, he would like people to say of him: "Paulo Freire lived, loved, and wanted to know."

Freire, in his poetic style, provided a simple and yet powerful message about the role of critical intellectuals. For Freire, critical intellectuals should live passionately their own ideas, building spaces of deliberation and tolerance in their quest for knowledge and empowerment. They love what they do, and they love those with whom they interact. Love, then, becomes another central element of the political project of intellectuals who are agonizing over producing knowledge for empowerment and liberation. Following Gramsci, critical intellectuals know that common sense always has a nucleus of "good sense." From this "good sense" of the common sense, critical intellectuals can develop a criticism of conventional wisdom, knowledge, and practices. In educational policy and planning, this "good sense" could be a starting point for a critique of instrumental rationalization (Torres, 1994c).

The lessons of Critical Social Theory for education are clear, and need to be remembered: Politics and education intersect continually—there is an inherent politicity of education. Power plays a major role in configuring schooling and social reproduction. Social change cannot be simply articulated as social engineering from the calm environment of the research laboratory or the corridors of a ministry building. Social change needs to be forged in negotiations and compromise, but also through fights in the political system; it needs to be struggled in the streets or online with the social movements; it needs to be conquered in the schools struggling against bureaucratic and authoritarian behavior, defying the growing corporatization of educational institutions, particularly in higher education, and striving to implement substantive rationality through communicative dialogue; and it needs to be achieved even in the cozy and joyful environment of our gatherings with our family and friends. Dialogue and reason cannot take vacations if one pursues the dream of social justice education and peace. In the next chapter, I will discuss some of the reasons why the original intent of Paulo Freire, this pedagogy of consciousness of the 1960s, is still viable and useful in the 21st century.

Frei Betto's analysis of Paulo Freire provides us with fitting last words for this chapter:

> He was the one who furnished us with the "road map." The people build the road, but the person who gave us the map of how "the little ones" can become the subject of history, how a simple peasant, a simple worker can become a great political leader, was Paulo Freire. (Borg & Mayo, 2007, p. 35)

APPENDIX TO CHAPTER 10: 50 YEARS OF ANGICOS AND THE NATIONAL LITERACY PROGRAM

Chronology

1958: **July 9–16:** Paulo Freire presents the theoretical foundations of his adult literacy system at the Second National Conference on Adult Education, held in Rio de Janeiro. He was the coordinator for the report on "Adult Education and Marginal Populations: The Problem of the Shanties." This report "is the germ of all ethic-political-critical literature of Paulo's on education for transformation" (Freire, 2006, p. 126).

1959: Paulo Freire applies for the chair of History and Philosophy of Education at the School of Fine Arts in Pernambuco. His thesis, entitled *Education and Brazilian Actuality*, is the "first systematic elaboration" of his thoughts, whose "axes and categories would pervade all his work" (Romão, 2001, p. XIII).

1960: **May 13:** Foundation of the Popular Culture Movement (MCP) in Recife under the administration of newly elected mayor Miguel Arraes. Germano Coelho is one of its founders, and Paulo Freire is one of its most active members. The ideals of MCP spread rapidly through several northeastern states. MCP fuses popular culture with political struggle, increasing people's consciousness and promoting literacy through cultural circles. The first experience of the Paulo Freire System is hosted at the Centro Dona Olegarinha in 1962, and the first National Literacy and Popular Culture Meeting is sponsored by the Ministry of Education in 1963.

1961: **February:** Secretary of Education Moacyr de Góes launches his campaign, "Barefoot on the ground one also learns to read," in Natal. This happens during the administration of Mayor Djalma Maranhão, who understood education and culture as tools of liberation.

1961: **March 21:** The Grassroots Education Movement (MEB) is formed through an initiative of the Catholic Church. This is a partnership between the federal government and National Conference of Bishops of Brazil (CNBB) to contribute to the process of adult literacy and help develop communities.

1961: **April:** The National Union of Students (UNE) creates the Popular Center of Culture (CPC), paving the way for the politicization of social issues. UNE's goal is to create and disseminate a revolutionary popular art, supporting the political engagement of artists to overcome people's alienation and naïve consciousness. In order to achieve this goal, they promote the staging of critical plays in factories and on the streets.

1961: Aluísio Alves takes office as governor of the state of Rio Grande do Norte.

1961: **August 25:** Jânio Quadros resigns from the presidency he has held since January 31, 1961.

1961: **September 7:** Inauguration of President João Goulart, who serves until April 1, 1964, when a military coup takes place.

1962: **January:** Paulo Freire and his team at the University of Recife advise the Campaign for Popular Education of Paraíba (CEPLAR), created in João Pessoa by college students and professionals trained to work in adult literacy programs.

1962: **April 13:** João Goulart signs the Brazil–USA Agreement on the Northeast.

1962: **September 18:** Darcy Ribeiro takes office at the Ministry of Education until January 23, 1963.

1962: **September (mid):** Calazans Fernandes, secretary of education of the state of Rio Grande do Norte and coordinator of the Office of Cooperative Education of Rio Grande do Norte (SECERN), and Maria José Monteiro, a former student of Paulo Freire's, meet with Paulo Freire at the University of Recife to discuss the Angicos Literacy Project.

1962: **September (late):** Aluísio Alves, Calazans Fernandes, and Maria José Monteiro meet with Paulo Freire at his house to discuss conditions of the project, as follows: autonomy to hire coordinators and teachers, and no political-academic and ideological interference. This is because Paulo Freire feared that resources were coming from the Alliance for Progress that could interfere with his work.

1962: **December:** Marcos Guerra, a law student and president of the national Union of Students, forms a team of teachers (facilitators) for the Angicos Literacy Project. Thus, the project becomes a partnership between SECERN and the Cultural Extension Service of the University of Recife (SEC/UR) while being directed by Paulo Freire. The work begins with a survey of the number of illiterates in Angicos and a study of people's specific vocabulary (words and generative themes).

1962: **December 3:** Signing of the agreement among the Ministry of Education, the Superintendence for the Development of the Northeast (SUDENE), the state of Rio Grande do Norte, and the U.S. Agency for International Development (USAID) within the guidelines set forth by the Alliance for Progress.

1963: **January:** Selection of the 21 coordinators (facilitators) for the cultural circles: among them Madalena Freire (Freire's oldest daughter) and his supervisor Carlos Lyra. Training of staff takes place in collaboration with Elza Freire (Freire's wife).

1963: **January 18:** Launch of the project and the inaugural class of the Angicos Literacy Program. The inauguration is attended by Aluísio Alves. Three hundred eighty residents begin their literacy program.

1963: **January 24:** The first class of the project, "Anthropological Concept of Culture," marks the start of the "Forty Hours of Angicos."

1963: **January 28:** First literacy class starts with the generative word *belota*, which means "political cabal" or "clique."

1963: **February–March:** Classes take place at the same time as the meetings for the training of coordinators in the cultural circles.

1963: **April 2:** The final, 40th hour of the program is taught by President João Goulart. This is attended by several governors in the northeast and representatives of the Alliance for Progress. Aluísio Alves, Paulo Freire, and former illiterate Antonio Ferreira also share their experiences in this class. The oldest student, Maria Hermínia, gives the president a letter written by participants of the course. This is the first graduating class of Angicos. General Humberto de Alencar Castelo Branco, commander of the Military Region in Recife, attends the meeting and tells Calazans Fernandes, "Young man, you're fattening rattlesnakes in this area."

1963: **April:** The experiment ends. The evaluation results of the Angicos Literacy Project are released: Three hundred participants are considered literate, with a 70% success rate on the Literacy Test and 87% success rate on the Test of Politicization.

1963: **April–June:** The magazine *University Studies* of the University of Recife publishes the first studies on the Paulo Freire System. These papers are authored by Jarbas Maciel, Jomar Muniz de Britto, Aurenice Cardoso, Pierre Furter, and by Paulo Freire himself who, in his article "Awareness and Literacy," refutes criticism from the conservative media that accuse him of confusing literacy with politicization.

1963: **May:** The city of Angicos has its first strike. Landowners call the experience of Paulo Freire a "communist plague."

1963: **May 29:** In a letter to Aluísio Alves, U.S. Ambassador Lincoln Gordon recommends that the "Angicos program for the end of illiteracy" be adopted in all states.

1963: **June:** Launch of the movie *The Forty Hours of Angicos*, directed by Luiz Lobo and a production of the Office of Cooperative Education of Rio Grande do Norte (SECERN), describing the Angicos Literacy Project as a "first phase" of the literacy program through a "simple, clear, and efficient method" to "transform Angicos into a strong conscious and entrepreneurial community," that trains people to "contribute to the larger decisions of the homeland."

1963: **June 2:** The *New York Times* publishes a report on the experience of Angicos, spurring greater international attention. Reporters from well-established publications such as *Time* magazine, *Herald Tribune*, *Sunday Times*, *Associated Press*, and *Le Monde* also travel to Angicos to cover the project.

1963: **June 18:** Paulo de Tarso Santos takes office at the Ministry of Education until October 21, 1963. Per the recommendation of his predecessor, Darcy Ribeiro, he invites Paulo Freire to Brasília to create a National Literacy Program based on the Angicos experiment.

1963: **July 16:** Ministerial Ordinance #195 establishes the Committee of Popular Culture within the Office of the Ministry of Education in order "to deploy, nationwide, new educational systems eminently popular, to cover areas not yet reached by the benefits of education." Paulo Freire is appointed chairman of this committee. His first task is to survey the national number of illiterates to support the future National Literacy Program. The number of illiterates between 15 and 45 years of age totals 20,442,000—out of a total population of 79,599,340.

1963: **July:** Celso Beisiegel, a teacher of the Regional Center for Educational Research (CRPE) of São Paulo, visits the Angicos Project in order to replicate a similar experience and method in the municipality of Osasco (state of São Paulo).

1963: **September 15–21:** The first Literacy and Popular Culture National Meeting is held in Recife, convened by the Ministry of Education, with the participation of educators, artists, politicians, students, workers, trade union and religious leaders, among other actors.

1963: **October:** An envoy of U.S. ambassadors visits Governor Aluísio Alves in Natal to prepare for the visit of President John F. Kennedy to Angicos, scheduled for December 1963 (but Kennedy is assassinated on November 22).

1963: **October 21:** Júlio Furquim Sambaqui takes office at the Ministry of Education until April 6, 1964.

1963: **Second semester:** Similar projects spread to other cities: Quintas, Mossoró, Caicó, Macau, Ubatuba, Osasco, Rio de Janeiro, Brasília, Aracaju, Porto Alegre, and others, as an experiment of the National Literary Program. Paulo Freire travels throughout the country to help structure the National Literacy Program.

1964: **January 21:** Decree #53.465 formally establishes the Programa Nacional de Alfabetização National Literacy Program (PNA) and enshrines the "Paulo Freire System for literacy in quick time." The PNA oversees the "cooperation and services" of professional and student associations, sports clubs, neighborhood and local associations, religious entities, government, civilian and military organizations, employers associations, private companies, broadcasting agencies, teachers and all possible sectors. From his early writings and his political-pedagogical praxis, Freire has advocated the need for popular participation in the fight against illiteracy. The program intends to create 60,870 cultural circles, each lasting 3 months, throughout Brazil to teach 1,834,200 illiterates between the ages of 15 and 45 years. Its implementation is accomplished through pilot projects in the south, southeast, and northeast regions. PNA is a success compared to previous campaigns.

1964: The Ministry of Education appoints Paulo Freire and other members of the Angicos Literacy Project to the Special Committee of the National Literacy Program, chaired by the minister, via Ordinance #72. Subsequent Ordinance #92 appoints Paulo Freire to replace the minister as chair of the committee whenever necessary.

1964: **March 10:** Police in Guanabara, Rio de Janeiro, seize a book entitled *To Live Is to Struggle*, published in 1963 by the Grassroots Education Movement MEB.

1964: **April 14:** Decree #53.886 extinguishes the National Literacy Program as a reaction to the coup of April 1. President Ranieri Mazzilli abolishes the program in order to "preserve institutions and the traditions of our country." President João Goulart had scheduled the official inauguration of the program, symbolically, on May 13 in the main square of Caxias, Rio de Janeiro.

1964: **April 15:** Inauguration of General Humberto de Alencar Castelo Branco as president of the republic.

1964: **June 16:** Paulo Freire is arrested and spends 70 days in jail in Olinda. He is accused of being "subversive and ignorant."

1964: **September:** Paulo Freire goes into exile in Chile to work at the Training and Research Institute of Agrarian Reform (ICIRA), where he remains until 1969. He does not return to Brazil until 1979.

1983: **May 21:** In an interview, Paulo Freire says, "I do not accept anything from the Alliance for Progress, but I have nothing against using the money they think is theirs but is not. In fact, the money from the Alliance for Progress was the money returned to Brazil, as if it was a favor, and is our money, money of this underdeveloped area, which is underdeveloped only because it is exploited and dominated. So why not to take advantage of this money in return, provided we could secure what to do with it? My position is this: if I have authority over what the project will do, I do not want to know if this money comes from the Alliance or comes from the Japanese" (Lyra, 1996, p. 182).

1993: **August 28:** Paulo Freire and his second wife (his first wife died in 1987), Ana Maria Araújo Freire, along with two founders of the Paulo Freire Institute (founded in 1991), Carlos Alberto Torres and Moacir Gadotti, visit Angicos and meet with former students and teachers, including Marcos Guerra and former illiterate Antonio Ferreira, who spoke on behalf of his colleagues during the historic visit of João Goulart.

2002: Analyzing the "long term effects of literacy method" of the Angicos experience, Nilcéa Lemos Pelandré (2002), after interviewing students who learned to read and write in 1963, shows that participants learned to write single words and short sentences, and that some even wrote according to their own rules. In addition to literacy, the most significant outcome was the increase in their self-esteem and the feeling of inclusion in the literate world. Pelandré concludes that the effectiveness of the project stems from the employment of human promotion, trained and motivated teachers, and intensive immersion.

2005: **September 3:** President Luiz Inácio Lula da Silva attends the ceremony to endow a certificate of literacy to 3,000 students of the MOVA-Brazil Project in Angicos. The project is a partnership between Petrobras, the Federation of Oil Workers, and the Paulo Freire Institute.

2012–
2014: Celebration of the 50th anniversary of the Angicos Literacy Project and the National Literacy Program.

Sources

Beisiegel, C. de R. (1974). *Estado e educação popular.* São Paulo, Brazil: Pioneira.

Fernanes, C., & Terra, A. (1994). *40 horas de Esperança: o método Paulo Freire, política e pedagogia na experiência de Angicos.* São Paulo, Brazil: Ática.

Freire, A.M.A. (2006). *Paulo Freire: Uma história de vida.* Indaiatuba: Villa das Letras.

Gadotti, M. (Org.). (1996). *Paulo Freire: Uma biobibliografia.* São Paulo, Brazil: Cortez/Instituto Paulo Freire.

Gerhardt, H. P. (1983, May). Angicos—Rio Grande do Norte—1962/63. In *Revista Educação & Sociedade*, 4 (14), 1983. São Paulo, Brazil: Cortez/Unicamp.

Lyra, C. (1996). *As quarenta horas de Angicos: uma experiência pioneira de educação.* São Paulo, Brazil: Cortez.

Manfredi, S. M. (1981). *Política e educação popular: experiências de alfabetização no Brasil com o Método Paulo Freire—1960/1964.* São Paulo, Brazil: Cortez.

Pelandré, N. L. (2002). *Ensinar e aprender com Paulo Freire: 40 horas 40 anos depois.* São Paulo, Brazil: Corte/Instituto Paulo FreireFreirean.

Romão, J. E. (2001). Paulo Freire e o pacto populista (contextualização). In P. Freire, *Educação e atualidade brasileira* (pp. XIII–XLVIII). São Paulo, Brazil: Cortez.

Rosas, P. (Org.). (2002). *Paulo Freire: Educação e transformação social.* Recife: Centro Paulo Freire/UFPE.

ELEVEN

Reinventing Paulo Freire in Democracy: Freire's Political and Pedagogical Currency as a Universal Thinker

If the people's schools do what the State should do, then the State can sleep in peace and my political thesis is the following: we cannot let the State sleep in peace. Civil society has to censure the State daily so that it never has a chance to sleep.

(Freire & Quiroga, 1995, p. 27)

FREIRE, DEMOCRACY, AND EDUCATION

Karl Marx, in one of the most lucid passages of his *Contribution to the Criticism of Hegel's Philosophy of Right*, wrote: "All the other forms of the State are definitive, distinct, and particular. In democracy, the formal principle is simultaneously the material principle. Therefore, only democracy truly unites the general and the particular" (quoted in Tucker, 1978, pp. 21–22).

This sentence of Marx's, which could make way for a veritable treatise on the nature of democracy, invites us to think of all the difficulties inherent in democratic forms as processes of participation and political representation—and, of course, the new difficulties that arise when democracy and capitalism are linked. The democratic forms of government represent the only possible formulation where the rights and liberties of individuals and communities—national as well as in the context of the world system—can be linked as an effective way of joining general and private interests.

This is actually why Paulo Freire was always thinking and writing about social classes, criticizing and celebrating democracy at the same time, something that today continues to be a fundamental normative and analytical principle of Critical Theory. In a private conversation we had at his house in São Paulo in the mid-1990s, Freire told me, with a trace of sadness, that sometimes he did not really understand why he was criticized for not putting enough emphasis on questions of class and for being considered a liberal democratic thinker defending democracy.

When he visited Chile 20 years after he had written *Pedagogy of the Oppressed* there, he found that many of those who had bitterly criticized him in the 1960s for his defense of democracy and for his limited analysis of social classes, had completely stopped their analysis from the point of view of class struggle and become fervent defenders of a neoliberal democratic model. Freire concluded his lament with the following, "Carlos, I have always been consistent in simultaneously postulating an analysis of class struggle with an analysis of democracy."

His belief in the need to work the analysis of the class struggle in democracy and its importance for education linked to the analysis of the state is, perhaps, one of the primary teachings of the early and the late Freire as well. As the epigraphic sentence in this section intimates, such an analysis should take into account gender, race, ethnicity, and other forms of social discrimination.

The *International Herald Tribune* of May 23, 2005. ran the obituary of the French philosopher Paul Ricoeur, who died peacefully in his sleep on May 19, 2005, at the age of 92, at his house in Chatenay-Malabry, in the west of Paris. Paul Ricoeur (1974), professor at the Sorbonne, the University of Chicago, and so many other universities as well as a member of the French socialist party, was one of the most important humanists and phenomenological philosophers of the 20th century. His contributions to Critical Theory, biblical studies, and human perception were numerous (Ricoeur, 1978, 1984, 1985, 1988). However, I want to emphasize one of his most suggestive intuitions, when he argued something that Freire always proclaimed: the importance of developing a logic of suspicion—that is, to suspect that all cultural relations involve an aspect of domination. If Ricoeur and Freire are correct, can we contemplate an education for freedom that, as cultural politics, does not involve an aspect of domination?

This is another of the themes that cannot be resolved in a few pages because it calls for a very detailed treatment, both historical and theoretical. But we could initiate a response imagining which conditions would fulfill what Freire included in his definition of education as a possible dream and what kinds of teachers would be able to make this liberating education feasible.[1]

EDUCATION AS THE POSSIBLE DREAM: THE QUESTION OF TEACHERS' EDUCATION

> *Maybe what's important is to remain attentive, to pay attention to what we are doing, to constantly question ourselves about what we are doing, and to doubt, to doubt deeply and systematically, without fear, without worrying about offending anyone. (Gadotti, 2004, p. 169)*

Paulo Freire was one of the first to argue that there are two moments in revolutionary education: education as cultural action for freedom (Freire, 1968a), which is constructed in opposition to the state, and pedagogy of the oppressed, which is constructed in harmony with the cultural revolution and a new state, although by no means accepting all the precepts of the state's authority even if it is a new revolutionary state. In this sense, Freire was always a typical libertarian (or perhaps anarchistic) thinker, and some of his quotes included in this section offer creditable evidence of this.

Karl Marx in his *Thesis on Feuerbach* (1888) asked a reasonable question: Who would educate the educators, themselves the products of a system, so that the system could be transformed? This theme has remained a nagging question in the cultural politics of revolutionary educational transformation.

In an interview I conducted with Paulo Freire in 1990, I asked him:

> Certain people have questioned your positions, at times saying that Paulo Freire is such a gifted teacher, such a brilliant facilitator, that it's not fair to ask that everyone who has embraced the profession, no, the vocation of teaching, should be like him. That they should have the same confidence to be themselves. That they should have the same thirst for knowledge. That they should be politically as competent as he is. That they should be as technically competent as he is. What would you say to those who question whether such teachers will ever exist and say, therefore, that we must work with those who we have at hand? (Torres, 1995c, p. 179)

Paulo answered me with his proverbial smile while his hands sculpted the air as if wanting to capture the spirit of our dialogue:

> Really it's not easy to have this kind of teacher. But I think I would like to begin to respond to your question with another question that I ask myself, and that is: Really, is it easy to have, to find, to train good social scientists, good physicists, serious, honest, competent people, dedicated people, loving people? It isn't easy. It's all very difficult to do. But that isn't the real question.
>
> The question for me is if it's possible or impossible. To what degree is it an impossible or a possible dream? First, for me, it's a possible dream. Second, when one knows that this kind of dream is possible, then one has another question: Is this possible dream for today or for tomorrow? (Freire, quoted in Torres, 1995d, pp. 179–180)

Paulo Freire's answer is even more important these days, when we are struggling against neoliberal models of education that have been implanted or attempted in different parts of the world because, I would argue, pursuing his legacy, that not only is it possible and desirable to count on highly technically qualified, politically committed and loving teachers but, also, that the demands of the hour urgently admonish us to finish the job of educating this kind of teacher. This leads us ineluctably to a discussion of the connection between politics and education, not from an activist and populist commitment but, rather, from a radical democratic one, as I (1998a) once proposed:

> Without a serious exploration of the intersections between cultural diversity, affirmative action and citizenship, the plural bases of democracy and democratic discourse per se will find themselves at risk. Without a theory and practice of radical, democratic and multicultural citizenship which is simultaneously technically competent, ethically solid, spiritually committed and politically practicable, the nation will die. As it is written in the Book of Proverbs, "where there is no vision, the people perish." (p. 259)

THE CONNECTIONS BETWEEN EDUCATION AND POLITICS

> *To all of you who have received honors, scholarships and distinctions, I say: well done! And to the students who received "C" I tell you, you too can be President of the United States!*
>
> *(Bush, quoted in Gerstenzang, 2003, p. A18)*

George W. Bush's epigraph, which opens this section, may be shocking to educators who believe in the technocracy, meritocracy, and in education's selective role. This paragraph gives more weight to opportunity and luck than to tenacity and study. The truth that shines through this epigraph is that education does not only reproduce social inequality, as social reproduction theories have amply demonstrated, but it also legitimates privilege. That education can advance social mobility within certain limits is something that has been very well documented in the economy of education. Moreover, this "joke" by the president of the United States reminds us that race, class, and gender count—and count a lot—when you reach the highest rungs of the political ladder in a society that calls itself bureaucratic and rational like the United States.[2]

In this section, I will postulate the hypothesis that, from a normative and analytical perspective and pursuing the legacy of Freire, the establishment positions (liberals, conservatives, neoconservatives, and neoliberals) are cheek by jowl and in marked contrast to the positions of the New Left.

The establishment vision is that politics and education represent two kinds of clearly separated practice that cannot and ought not to connect with one another. Education should remain objective in theoretical terms (because the truth can be presented objectively); neutral in political terms (because educators don't take sides, politically speaking); and above all apolitical, considering the normative and political options at play. Education is apolitical in the vision of the establishment because politics habitually involves the practice of fighting for ideological positions, defending social or private interests, while education is a practice of noble stamp that seeks the common interest of all those involved.

Thus, the establishment sees academics, teachers, and decisionmakers divesting themselves of their political clothes (whether these be political affiliations, doctrines, or ideologies) at the threshold of the classroom or at a certain distance from their research laboratories and decisionmaking. Otherwise, in the vision of the establishment, mixing politics and education invariably results in the manipulation and ideologizing of the contents and practice of education. Decent, benevolent educators will practice an education that is value neutral. However, for the establishment, education is or ought to be dispossessed of political interests and ideology. And thus, it is despite the fact that the normative vision of the establishment recognizes that there are disparities and inequalities in the world—in other words, discriminatory processes. But these can be prevented by social engineering and the application of the law. This is why "quality education," when it is documented by proof of performance and accountability and when it is understood and practiced scientifically—meaning informed by rigorous empirical research—becomes a central pillar for the construction of a more efficient and equitable society.

For the New Left, the story is much more complex. Politics is intimately connected to power. Politics refers to the control of the means of production, distribution, consumption, and accumulation of symbolic resources and materials. Political activities take place in private as well as public spheres and are connected to all aspects of human experience that involve power (Ginsburg, 1995).[3] That is why, following Freire and all the critical pedagogues, politics is conceived of as a group of forceful relationships in a society and it is from this perspective that we must examine the connections between politics and education.

Paulo Freire taught us that domination, aggression, and violence are intrinsic to human social life. Freire argued that very few human encounters are exempt from oppression of one kind or another. By virtue of class, race, or gender, people tend to be victims or perpetrators of oppression. Freire pointed out that classism, racism, and class exploitation are the most salient forms of domination and oppression, but he also recognized that oppression is found in religious beliefs, sexuality, political affiliation, and a variety of other aspects, including attitudes about origin, size, age, and physical or intellectual disability. Setting out from a psychoanalytical perspective on oppression and influenced directly or indirectly by the work of psychotherapists such as Freud, Jung, Adler, Fanon, and Fromm, Freire developed in his pedagogy of the oppressed one of the most provocative analyses of the connections between politics and education in the 20th century. Extracted from a much later book than *Pedagogy of the Oppressed,* his analysis is so pertinent to the matters we are discussing that it deserves extensive quotation:

> Understanding the limits of educational practice requires political clarity on the part of educators with respect to their project. This demands that the educator accept the political nature of his or her practice. It is not enough to say that education is a political act, just as it is not enough to say that political acts are educative. It is truly necessary to accept the political nature of education. I cannot consider myself progressive if I believe that school spaces are neutral with a limited connection, or no connection

> at all, to the class struggle; spaces where students are seen as apprentices of limited domains of knowledge to which I grant a magical power. I cannot recognize the limits of the politico-educative practice in which I am involved if I do not know or if I am not clear about in whose favor I work. To clarify the question of in whose favor I practice education not only places me in a position which is necessarily a position of class, it also obliges me to be clear about against whom I practice and for what reason I practice education. (Freire, 1998b, p. 46)

TWENTY LESSONS FROM FREIRE

When Freire passed away on May 2, 1997, my former student Daniel Schugurensky, now professor at Arizona State University, published an essay entitled "Paulo Freire: A Man Who Lived, Loved and Tried to Know" in the journal *Taboo* (Schugurensky, 1997). Schugurensky has also reproduced these pages in his recent book (Schugurensky, 2011). Daniel Schugurensky offers a very personal assessment of the lessons he learned by engaging with Freire's words and world. It is worth to quote it *in extenso* to show why Freire's thought is still so relevant:

1. I learned that education is not neutral: it can be used to reinforce structures of domination, but it can also be used to promote social transformation.
2. I learned that oppressed people have part of the oppressor within themselves.
3. I learned that people learn faster and are happier when educational content is relevant to their lives and when the method is based on dialogue and respect.
4. I learned that ignorance is a relative concept because all humans have considerable knowledge, experience, skills and values. At the same time, I learned that rejection of popular knowledge is as dangerous as its exaltation or mystification.
5. I learned that the authoritarianism of many schools is part and parcel of larger societal dynamics and that an emancipatory education can contribute to the development of a more democratic society.
6. I learned that implementing an educational model promoting democracy and critical thinking is sometimes frustrating and usually takes longer than traditional models. Consequently, temptation to return to the banking approach in which the teacher talks and the students listen is always present.
7. I learned that teachers can proclaim—and sometimes believe—themselves to be implementing an emancipatory pedagogical model, and yet in practice impose a traditional banking education.

8. I learned the importance of being consequent to core principles and values while being flexible enough to accept mistakes and change ideas and practices accordingly.
9. I learned that both the content and the method are important. A progressive content imposed through an authoritarian method is antithetical to a genuine learning process. An interactive method that avoids critical reflection and transformative action is antithetical to a liberating education.
10. I learned that it is possible to reconcile apparently contradictory concepts: reason and passion, teaching and learning, education and organization, technical skills and political activism, reflection and practice, leadership and humility, knowledge and love, academic rigor and compassion, structural analysis and individual anecdotes, religiosity and Marxism, intellectual freedom and social commitment, and denunciation of present conditions and annunciation of a better future.
11. I learned of the dangers of both voluntarism (a kind of idealism that attributes to the will of the individual the power to change everything) and determinism (a sort of mechanistic structuralism that downplays the role to human agency in the historical process), because each of these approaches alone is incapable of resolving the tension between consciousness and the world.
12. I learned that it is possible to reject a loan from an international financial institution when it imposes unfair conditionalities and priorities, and when it places an unnecessary burden on the next generations. Paulo suggested that something was wrong when a country like Brazil needed financial assistance to educate its own citizens.
13. I learned that educational processes can be directive without being authoritarian or manipulative: directiveness can be compatible with dialogue and respect for differences in ideas and opinions.
14. I learned that education is communion: "I cannot think authentically unless others think. I cannot think for others, or without others."
15. I learned that the curriculum is not something given, a universally accepted truth to be transmitted, but a social construction in which the word of the oppressed is seldom included.
16. I learned of the importance of recognizing both the political dimension of education and the pedagogical dimension of politics.
17. I learned that any process of social change starts with the hope that history can be modified and the belief that oppressors are not invincible, and that it progresses with the development of an "inédito viável," a sort of untested feasibility or possible dream.
18. I learned about the urgency of building "democratic radicalness", which calls for a new ethics and a new educational practice based on respect

and emancipation, and aims at assisting subordinated groups to develop political determination.

19. I learned the potential of a work that is genuinely interdisciplinary and combines theory and practice.
20. I learned that if your ideas challenge domination and oppression, and you stand for those ideas in your everyday practice, you are likely to be persecuted by the powerful, and you must be prepared to face jail, exile, and censorship. At the same time, I learned that despite suffering hardship, you are going to be supported and encouraged by the oppressed and disenfranchised, and by those whose ethics value social justice and solidarity. (Schugurensky, 2011, pp. 4–6)

This testimony can be reproduced by the thousands of people who have learned these lessons and many more from engaging Freire's ideas seeking, in the words of Freire's handwritten manuscript of *Pedagogy of the Oppressed*, "a world in which it will be easier to love."[4]

FOR CRITICAL EDUCATORS, ANOTHER GLOBALIZATION IS POSSIBLE

> *History is there, waiting for us to do something with it, waiting for us to confront immobilizing, neoliberal fatalism that maintains, for example, that the number of people unemployed in the world is a fin du siècle fatality. . . . How is it possible for people in universities to claim that world unemployment is destiny? What did they read? How do they reason? No. In the world of culture, there is nothing fatalistically determined.*
>
> *(Freire, "The Gentle Scream," in* Pedagogy of the Oppressed, *p. 70)*

Having located the theoretical axes of the connection between politics and education from the perspective of Critical Theory in general and of Freire in particular and then shown its currency, I will now attempt to confront these suppositions with some aspects of the dynamics of the global and the local in the context of globalization and the new imperatives imposed on education.

In a book with Nicholas C. Burbules (Burbules & Torres, 2000), we argued that the term *globalization* is polyvalent. For some, it signifies fundamentally the outgrowth of supranational institutions whose decisions determine and restrict the political options of any nation-state; for others, globalization principally assumes the devastating impact of social and economic processes, including those of production, consumption, market, capital flow, and monetary interdependence. For others, it means before anything else the summit of neoliberalism as a discourse of hegemonic politics; and, for still others, globalization signifies, primarily, the birth of new global forms of culture, media, and communication technologies that model relations of affiliation, identity, and interaction inside and outside of the local cultural boundaries. There are even some people for whom globalization is fundamentally a group of perceived changes, a term utilized by state politicians responsible for inspiring support and repressing opposition to the changes (Burbules & Torres, 2000).

In a critical work about what is called "corporate globalization," Cavanaugh et al. claimed that the model has various central aspects, among them:

> - promotion of hyper-growth and unrestricted exploitation of the environment and its resources to sustain such growth;
> - privatization and mercantilism of public services and their remnant aspects, globally and communally;
> - cultural homogeneity, global economy, and intense promotion of consumerism;
> - integration and conversion of national economies, including those that have been self-sustaining, into economies oriented toward production for exportation, affecting the environment and the society itself;
> - corporate deregulation and unrestricted movement of capital across borders;
> - dramatic increase in corporate concentration;
> - dismantling of systems of public health, and the social and environmental programs that still exist; and
> - replacement of the traditional powers of democratic nation-states and local communities by global corporate bureaucracies. (Cavanaugh et al., 2003)

The worldwide expenditure on educational systems exceeds $2 trillion and the cost of public health exceeds $3.5 trillion. Therefore, it is not surprising that global corporations are trying to privatize both services (Cavanaugh et al., 2003).

Looking at the United States, Hank Levin (2011) tells us why the field of education is second only to health care in terms of a new frontier for capital to colonize and profit from:

> The United States and most other countries devote a huge share of their resources to education. In 2008–09 the U.S. spent considerably more than one billion dollars in institutional expenditures on education from kindergarten through higher education (National Center for Education Statistics, 2010). What is notable is that this figure does not include pre-school or spending on education and training by businesses or the military. Nor does it include private tutoring or the types of specialized lessons provided to children and adults by public and private entities such as the YMCA, Boys and Girls Clubs, and after-school academies. Even so, the official spending statistics

> accounted for almost 8% of Gross Domestic Product, a percentage that would surely rise to over 10% if all educational spending were included, more than one of every ten dollars of national income. This amount exceeds considerably the spending on the military and is second only to the health care sector. Moreover, this spending has doubled in real terms (adjusted for price level inflation) between 1986–87 and 2008–09. (Levin, 2011, p. 395)

Faced with this increased process of cultural homogenization and considering the local battles for quality education that respects the cultural legacies of communities and individuals, the work of schoolteachers and their social responsibility are magnified.

Thinking of the Freirean key, *another globalization* is a possible dream, and a possible dream today and not tomorrow. Imagining men and women educators socially committed to their political-pedagogical practices—capable of confronting the deleterious tendencies of globalization, of taking advantage of its technological advances, and, especially, of working with their students, with their students' parents, with substantively democratic governments and political parties as well as with labor unions and social movements—it is possible to make this possible dream a reality. The manifold manifestations of these criticisms of neoliberal globalization from the Occupy Wall Street Movement to the Arab Spring are indications that there is growing resistance and attempts at social transformation, facing the perils of neoliberal globalization (Byrne, 2012; Torres, 2009a, 2009b).

For these purposes, it is necessary to think theoretically and practically, utilizing the developments of Critical Theory and Critical Pedagogy in the construction of a democratic and multicultural citizenship (Rexhepi & Torres, 2011). What would be the civic virtues of teachers in the construction of this possible dream of a liberating education? (A systematic analysis of the connections between education, democracy and multiculturalism can be found in Torres, 1998a.)

The first virtue coincides with one of the most important contributions of liberalism, one that, since 9/11, is more than at risk the world over: the virtue of tolerance. Liberalism arose as an anti-authoritarian political philosophy to rescue the notion of liberty as a categorical imperative in complete opposition to despotism and absolutism. In the era that is ours to live, tolerance is, now more than ever, an important virtue that continually interweaves the lines of diversity in contemporary societies. Tolerance requires a continual process of self-vigilance and self-consciousness, revising the constitution of our own consciousness, something that can never be completed but is in permanent process until the end of our days. For instance, although individual racism can be confronted by means of the permanent educational discussion, to confront institutional racism—that is, practices, rituals, and routines that are much more widespread and subtle than sporadic individual acts—requires systematic vigilance, both legal/judicial and political, on the part of individuals, social movements, and communities.

As Freire explained to us about his learning in exile, tolerance is a revolutionary virtue. Tolerance requires knowledge and discipline as well—knowledge because it challenges ignorance, which is one of the foundations of prejudice, pertaining to class, gender, race, sex, and religion, and so on; and discipline, because only through a systematic exercise of introspection and investigation can we discover that, although social representations are constructed socially, they are based on historical processes that need to be examined as evidence for the knowledge.

The second virtue I propose is an epistemology of curiosity, as Freire suggested on innumerable occasions. This epistemology of curiosity must invite us to revive the questions of our childhood and adolescence—questions about the world as it touches our lives, questions about ourselves, questions about those who accompany us in the process of knowledge and of political transformation. Without curiosity, there can be no scientific discovery of any kind.

The third virtue I propose, following a proposal Freire made in his final book, published 40 days before his death, is an ethics of freedom that every teacher ought to adopt. Freire put it very simply: "The fundamental task of educators is to live ethically, to practice ethics daily with young people and children. This is much more important than the subject of biology, if we happen to be biology teachers" (Freire & Quiroga, 1995, p. 61).

From this position, Freire suggested the following 10 ethical principles in his book *Pedagogía de la Autonomía* (1998c):

1. To teach requires respect for the knowledge of our students;
2. To teach requires an aesthetic and an ethics;
3. To teach requires demonstrating with examples;
4. To teach requires respect for the students' autonomy;
5. To teach requires good critical judgment;
6. To teach requires curiosity;
7. To teach requires self-confidence, professional competence and generosity;
8. To teach requires liberty and authority;
9. To teach requires knowing how to listen;
10. To teach requires that we love our students.

(Quoted in Gadotti, 2002, p. 27)

The fourth virtue I want to propose in this chapter is the necessity of avoiding the symmetrically perverse positions of cynicism and of nihilism, defending at any cost the need to respect the principle of hope as the founding principle of all practices of teaching and learning. Hope—even when we feel or experience the cynical conviction that nothing can or will change. Cynicism is an anti-utopian philosophy of brutal adaptation to reality. The other side of the coin is nihilism, the morbid experience of abandoning the struggle, imagining that there is no hope of changing things. As the only antidote to cynicism and nihilism I propose the principle of hope.

The fifth virtue I would like to propose to educators who want to confront the dilemmas of globalization and the demands of the local, is a secular or nonreligious spirituality of love. Nothing is stronger than love to guide our decisionmaking, based on the notions of community and compassion. A spirituality of love, as Erich Fromm suggested more than 40 years ago, does not have to be based on faith, on the transcendent, but it does need to be based on faith in human nature and in the necessity of reconciling passion and reason in our actions.

The sixth virtue is dialogue, our ability to dialogue, dialogue as a method. This includes dialogue when people's positions are diverse and even diametrically opposed, as it does when there may be incommensurability in their discourses. This idea of dialogue is one of the basic principles of Jürgen Habermas and his social construction of the principle of the ideal conversation and communicative rationality (Morrow & Torres, 2002). Three notions intercede in the notion of dialogue as communicative rationality: (1) the notion of intersubjectivity in the affirmations of validation—that is, the position of the speaker is fundamental; (2) the mode of argumentation—which varies according to disciplines, professions, and so forth; and (3) the possibility of reaching a rational accord among the dialogue's participants, beginning with a principle of discursive intelligibility.

In other words, the currency of the Freirean arrangement is evident because he has historically postulated the shaping of critical educators, proposing an anticlassist, antisexist and antiracist philosophy based on tolerance, on an epistemology of curiosity, on the rejection of cynicism and nihilistic positions, and on reaffirming the principle of hope, in a secular spirituality of love and the ability to connect intersubjectively through dialogue as a method and also as a cognitive process.

PAULO FREIRE, A PILGRIM OF UTOPIA

For me, it's impossible not to read Paulo Freire.
(Freire, quoted in Freire & Quiroga, 1995, p. 61)

Those who have fought against injustice, the lack of love and tenderness, avarice, measureless ambition, intolerance, exploitation, oppression, and domination—in sum, against all the evils of the cultures—know that they live in a very precarious and certainly marginal position with respect to the elites of power and politics in the hegemonic culture. But, curiously, this marginality invites us to broaden our commitment to this life of struggle against the oppressive living conditions of the majority of the world's people.

The very notion of anger, defined as existential disgust with these evils, constitutes a political instrument for social movements, communities, and individuals. However, Freire, despite having been made into a living icon of the educational left, always defended the notion of utopia as the ultimate horizon of educative practice, advising us to be careful not to fall into the trap of self-victimization, always blaming others for our mistakes, losses, or misfortunes because the notion of a utopian marginality coalesces with a notion of individual responsibility that must be honored.

Therefore, this notion of utopian marginality that Freire appropriated by declaring himself a "utopian traveler" is founded on a model of spirituality that is itself utopian.

It is utopian because, as poets have suggested in countless verses, utopia is that distant horizon, a horizon that one always wants to reach but can never approach. One takes two steps toward this horizon and it recedes another two paces. What, then, is the advantage of utopia, we might ask? As a rational and spiritual model guiding our desire, it helps us to keep moving (Galeano, n.d.).

But when we speak of utopian marginality, it is in another sense of the word, in the biblical and prophetic sense of utopia: the utopia of denouncing the causes of exploitation, of oppression, of inequalities—a very important part played by pedagogical and political criticism—at the same time that we announce the coming, not of the Messiah but, rather, of the possibility of a better world or, as Paulo Freire put it, a world in which it is possible to love.

Freire continues to be as relevant or more so today than at the time of his early contributions. His prophetic voice still powerfully resonates in the struggle for social justice education:

> The prophets are not badly dressed men and women, with long, dirty, unruly hair and beards, carrying staffs. The prophets are those who submerse themselves in the waters of their culture, of their history, of the history of their oppressed people. The prophets are those who know the here and now, and may not be able to see the future because they are making it. (Quoted in Gadotti, 2002, p. 27).

Perhaps we should leave the last word to Freire. Twenty years ago, in one of our conversations I asked what he thought his legacy would be. His answer is vintage Freire:

> What is my legacy? I think that it is just one. I think that it is possible to be said about Paulo Freire, when I die [that] "Paulo Freire was a man who loved, who could not understand a life existence without love and without knowing. Paulo Freire lived, loved and tried to know. Paulo Freire was constantly curious and asking questions to himself." Do you see that this is not a very personal legacy? This is the legacy which all people in the world, with a minimal of good sense, leave to the other, to the next generations. And this is what I hope can be said about me, even when what I thought about education lost meaning. But that I loved, it can never lose meaning." (Freire, quoted in Torres, 1995c, p. 181)

Notes

Preface

1. Coordinated by José Eustaquio Romão, with the collaboration of Moacir Gadotti and myself, in 2013, the year of the celebration of 50 years of the experience of Angicos, we published the original manuscript of *Pedagogy of the Oppressed* (handwritten by Freire in Portuguese). See Freire, Brazil, 2013.

2. This is the most comprehensive study of its kind in the world. It includes an international bibliography about Paulo Freire and more than 100 short analytical contributions discussing the work of Freire and his influence in contemporary pedagogy. First edition in Portuguese. Spanish edition, Mexico: Siglo XXI Editores, 2001.

3. This critique has been considered by some people the first academic criticism of Freire's work in Brazil but this view overlooked my own more sympathetic criticism of Freire's work published in 1978 and 1979 in Spanish and Portuguese. See Moacir Gadotti's Foreword in this book.

4. For an alternative analysis, see Carlos A. Torres (1979, 1981) and the work of Moacir Gadotti (1989).

5. I have narrated this episode in several texts, particularly in my book *Education and Neoliberal Globalization* (2009b). Because that book has been printed only in hardcover, however, and may not be fully accessible to all individuals, I choose to reproduce this conversation here again.

6. Written in the Paulo Freire Institute, São Paulo, May 2, 1998.

Chapter 1

1. Though it would be fair to say that Freire was not interested in studying the connections between education and work, it is also fair to argue that his contribution to literacy training, from his job in 1947–1958 in the Serviço Social da Indústria, (SESI) in Brazil to his work in Chile (1964–1970) on the process of agrarian reform, had formidable implications for economic development in both countries and internationally.

2. Documents issued by the Conference of Catholic Bishops of Latin America (CELAM), at its meeting in Medellin in 1968, launched an attack on international capitalism, poverty, and social injustice. Although they were condemned by some as the work of radical leftist groups, the Medellin documents gave a profound boost to supporters of the emerging Theology of Liberation.

3. Freire's dissertation was published posthumously. It included a preface by the founders of the Paulo Freire Institute in São Paulo, Brazil, including Moacir Gadotti, Carlos Alberto Torres, Walter Garcia, Francisco Gutiérrez and José Eustaquio Romão. It includes a historical study contextualizing the work of Freire by José Eustaquio Romão (Freire, 2001). Technically it may not be considered a doctoral dissertation because Freire was never enrolled in a Ph.D. program. In fact, it was written for competition for an academic position in the Escola de Artes do Recife that later would become part of the Universidade Federal de Pernambuco (Federal University of Pernambuco). The Portuguese tradition in higher education has a system known as Provas de Agregação that in Brazil was called Livre Docência, a practice that no longer exists in the federal universities, except at the Universidade de São Paulo, USP, Universidae de Campinas, UNICAMP, and Universidade Estatal Paulista, Unesp. This evaluation, if it is conducted following the traditional Portuguese university model, implies that the candidate provides and defends his or her curriculum vitae in public, write an original piece of academic work (e.g., what is now considered Freire's thesis), defend this in a discussion with an evaluation committee, and present a public lecture to be considered for an academic position and/or promotion to full professor. Freire competed with another candidate for a teaching position and lost because the other candidate obtained a better grade in the evaluation.

4. To quote from the original: "*O Brasil age como se não houvesse mais possibilidade de descobrir novos caminhos. O país produziu o método Paulo Freire de alfabetizacão, que foi estudado e se tornou famoso no mundo. Ele foi deixado de lado e, em vez de usar a cultura popular para melhorar o ensino, como propunha Paulo Freire, recorre-sé as formulas estrangeiras, que nem sempre ajudam*" (2000).

5. Freire died of heart failure on May 2, 1997.

6. In this study, Gadotti (2008a) quotes Leonardo Boff: "The category sustainability is central for the ecological cosmos vision and possibly constitutes one of the bases of a new civilization paradigm that searches to harmonize human beings, development and Earth, understood as Gaia." See http://www.acervo.paulofreire.org:8080/xmlui/bitstream/handle/7891/3080/FPF_PTPF_12_077.pdf

7. We speak of Freire's intuition, in terms of both its normative and analytical dimensions. Carl G. Jung (1968) identified a number of functions in consciousness, and also distinguished the ectopsyche and the endopsyche. When he spoke of the ectopsychic functions ("a system of relationships between the contents of consciousness and facts and data coming in from the environment," p. 11), he described the functions of sensation, thinking, feeling, and intuition. Intuition, then, although mystical in the view of many, is very practical. Jung argued: "Whenever you have to deal with strange conditions where you have no established values or established concepts, you will depend upon that faculty of intuition" (p. 14). Jung was referring to anticipatory dreams or telepathic phenomena, but also to intuition in day-to-day interactions with people, things and animals. Freire was able to let his intuition guide his theorizing, and we believe that much of what we learn in our lives is as connected to intuition as it may be connected to sensations, thinking, or feeling.

8. For an analysis of some of these works, see Gadotti, 1994, pp. 109–143, and Schugurensky, 2011.

Chapter 2

1. In total this research agenda resulted in four books: *Paulo Freire: Educación y Concientización* (*Paulo Freire: Education and Consciousness Raising*) (Torres, 1980b); *Paulo Freire en América Latina* (*Paulo Freire in Latin America*) (Torres Novoa, 1978c) (Portuguese translation: *Leitura Crítica de Paulo Freire* (*A Critical Reading of Paulo Freire*) [1981a]); *La Praxis Educativa de Paulo Freire* (*The Educational Praxis of Paulo Freire*) (Torres Novoa, 1978b) (Portuguese translation: *Consciência e História: A Práxis Educativa de Paulo Freire* (*Conscience and History. The Educational Praxis of Paulo Freire* [1979]); and *Entrevistas con Paulo Freire* (*Conversations with Paulo Freire*) (Torres Novoa, 1978a).

2. In an essay written with Raymond Allen Morrow, I draw a brief biographical profile of Freire's trajectory and his impact, especially in the First World and the United States (2002b, pp. 57–70, 459–460).

3. I want to pay homage here to one of the most enlightening and committed social scientists of Latin America, Dr. Atilio Alberto Boron, who was the general secretary of the Consejo Latinoamericano de Ciencias Sociales (CLACSO). Atilio was the director of my master's thesis and it was in his classes and in countless hours of private conversation in Mexico City that I developed my taste for political science. Above all, I want to thank him for his unconditional support in what were very difficult years for me. After I left Argentina, to which I would not return until after democracy was reestablished in 1984, I was living in very humble, very difficult conditions as a married graduate student with three small children. My partner at the time, and the mother of my children, María Cristina Pons, also deserves recognition. Without her support, love and solidarity, I would never have been able to survive the hardships of our daily life, all while attempting to understand the complexities of theoretical thought in the social sciences and analyzing the surly and difficult reality of Latin America.

4. This became known as the Rodrigazo, with the political ascension of the engineer Celestino Rodriguez, who tripled the price of gasoline, drastically devalued the peso, and substantially raised taxes on public services. This provoked the first general labor strike against a Peronista government, on July 7, 1975.

5. For an analysis of the links between religion and hegemony in Latin America and my observations as a participant in the nascent Theology of Liberation, see Torres (1992a).

6. Similar experiments in the United States occurred in many states, not only in terms of the link with nature through ecological production—e.g., the Permaculture movement—but also in movements to expand the production of adobe and straw-bale houses, considered economical and ecological because of the energy they saved.

7. The emblematic book of this period is Paulo Freire (1978), *Pedagogy in Process: The Letters to Guinea Bissau*. New York, NY: The Seabury Press. This book shows Freire's Marxist orientation.

8. See the book written by Adriana Puiggrós (2010), a distinguished historian of education and daughter of Rodolfo Puiggrós.

9. Documentation having to do with Operation Condor can be found in many places on the Internet.

10. Dr. Emilio Mignone was a distinguished Argentinean lawyer and educator who was undersecretary of education and also a functionary of the Organization of American States (OAS) and first chancellor of the University of Lujan. He would also be one of the founders, along with his wife, of the Mothers of the Plaza de Mayo organization and of a human rights institute, el Centro de Estudios Legales y Sociales. Both organizations were among the first to confront the violence of the state, putting their members' lives at enormous risk as they searched for sons and daughters who had disappeared and attempted to get to the bottom of the monstrous operation of state violence run by the military governments from 1976 to 1983.

11. Such *Grupos de Tareas* of the Argentinean armed forces combined military, navy, air force officers, coast guards, border protection agents, members of the federal and provincial jail systems, and provincial and federal police.

12. Along with five other Argentinean students, I was awarded a scholarship to travel to Mexico and participate in the first master's program that had opened after the Chilean military coup of 1973 forced FLACSO to move its educational center first to Argentina and then to Mexico.

13. It is worth mentioning, and not just as a historic curiosity, that the archives of the CIDOC—Intercultural Documentation Center—created by Ivan Illich in Cuernavaca and frequented by radical thinkers such as Paulo Freire, Everett Reimer, Erich Fromm, and so many others, are now stored in the Colegio de México's excellent library in Ajusco, Mexico City.

14. See the preface especially prepared for this book by Moacir Gadotti, Freire's principal biographer and one of the best philosophers of education in Latin America. The director and founder of the Paulo Freire Institute in São Paulo, Brazil, he is one of those few extraordinary friends with whom we can entrust our very lives.

Chapter 3

1. I have criticized the theoretical confusion of identifying Paulo Freire's thought with "permanent education" or the paradigm of lifelong education (Torres, 1980b).

2. See my comparative analysis of Freirean and Hegelian dialectics (Torres, 2009a, pp. 131–151).

3. Martin Heidegger (1889–1976) was one of the most important philosophers of the 20th century. His main book, *Being and Time*, altered the ontological understanding of being, impacting several domains, including phenomenology, existentialism, hermeneutics, theology, psychology, and political theory.

4. Emmanuel Mounier (1905–1950) was the creator of personalism and founder and director of the famous journal *Sprit*. His emblematic book is *The Personalist Manifesto*. His orientation was related to the Catholic Work Movement in France.

5. Pierre Teilhard de Chardin (1881–1955) was a Jesuit philosopher trained as a geologist and palentologist. His book, *The Phenomenon of Man*, censured by the Vatican, was a very important work in the nascent Theology of Liberation in Latin America. The reach of his thought, thinking of the universe as a "living host," would qualify as one of the earlier eco-pedagogy theses.

6. Gabriel Marcel (1889–1973), a leading French Christian philosopher and playwright, was considered by many the first French existentialist. His two-volume book *The Mistery of Being* was well read by Freire (see Freire's personal library in the Paulo Freire Institute, São Paulo, Brazil).

7. Karl Jaspers (1883–1969) was a German physician and psychiatrist who became a philosopher and was influential in the transition from Nazism to liberal Germany.

8. Edmund Husserl (1859–1938), a German philosopher and mathematician, is credited as the founder of the 20th-century school of phenomenology.

9. Franz Clemens Honoratus Hermann Brentano (1883–1917) was a German philosopher and psychologist who influenced Sigmund Freud and Edmund Husserl, among others.

10. Karel Kosic (1926–1963) was a Czech neo-Marxist philosopher who, linking Marx and Heidegger, produced a book called *Dialectics of the Concrete* that influenced a whole generation of Latin American intellectuals, Paulo Freire included.

11. Max Scheller (1874–1928), a German philosopher who worked on phenomenology, ethics, and philosophical anthropology, expanded upon the work of Husserl.

12. Nicolai Hartmann (1882–1950) was a Russian philosopher of German descent who worked extensively on the question of philosophies of consciousness, influencing Hans-George Gadamer and Freire in particular.

13. Georg Wilhelm Friedrich Hegel (1770–1831) was a German philosopher who, jointly with Emmanuel Kant, should be considered the heart and soul of Western and Continental philosophy, heavily influencing both Marxism and Freire.

14. Without getting into the dispute between Althusser and Garaudy on "Marxist humanism," Marcuse and Fromm insist on pointing out many elements of "humanist" thought in Karl Marx's *Economic and Philosophical Manuscripts of 1844.*

15. For my previous work more than 35 years ago, see my article (Torres, 1976a) in Portuguese.

Chapter 4

1. Freire's theological background has a profound incidence in Latin American studies that were influential at the beginning of the Theology of Liberation—for instance, Ruben Alves, 1971. One of the emblematic authors of the Theology of Liberation, the Argentine Mexican theologian, historian, and philosopher Enrique Dussel recognizes the paternity of Paulo Freire to the emerging new theological model in an interview with Freire in Mexico (Dussel, 1971), in which Dussel reaffirms the deep Freirean influence in the nascent theology of liberation. See also Dussel, 1985, pp. 95–98. For the analytical and political convergence of Freire and Dussel see Jose Pedro Boufleuer, 1991.

2. For a contemporary rendition of the debates among philosophers of liberation in Latin America, many of them influenced by Freirean analysis, see Vanessa de Oliveira Andreotti, 2011.

3. In my book *Paulo Freire: educación y concientización*, I have thoroughly analyzed Freire's sociological evolution, especially the qualitative leap that occurs between *Education as the Practice of Freedom* and *Pedagogy of the Oppressed.*

4. To broaden our argument about the intimate relations between the Hegelian dialectic and the pedagogical dialectic of the oppressed, in an article entitled see *"La dialéctica hegeliand y el pensamiento lógico-estructural de Paulo Freire,"* which appeared in the *SIC Review* (*Centro Gumila*), Vol. XXXIX, Number 383, March 1976, pp. 116–120. See also *SINTESE Review* (Volume III, Number 77, April/June 1976, pp. 61–78) for an update of the same article.

5. Mouvement International de la Jeunesse Agricole et Rural Catholique (MIJARC) (1969), Comment Paulo Freire voulait changer les brésiliens, *Terre et Culture, 34* is very illustrative in terms of historical analysis to consult Marcio Moreira Alves's excellent book, *Un grano de mostaza. El despertar de la revolución brasileña.* Premio testimonio 1972, Casa de las Américas. Ediciones CEPE, Buenos Aires, 1974), or, finally, Arme Mareland's paper, Paulo Freire: On Education and Conscientização, Lutheran campus Ministry, Utah, mimeographed, 1970, 12 pages.

6. To understand the relationship of education and politics in the theoretical beginnings of the method, we suggest that the reader consult Francisco C. Wefort's excellent essay, "Education and Politics (Sociological reflections on Education for Freedom)" which serves as the Introduction to Freire's book *Education: An Exercise in Freedom*, translated by Loretta Slover in June 1969. The reader might also consult the brief but suggestive work of Janice Farmer Weaver, "Paulo Freire and Education: A Sociological View," a presentation at the AESA Conference at the Chicago Circle of the University of Illinois, on February 23, 1972. The key book from Freire is *Politics and Education.*

7. This argument has been made in a very didactic way by Julio Barreiro (1974) in *Educación popular y proceso de concientización.* As we have already indicated, while Julio Barreiro is the listed author of the book, the actual author, whose identity Barreiro tried to protect from the brutalities of the Brazilian dictatorship is Brazilian anthropologist Carlos Rodrigues Brandão.

8. See Adwinkie, 1954, in which Adwinkie argues that scientific concepts are really mythic as well and that there would not be a myth versus logic opposition if humans were not "mythological" beings. On the other hand, Enrique Dussel's reflections in a series of articles entitled "Latin America, Liberation or Dependency" are very suggestive, especially when he discusses, following Mircea Eliade, that "all civilizations have an ethical-mythical nucleus, on which all their culture feeds." In this, Dussel is still very much under the Christian existentialist influence of Paul Ricoeur. In subsequent work, he has abandoned these themes in favor of a more dialectical-historical treatment of culture.

9. The underlying analysis of Freire is reflected in proposals of a Critical Theory of society, particularly the contributions of Herbert Marcuse. It is illustrative to consult Marcuse's fundamental books, including his doctoral thesis, *Hegel's Ontology and Theory of History*, edited in 1933 (re-edited in Spanish by Martinez Roca, Barcelona, 1969) and *Reason and Revolution* from 1941 (published in Spanish by Editorial Alianza). See also *Eros and Civilization* (1955) and *The One Dimensional Man* (1964), which go beyond his 1958 Soviet Marxism. Marcuse develops the thesis that in advanced industrial societies, the power of reason becomes one-dimensional as a negative critical force and winds up expressing

itself with the development of capitalism as the ideological totality of the consumer society (implementing mind-control techniques), endeavoring to make the irrational rational in the society at the same time subverting the rational by negating it as societal irrationality. In other words, the explicative immutability of science can be utilized as a dominating factor, even within highly developed social formations (without forgetting that, in dependent social formations, the words *science* and *scientific* are used to mystify and manipulate ahistorical content far removed from the social context where such "scientific" practices take place).

10. Due to the deep divergences that this arrangement provoked in the Second Vatican Council, the final documents express that the Spirit acts wherever it wishes and in ways known only to Itself, thus manifesting the impossibility of completely circumscribing what is subjectively and objectively correct in terms of social action, including everything from playing the piano to the practice of faith. In other words, it attempts to understand and respect the tremendous wealth of human action, from the high-fidelity perspective of salvation.

11. For the Greeks, the expression drama means action.

12. For example, the works of Rodolfo Kusch and the preconceptions inherent in some of the developmentalist theories (in Torres, 1981a, pp. 139–155).

Chapter 5

1. Freire used the word *problematização* to refer to a "problem-posing" approach to language learning that took into consideration the psychosocial and political contexts of adult learners' lives.

2. See Vachet (1972), who in basic texts, reconstructs the entire liberal ideology—its major themes, logical arguments, and historic conditioning. If we transcribe the proposals of the liberal political philosophy to the analysis of the aforementioned educational paradigm, we will find the same theoretical determinants coated in pedagogical rhetoric.

3. The excellent work of Herbert Marcuse entitled *Toward a Critical Theory of Society* analyzes, in its central chapters, the conversion of liberal theory into the progressive theory of an ascending social class (the bourgeoisie) versus the conservative theory of an entrenched class with consolidated power, preoccupied that the proletariat in its antagonistic contradiction might eliminate it in an attempt to create a classless society.

Chapter 6

1. This occurred on November 16, 1889.

2. Here, the irrational represents the group of blind forces that go against the grain of historical reason. Freirean analysis is nourished by the dichotomy between rational development (adequate to the idea of reason that must be preserved in a society that bases its ascension on superior kinds of cohabitation) and irrational development (adequate to the idea of the centrifugal forces that control—according to Freire, starting with a kind of "emotionality"—societal development, thereby reversing this process of ascension,

dichotomizing it, divesting it of the elements that give it value and universality, and reducing social space to the political will of a single social sector). We cannot discuss Freire's analysis of rationality at greater length.

Chapter 7

1. I have translated the word literally from the Spanish *alfabetización* rather than using the English *literacy*, which has nothing to do with the art of teaching people, particularly adults, to read and write their native language.

2. We explore this further in Chapter 9, "The Methodology of the Thematic Investigation."

3. We refer to the cultural circles that Freire and his literacy training facilitators set up in several northeast Brazilian coastal cities, including Recife, Natãl, João Pessoa, and Maceió. The groups comprised fishermen and day laborers, and in the tiny hamlet of Angicos, in the dry backlands of the neighboring state of Rio Grande do Norte, Freire and his facilitators taught 300 peasants to read and write basic Portuguese in 40 hours.

4. As already stated, the book attributed to Julio Barreiro was in fact written by anthropologist Carlos Rodrigues Brandão, but was published under Barreiro's name to protect the integrity of Rodrigues Brandão, who at the time was living under the dictatorship in Brazil.

Chapter 8

1. See my book with Raymond Morrow (Morrow & Torres, 2002), in which we discuss the similarities and differences between Freire and Habermas.

2. We have explained the value of the term *utopia* to Freirean thinking in Morrow and Torres, 2002. Paulo Freire makes distinct statements about the idea that sustains "utopia," which is of inestimable value to his analytical goals.

3. Although it became known as a psychosocial method of adult literacy, Freire's work should be better defined as theoretical and methodological insights toward literacy training rather than as a method per se. However, for the sake of the argument, we may refer from time to time to the Paulo Freire Method.

4. See, in respect to the critique Marx makes of Hegel for conceiving of man as if his essence was the workforce on one hand and self-consciousness on the other (Rubel, 1970, pp. 50–69).

Chapter 9

1. In Marx's definition in the *Grundisse*, the real-concrete is the synthesis of multiple determinations, hence unity in diversity. Submitted to the arbitration of the senses, even though it is not reduced to the empirical (in spite of being the point of departure of the intuition and of representation), it implies a certain connection with meaning that is, at times, occult and at times manifests in empirical phenomena.

2. See the fourth chapter of our aforementioned book *Paulo Freire: Educación y concientización*, where, following the excellent analysis of Thomas S. Kuhn, we discuss pedagogy as multiple scientific paradigms.

3. I have analyzed comparatively the question of communication in the constitution of the public sphere in Freire and Habermas in my work with Raymond Morrow (Morrow & Torres, 2002).

4. We recommend that readers who want a more complete vision of the process of thematic investigation and can read Spanish consult José Luis Fiori (1969, November), *Dialéctica y Libertad: Dos Dimensiones de la Investigación Temática*, MIEC, JECI, Servicio de Documentación, Serie 2, Documento 8, Uruguay, pp. 12–18. See also the second chapter of our *Paulo Freire: Educacion y concientización*, where we discuss the didactic-methodological dimensions. In English, a most welcome addition to the bibliography is Daniel Schugurensky's *Paulo Freire* (2011).

5. Freire advises that this group of specialists should include at least a psychologist, one or two educational specialists (for instance, sociologists or educators), and a pedagogue. The ideal group would add to these specialists a linguistics expert, a communications specialist, and a specialist in group theory.

6. The circle of investigation is responsible for "phase one" of the thematic investigation and is the antecedent, from a research perspective, of the constitution of the cultural circle.

7. *Epochal themes* is a lovely term that Freire employs to identify the hopes, doubts, dreams, problems, struggles, conflicts, and projects of the alphabetizing community.

8. The culture circle replaces traditional schooling. It is the place where problem-posing dialogue is exercised with a debate coordinator and where thematic decodification takes place.

9. I have dedicated this book, and many other books discussing literacy training to three dear friends: Monica Mignone and César and María Marta Lugones, who were among the first to be "disappeared"—that is, kidnapped, tortured, and assassinated in Argentina in October 1975 because they were practicing liberation pedagogy in a shantytown, teaching people to read and write, and trying to organize the oppressed against the establishment. We learned that Freire's model of literacy training is very efficient but needs a certain milieu for its implementation—a democratic framework in which human rights are protected. The presence of social movements, community organizations, or political parties may help to this end, but certainly, in the context of the class struggle of Argentina 1975, with guerrilla warfare in the street, a weakened democratic state, and the presence of right-wing paramilitary groups freely kidnapping and killing the political opposition and social activists, resulted in a great national tragedy that was completed, as I tried to explain in the Introduction, with the onset of the military dictatorship that scaled up the process of repression. For the original investigation on the Argentinean genocide, see the National Commission on the Disappearance of Persons (Spanish: Comisión Nacional sobre la Desaparición de Personas, CONADEP) and consult the report in the book *Nunca Más* (*Never Again*).

Chapter 10

1. See the Appendix to this chapter for a chronology of the period. I would like to thank Moacir Gadotti for preparing the chronology that informs this section of the chapter and for his willingness to share with the reader in this book. Dr. Jaana Flavia Fernandes Nogueira translated the selection from Portuguese. I am very grateful to her.

2. The Alliance for the Progress was the U.S. response to the revolutionary trends emerging from the installation of the Cuban Revolution and Cuba's definition as a socialist state. Using substantial funds to be lent to the Latin American countries, which were to be repaid later—resembling to some extent the Marshall Plan that was implemented in postwar Europe—the Alliance for the Progress sought to create solid markets and formally democratic governments, including planned agrarian reforms, fiscal reforms, reindustrialization, and models of democratic governance. However, once the rising tensions, guerrilla warfare, and radical social movements began to impact and challenge the conservative or modernizing governments in the region, the model of development exemplified in the Alliance for the Progress took a nasty turn, supporting the advent of the new authoritarianism in Latin America, considered a preferable option to the "totalitarian" governments that were closely connected, in the view of U.S. policymakers, to the Soviet Union. There were many other instances in which the "interests" of the United States in the region were preserved by projects such as Operation Condor or the training of Latin American officers in Panama under U.S. military personnel and with a furious anti-Marxist, Cold War ideology. The first experience of neoliberalism implemented by Pinochet in Chile emerged as another response to what was perceived as a socialist threat in the region.

3. The concept of a Paulo Freire System was already part of the conversation of people very close to Freire. See for instance: *Fundamentação teórica do Sistema Paulo Freire de Educação* (Theoretical Foundations of the Paulo Freire System of Education), written by Jarbas Maciel (1983) fourth volume of the *Revista de Cultura* of the University of Recife, published in April–June 1963 (pages 25–58). Likewise *Conscientização e alfabetização: Uma visão prática do Sistema Paulo Freire* (Conscientization and Literacy: A Practical Vision of the Paulo Freire System), written by Aurenice Cardoso (1983, pp. 71–79).

4. For a chronology of events, see the Appendix to this chapter.

5. These articles can be found in Osmar Fávero (1983), *Cultura popular, educação popular–memória dos anos 60*, Rio de Janeiro, Brazil: Editora Graal. All of them were published under the section titled "The Paulo Freire System."

6. *Every idle word God will notice.*

7. Excepticism is the luxury of a minority.... To the rest we will serve a well-cooked happiness, and the humanity will gobble up that divine garbage

8. In the sixties three processes were deem fundamental for the modernization of traditional societies, including urbanization, industrialization and literacy (see Torres, 1977).

Chapter 11

1. Henry Giroux has postulated the need for teachers to become public intellectuals. Others have insisted that it is necessary for teachers to be organic intellectuals of the working classes and popular sectors. This is not the place for a treatment of these positions, and there are some extremely suggestive books on the subject, such as Sarlo's (2001) *Tiempo Presente: Notas sobre el intercambio de cultura*. Another interesting book is *Paulo Freire on Higher Education. A dialogue at the National University of Mexico*. In the Introduction to this book, I discussed some of the postures connected to traditional intellectuals, Gramscian intellectuals, and institutional intellectuals (Torres, 1994c).

2. I have developed this analysis in chapter 18 of Arnove, Torres, and Franz (2013).

3. For an analysis playing with the limits between fiction and reality in the politics of education, see C. A. Torres (1995a), Fictional Dialogues on Teachers, Politics, and Power in Latin America. In M. Ginsburg (Ed.), *The Politics of Educators' Work and Lives* (pp. 133–168). New York, NY: Garland.

4. See manuscript of *Pedagogy of the Oppressed*, in its Portuguese original version. Not surprisingly, the original version in Portuguese doesn't correspond into too many of the translations that I have been able to read.

References

Adames, R. (1971). Concientización: Hacia una presentación del problema. *Estudios Sociales, 4*, 206–216.

Adwinkie, R. F. (1954). Myth and symbol in contemporary philosophy and theology. *The Journal of Religion, 34.*

Alves, R. (1971). *Religión: Opio o instrumento de liberación.* Lima, Peru: CEI.

Aricó, F. (1988). *La cola del diablo.* Caracas, Venezuela: Nueva Sociedad.

Arlt, R. (2013) *Los siete locos.* Buenos Aires, Argentina: Editorial Modernito.

Arnove, R. (1994). *Education as contested terrain: Nicaragua, 1979–1993.* Boulder, CO: Westview.

Arnove, R., Torres, C. A., & Franz, S. (Eds.). (2013). *Comparative education. The dialectics of the global and the local* (4th ed.). Lanham, MD: Rowman & Littlefield.

Arregui, J. J. H. (1960). *La formación de la conciencia nacional.* Buenos Aires, Argentina: Hachet.

Ayer, A. J. (Compiler). (1963). *El positivismo lógico.* Mexico City, Mexico: Fondo de Cultura Económica.

Banks, J. A. (2003). *Handbook of research on multicultural education* (2nd ed.). San Francisco, CA: Jossey-Bass.

Banks, J. A. (2004). *Diversity and citizenship education: Global perspectives.* San Francisco, CA: Jossey-Bass.

Barreiro, J. (1974). *Educación popular y proceso de concientización.* Buenos Aires, Argentina: Siglo XXI Editores.

Barreiro, J. (1980). *Los molinos de la ira. Pronóstico sobre la situación de América Latina.* Mexico City, Mexico, Siglo XXI Editores.

Barreiro, J., de Santa Ana, J., Cetrulo, R., & Gilbert, V. (1974). *Conciencia y revolución: contribución al proceso de concientización del hombre en América Latina: Ensayos sobre la pedagogía de Paulo Freire.* Buenos Aires, Argentina: Schapire/Tierra Nueva.

Beisiegel, C. de R. (1974). *Estado e educação popular.* São Paulo, Brazil: Pioneira.

Bobbio, N. (1985). *Estudios de historia de la filosofía: De Hobbes a Gramsci.* Madrid, Editorial Rebate.

Bohorquez, I. (2008). Untested feasibility in Paulo Freire: Behind the profile of a dream. In C. A. Torres & P. Noguera (Eds.), *Social justice education for teachers: Paulo Freire and the possible dream* (pp. 177–189). Rotterdam, Netherlands, and Taipei, Taiwan: Sense Publishers.

Borg, C., & Mayo, P. (2007). *Public intellectuals, radical democracy, and social movements: A book of interviews.* New York, NY: Peter Lang.

Borges, J. L. (1999). *Selected poems* (A. Coleman, Ed.). New York, NY: Penguin.

Bosco Pinto, J., et al. (1970). *Metodología de la investigación temática, supuestos teóricos y desarrollo, IICA-CIRA*, (OEA), Didactic material, no. 147, Bogotá, Colombia.

Boudon, R., & Lazarsfeld, P. (1974). *Metodología de las ciencias sociales.* Barcelona, Spain: Editorial Laia.

Boufleuer, J. P. (1991). *Pedagogia Latino-Americana: Freire e Dussel.* Ijuí, Brazil: UNIJUI Editorial.

Britzman, D. (n.d.). *Britzman on Freire and psychoanalysis.* [Video.] Retrieved from http://vimeo.com/31747556

Brown, C. (1978). *Literacy in 30 hours: Paulo Freire's process in northeast Brazil.* Chicago, IL: Alternative Schools Network.

Burbules, N. C. (1993). *Dialogue in Teaching. Theory and Practice.* New York, NY: Teachers College Press.

Burbules, N. C., & Torres, C. A. (Eds.). (2000). *Globalization and education, critical perspectives.* New York and London: Routledge.

BusinessDictionary.com. (2013). System. Retrieved from http://www.businessdictionary.com/definition/system.html

Byrne, J. (Ed.) (2012). *The occupy handbook.* New York, NY: Back Bay Books.

Cândido, M. (1996). *Memento dos vivos. A esquerda católica do Brasil.* Rio de Janeiro, Brazil: Templo Brasileiro.

Cardoso, A. (1983). Conscientização e alfabetização: uma visão prática do sistema Paulo Freire. In Osmar Fávero (Ed.), *Cultura popular, educação popular: Memória dos anos 60* (pp. 161–172). Rio de Janeiro, Brazil: Editora Graal.

Castells, M. (1968). *Metodología de la práctica sociológica.* Santiago, Chile: FLACSO.

Cavanaugh, J. et al. (2003). *Alternatives to economic globalization, a better world is possible.* San Francisco, CA: Berrett-Koehler.

Collier, David et al. (1979). *The new authoritarianism in Latin America.* Princeton, NJ: Princeton University Press.

Concatti, R. (1970). Profetismo y política. *Enlace,* 10, 5–17.

De Kadt, E. (1970). *Catholic radicals in Brazil.* London, UK: Oxford University Press.

de Lima, V. A. (1981). *Comunicação e cultura: as idéias de Paulo Freire.* Rio de Janeiro, Brazil: Paz e Terra.

Della Volpe, G. (1963). *Rousseau y Marx.* Buenos Aires, Argentina: Editorial Platina.

Dewey, J. (1916). *Democracy and Education.* New York, NY: McMillan.

de Santa Ana, J. (1974). De la conciencia oprimida a la conciencia crítica. In J. Barreiro, J. de Santa Ana, R. Cetrulo, & V. Gilbert, *Conciencia y revolución* (pp. 37–56). Buenos Aires, Argentina: Editorial Tierra Nueva.

Donghi, T. H. (1987). *El espejo de la historia: Problemas argentinos y perspectives latinoamericanas.* Buenos Aires, Argentina: Sudamericana.

Dussel, E. (1971, July 22). Interview with Paulo Freire. *Vida Nueva, 842,* 12–20.

Dussel, E. (1972). *La dialéctica hegeliana: Supuestos y superación.* Mendoza, Argentina: Editorial Ser y Tiempo.

Dussel, E. (1985). *Teología de la Liberación. Un panorama de su desarrollo.* Ciudad de Mexico, Mexico: Potrerillos Editores S.A. de C.V.

Dussel, E. (1997). The architectonic of the ethics of liberation: On material ethics and formal moralities. In D.E.A. Batstone (Ed.), *Liberation theologies, postmodernity, and the Americas* (pp. 273–304). London, UK, and New York, NY: Routledge.

English, L. M., & Mayo, P. (2012). *Learning with adults: A critical pedagogical introduction.* Rotterdam, The Netherlands and Taipei, Taiwan: Sense Publishers.

Fávero, O. (Ed.). (1983). *Cultura popular, educação popular: memória dos anos 60.* Rio de Janeiro, Brazil, Editora Graal.

Feinberg, W., & Torres, C. A. (1995). Democracy and education: John Dewey and Paulo Freire. In J. Zajda (Ed.), *Education and society* (pp. 59–70). Albert Park, Australia: James Nicholas Publisher.

Fernandez, C., & Terra, A. (1994). *40 horas de esperança: o método Paulo Freire, política e pedagogia na experiência de Angicos.* São Paulo, Brazil: Ática.

Fiori, E. M. (1973). Aprender a decir su palabra. El método de alfabetización del profesor Paulo Freire. In P. Freire, *Pedagogía del Oprimido* (Foreword). Buenos Aires, Argentina: Editorial Siglo XXI Editores.

Fiori, J. L. (1969, November). *Dialéctica y libertad: Dos dimensiones de la investigación temática.* MIEC, JECI, Servicio de Documentación, Serie 2, Documento 8, Uruguay.

Franco, F. (1973). *El hombre: construcción progresiva—La tarea educativa de Paulo Freire.* Madrid, Spain: Editorial Marsiega (Fondo de Cultura Popular).

Frazer, N. (2005). *Transnationalizing the public sphere.* Retrieved from http://www.republicart.net/disc/publicum/fraser01_en.htm

Freire, A. M. A. (2006). *Paulo Freire: uma história de vida.* Indaiatuba, Brazil: Villa das Letras.

Freire, P. (1959). *Educação e atualidade brasileira.* Recife, Brazil: Universidade Federal de Recife.

Freire, P. (1968a). *Acción cultural para la libertad.* Santiago de Chile, Chile: ICIRA.

Freire, P. (1968b). La concepción problematizadora de la educación y la humanización. In *Cristianismo y sociedad. Suplemento Especial-edición no comercial -ISAL*, Montevideo.

Freire, P. (1970a, May). The adult literacy process as cultural action for freedom. *Harvard Educational Review, 2* (40), 205–225.

Freire, P. (1970b). Cultural action and concientization. *Harvard Educational Review, 40*(3), 452–477.

Freire, P. (1970c). Cultural action for freedom. *Harvard Educational Review* (and Center for the Study of Development and Social Change). Cambridge, MA. Monograph, series #1.

Freire, P. (1970d). Education for awareness: A talk with Paulo Freire. *Risk Review, 6*(4), 9–12.

Freire, P. (1970e). *Pedagogy of the oppressed.* New York, NY: Herder and Herder.

Freire, P. (1972a). *Cultural action for freedom.* Harmondsworth, U.K.: Penguin.

Freire, P. (1972b). *Pedagogía del oprimido.* Montevideo, Uruguay: Editorial Tierra Nueva.

Freire, P. (1972c). *Sobre la acción cultural.* Santiago de Chile, Chile: Instituto de Capacitación e Investigación en Reforma Agraria.

Freire, P. (1972d). La misión educativa de las iglesias en América Latina. Mexico City, Mexico, *Contacto*, *9*(5), 1–13.

Freire, P. (1973a). Education, liberation and the church. *Study Encounter*, *IX*(1), 1–16.

Freire, P. (1973c). Indicaciones a los coordinadores de los círculos de cultura. In S. Sánchez, *Freire: Una pedagogía para el adulto* (pp. 55–58). Madrid, Spain: Editora Zero.

Freire, P. (1973d). *La educación como práctica de la libertad*. Buenos Aires, Argentina: Siglo XXI Editores.

Freire, P. (1973e). *Pedagogía del oprimido*. Buenos Aires, Argentina: Siglo XXI Editores.

Freire, P. (1974a). *Concientización*. Buenos Aires, Argentina: Editora Búsqueda.

Freire, P. (1974b, September 6). *Conscientization demystified by Freire*. Paper presented as part of the seminar Invitation to Conscientize and De-School: A Continuing Conversation, Department of Education, World Council of Churches, Geneva. [Published in Spanish in *Revista Sic-Centro Gumilla*, *374*, 164–166, April 1975.]

Freire, P. (1974c). *Las iglesias, la educación y el proceso de liberación humana en la história*. Buenos Aires, Argentina: Editora La Aurora.

Freire, P. (1975). *Acción cultural para la libertad*. Buenos Aires, Argentina: Editora Tierra Nueva.

Freire, P. (1976a). *La educación como práctica de la libertad* (14th ed.). Mexico City, Mexico: Siglo XXI Editores.

Freire, P. (1976b). *Education, the practice of freedom*. London, England: Writers and Readers Publishing Cooperative. (Original work published in 1967)

Freire, P. (1977, June). Political education in Africa, Latin American Research Unit (LARU). Toronto, Canada.

Freire, P. (1979). *Extensão ou comunicação?* (Prefacio de Jacques Chonchol). Rio de Janeiro, Brazil: Paz e Terra.

Freire, P. (1980). Quatro cartas aos animadores de círculos de cultura en São Tomé e Príncipe. In Carlos Rodrigues Brandão (Ed.), *A questão política da educação popular* (pp. 136–195). São Paulo, Brazil: Brasiliense.

Freire, P. (1981a). *Cartas à Guiné-Bissau. Registros de uma experiência em processo*. Rio de Janeiro, Brazil: Paz e Terra.

Freire, P. (1981b). The people speak their word: Learning to read and write in São Tomé and Príncipe (Trans. Loretta Slover). *Harvard Educational Review 51*(1), 27–30.

Freire, P. (1983). Conscientização e alfabetização: uma nova visão do processo. In O. Fávero, *Cultura popular, educação popular: memória dos anos 60* (pp. 99–126). Rio de Janeiro, Brazil: Editora Graal.

Freire, P. (1985). *The politics of education: Culture, power and liberation*. (Trans. D. Macedo). South Hadley, MA: Bergin and Garvey.

Freire, P. (1991). *Paulo Freire en Chile: conversaciones, conferencias y entrevistas*. Santiago, Chile: Centro El Canelo de Nos.

Freire, P. (1993). *Pedagogy of the City*. New York, Continuum.

Freire, P. (1994). *Pedagogy of hope: Reliving* Pedagogy of the Oppressed. New York, NY: Continuum.

Freire, P. (1998a). *Pedagogy of the heart*. New York, NY: Continuum.

Freire, P. (1998b). *Politics and education.* Los Angeles, CA: Latin American Center, University of California–Los Angeles.

Freire, P. (1998c). *Pedagogy of Freedom. Ethics, Democracy, and Civic Courage.* Lanham, MD: Rowman and Littlefield.

Freire, P. (2000). *Pedagogia da indignação, Cartas pedagógicas e outros escritos.* São Paulo, Brazil: UNESP.

Freire, P. (2001). *Educación y actualidad brasileña.* Mexico City, Mexico, Siglo XXI Editores.

Freire, P. (2002). *Pedagogía do Oprimido.* Rio de Janeiro, Paz e Terra, 32 edition.

Freire, P. (2013). *Pedagogia do oprimido (o manuscrito).* São Paulo, Brazil: Editora Ed., L. Uninove, and Ministério de Educação, Brazil.

Freire, P., & Betto, F. (1985). *Essa escola chamada vida.* São Paulo, Brazil: Editora Ática.

Freire, P., Ceccon, C., Darcy de Oliveira, M., Darcy de Oliveira, R. (1989). *Vivendo e aprendendo: experiências do IDAC em educação.* São Paulo, Brazil: Institut d'Action Culturelle.

Freire, P., Gadotti, M., Saúl, A. M., & Torres, C. A. (2005). *A educação na cidade.* São Paulo, Brazil: Cortez.

Freire, P., & Horton, M. (1991). *We make the road by walking: Conversations on education and social change.* Philadelphia, PA: Temple University Press.

Freire, P., & Illich I. (1975). *Diálogo Paulo Freire-Ivan Illich.* Buenos Aires, Argentina: Editorial Búsqueda- Celadec.

Freire, P., Illich, I., & Furter, F. (1974). *Educación para el cambio social.* Buenos Aires, Argentina: Editorial Tierra Nueva.

Freire, P., Quiroga, A. P. (1995). *Interrogantes y propuestas en educación. Ideales, mitos y utopias a fines del siglo XX.* Buenos Aires, Argentina: Ediciones Cinco.

Freire, P., & Torres, C. A. (1994). Learning to read the world: Paulo Freire in conversation with Carlos Alberto Torres. In C. A. Torres, *Education and social change in Latin America* (pp. 175–181). Melbourne, Australia: James Nicholas Publisher.

Furter, P. (1985). Profile of educators. *Prospects, 15,* 301–310.

Furter, P., & Fiori, E. (1975). *Educación Liberadora. Dimensión Política.* Buenos Aires, Argentina, Ediciones Búsqueda.

Gadotti, M. (1994). *Reading Paulo Freire: His life and work.* New York, NY: SUNY Press.

Gadotti, M. (2002). *Pedagogía de la tierra.* Mexico City, Mexico: Siglo XXI Editores.

Gadotti, M. (2004). *Os mestres de Rousseau.* São Paulo, Brazil: Cortez Editora.

Gadotti, M. (2008a). *Education for sustainability. A critical contribution to the decade of education for sustainable development.* São Paulo, Brazil: Paulo Freire Institute.

Gadotti, M. (2008b). *MOVA Por um Brasil Alfabetizado.* São Paulo, Brazil: Instituto Paulo Freire.

Gadotti, M. (2012, July 25–27). *Educação popular, educação social, educação comunitária, conceitos e práticas diversas, cimentadas por uma causa comum.* Keynote to the IV Congreso Internacional de Pedagogia Social. UNICAMP, UNISAL, USP, PUC-SP, MACKENZIE, Campinas.

Gadotti, M., Araújo Freire, A. M., Ciseski, A. A., Torres, C. A., et al. (Eds.). (1996). *Paulo Freire: Uma bio-bibliografia.* São Paulo, Brazil: Institute Paulo Freire, UNESCO, and Cortez Editores.

Gadotti, M., & Torres, C. A. (1991). Paulo Freire, administrador público. In P. Freire, *A educação na cidade* (pp. 11–17). São Paulo, Brazil: Cortez.

Gadotti, M., & Torres, C. A. (1992). *Estado e educação popular na América Latina.* Campinas, São Paulo, Brazil: Papirus.

Gadotti, M., & Torres, C. A. (Eds.). (1993). *Educación popular: Crisis y perspectivas.* Buenos Aires, Argentina: Miño y Dávila Editores.

Gadotti, M., & Torres, C. A. (Eds.). (1994). *Educação popular: Utopia latinoamericana (ensaios).* São Paulo, Brazil: Cortez Editores and Editora da Universidade de São Paulo.

Gadotti, M., & Torres, C. A. (2001). *Paulo Freire: Una bio-bibliografía.* Mexico City, Mexico: Siglo XXI Editores.

Gajardo, M. J. (1972). Introduction. *Sobre la acción cultural* (pp. 7–17). Santiago de Chile, Chile, Institute of Capacitation and Investigation of Agrarian Reform (ICIRA)

Galbraith, J. (1954). *The great crash, 1929.* Cambridge, MA: Houghton Mifflin.

Galeano, E. H. (n.d.). Quoted on *Goodreads.com.* Retrieved from http://www.goodreads.com/quotes/show/33846

Galtung, J. (1966). *Teoría y métodos de la investigación social.* Buenos Aires, Argentina: Eudeba.

Gerhardt, H. P. (1983). Angicos—Rio Grande do Norte—1962/63. A primeira experiência com o sistema Paulo Freire. *Educação & Sociedade, 4*(14). São Paulo, Brazil: Cortez/Unicamp.

Gerhardt, H. P. (1993). *Paulo Reglus Neves Freire: A Profile.* Manuscript of January 5, 1993. Retrieved from http://acervo.paulofreire.org/xmlui/handle/7891/2897#page/2/mode/1up

Gerstenzang, J. (2003, January 12). That retro feel to Bush's style: It's Reaganesque. *Los Angeles Times,* pp. A16–18.

Gibson, N. C. (2011). *Fanonian practices in South Africa.* New York, NY: Palgrave Macmillan.

Ginsburg, M. (1995). A personal introduction to the politics of educators' work and lives. In M. Ginsburg (Ed.), *The politics of educators' work and lives* (pp. xxv–xxxvii). New York, NY: Garland.

Goldmann, L. (1972). *Las ciencias humanas y la filosofía.* Buenos Aires, Argentina: Editorial Nueva Visión.

Gregorich, L. (1983). *La república perdida, crónica ilustrada de medio siglo de desencuentro argentino, 1930–1983.* Buenos Aires, Argentina: Editorial Sudamericana/Planeta.

Habermas, J. (1992). *Postmetaphysical thinking: Philosophical essays* (W. M. Honengarten, Trans.). Cambridge, MA and London: MIT Press.

Harasim, L. M. (1983). *Literacy and national reconstruction in Guinea-Bissau: A critique of the Freirian literacy campaign.* PhD dissertation, University of Toronto.

Hegel, G. W. F. (1931). *The phenomenology of mind.* (Trans. J. B. Baillie, rev. ed.). London: George Allen and Unwin.

Hegel, G. W. F. (1967). *The phenomenology of mind.* Harper and Row.

Hirschman, J. (Ed.). (2010). *In danger. A Pasolini anthology.* San Francisco, California: City Lights Books.

Horton, M., & Freire, P. (1990). *We make the road by walking: Conversations on education and* social change. Philadelphia, PA: Temple University Press.

Husserl, E. (1970). *Logical Investigations.* London and New York: Routledge and Paul Kegan.

Husserl, E. (1999). *Cartesian meditations. An introduction to phenomenology* (D. Cains, Trans.). Dortrech, Boston and London: Kluger Academic Publishers.

Instituto de Acción Cultural (IDAC). (1975). *Concientización y liberación: una conversación con Paulo Freire.* Buenos Aires, Argentina: Editorial Axis.

Jerez, C., & Pico, J. H. (1971, August–September). Paulo Freire y la educación: acción cultural liberadora. Un aporte latinoamericano a la democracia educacional y política. *Estudios Centro Americanos (ECA). 26*(273), 503–515.

Jung, C. G. (1968). *Analytical psychology: Its theory and practice.* New York, NY: Vintage Books.

Kuhn, T. (1962). *The Structure of Scientific Revolutions.* Chicago, Illinois: University of Chicago Press.

Lazarsfeld, P. (1968). Evidence and inference in social research. *Daedalus, 87,* 120–121.

Lei No. 12.612, de 13 de Abril de 2012. (Law Nº 12.612, April 13, 2012).

Levin, H. (2011). Economics of education. *Albany Government Law Review, 4,* 395–426.

Lewin, T. (2010, May 13). Citing individualism, Arizona tries to rein in ethnic studies in school. *New York Times.* Retrieved from http://www.nytimes.com/2010/05/14/education/14arizona.html?pagewanted=print

Lyra, C. (1996). *As quarenta horas de Angicos: uma experiência pioneira de educação.* São Paulo, Brazil: Cortez.

Maciel, J. (1983). Fundamentação teórica do sistema Paulo Freire de educação. In O. Fávero (Ed.), *Cultura popular, educação popular: memória dos anos 60.* Rio de Janeiro, Brazil: Editora Graal.

Mafra, J., Torres, C. A., & Gadotti, M. (2008). *Reiventando Paulo Freire no século 21.* São Paulo, Brazil: Instituto Paulo Freire.

Manfredi, S. M. (1981). *Política e educação popular: experiências de alfabetização no Brasil com o Método Paulo Freire —1960/1964.* São Paulo, Brazil: Cortez.

Marcuse, H. (1967). *Reason and revolution.* (Trans. Julieta Fombona de Sucre). Caracas, Venezuela: Instituto de Estudios Políticos, Facultad de Derecho, Universidad Central de Venezuela.

Marx, K. (1859). Preface. In Contribution to the critique of political economy. Retrieved from http://www.marxists.org/archive/marx/works/1859/critique-pol-economy/preface-abs.htm

Marx, K. (1888). *Theses on Feuerbach.* Retrieved from http://www.marxists.org/archive/marx/works/1845/theses/theses.htm

Marx, K. (1972). *Manuscritos de 1844—Economía, política y filosofía.* Buenos Aires, Argentina: Ediciones Estudio.

Marx, K., & Engels, F. (1947). *The German ideology.* New York, NY: International Publishers.

Mayo, M. (2005). *Global citizens: Social movements and the challenge of globalization.* London, England: Zed Books.

Morrow, R., & Torres, C. A. (1995). *Social theory and education: A critique of theories of social and cultural reproduction*. Albany, NY: State University of New York Press.

Morrow, R., & Torres, C. A. (2002). *Reading Freire and Habermas. Critical Pedagogy and transformative social change.* New York, NY: Teachers College Press.

Mounier, E. (1952). *Personalism*. (Trans. Philip Mairet). London, England: Routledge and Kegan Paul Ltd.

Muniz de Brito, J. (1983). Educação de adultos e unificação da cultura. In O. Fávero (Ed.), *Cultura popular, educação popular: memória dos anos 60*. Rio de Janeiro, Brazil: Editora Graal.

National Center for Educational Statistics, U.S. Department of Education. (2010, April). *Digest of Education Statistics: 2009*. NCES 2010-013. Washington, DC: U.S. Government Printing Office.

O'Cadiz, M. P., & Torres, C. A. (1994). Literacy, social movements, and class consciousness: Paths from Freire and the São Paulo experience. *Anthropology and Education Quarterly, 25*(3), 208–225.

O'Cadiz, M. P., Torres, C. A., & Wong, P. (1998). *Education and democracy: Paulo Freire, social movements, and educational reform in São Paulo*. Boulder, CO: Westview Press.

O'Donnell, G., & McGuire, J. (1988). *Bureaucratic authoritarianism: Argentina, 1966–1973 in comparative perspective* (R. Flory, Trans.). Berkeley: University of California Press.

Oliveira, R. D., & Dominice, P. Illich-Freire. (1975). Pedagogy of the oppressed. [Oppression of pedagogy. The pedagogical debate. Originally appeared as Document #8, Geneva, Institute of Cultural Action (IDAC). Published in Spanish in *Revista Cuadernos de Pedagogía*, Nos. 7/8, July/August, 1975.]

Oliveira Andreotti, V. (2011, September). (Towards) decoloniality and diversality in global citizenship education. *Globalisation, Societies and Education, 9*(3–4), 381–397.

Pelandré, N. L. (2002). *Ensinar e aprender com Paulo Freire: 40 horas 40 anos depois*. São Paulo, Brazil: Cortez/Instituto Paulo Freire.

Pescador, J. A., & Torres, C. A. (1985). *Poder politico y educación en México*. Mexico City, Mexico: UTHEA.

Puiggrós, A. (2010). *Rodolfo Puiggrós: Retrato familiar de un intelectual militante.* Buenos Aires, Argentina: Taurus.

Rexhepi, J., & Torres, C. A. (2011). Reimagining Critical Theory. *British Journal of Sociology of Education, 32*(5), 679–698.

Ricoeur, P. (1974). *The conflict of interpretations* (Trans. D. Ihde). Evanston, Illinois: Northwestern University Press.

Ricoeur, P. (1978). *The rule of metaphor: Multi-disciplinary studies in the creation of meaning in language* (Trans. R. Czerny, with K. McLaughlin & J. Costello). Toronto, Canada: University of Toronto Press. (Original work published 1975)

Ricoeur, P. (1984). *Time and narrative* (Vol. 1) (Trans. K. McLaughlin & D. Pellaver). Chicago, IL: University of Chicago Press.

Ricoeur, P. (1985). *Time and narrative* (Vol. 2) (Trans. K. McLaughlin & D. Pellaver). Chicago, IL: University of Chicago Press.

Ricoeur, P. (1988). *Time and Narrative* (Vol. 3) (Trans. K. McLaughlin and D. Pellaver). Chicago, IL: University of Chicago Press.

Rocco, R. (1990). The theoretical construction of the "Other" in postmodernist thought: Latinos in the new urban political economy. *Cultural Studies 4*(3), 321–330.

Rocco, R. (1997). Citizenship, culture and community: Restructuring in southeast Los Angeles. In W. V. Flores & R. Benmayor (Eds.), *Latino cultural citizenship: Claiming identity, space, and rights.* Boston, MA: Beacon Press.

Rocco, R. (1999). The comparative study of clientelism and the changing nature of civil society in the contemporary world. In L. Roniger & A. Gunes-Ayata (Eds.), *Democracy, clientelism, and civil society.* Boulder, CO: Westview Press.

Rocco, R. (2002). Citizenship, civil society, and the Latina/o city: Claiming subaltern spaces, reframing the public sphere. In C. Vélez-Ibáñez & A. Sampaio (Eds.), *Transnational Latina/o communities: Politics, processes, and cultures.* Lanham, MD: Rowman and Littlefield.

Rocco, R. (2010). The structuring of Latino politics: Neoliberalism and incorporation. *NACLA Report on the Americas, 43*(6): 40–43.

Rocco, R., & Garcia Selgas, F. (Eds.). (2006). *Transnationalism: Issues and perspectives.* Madrid, Spain: Editorial Complutense.

Rodrigues Brandão, C. (Ed.). (1980). *A questão política da educação popular*. São Paulo, Brazil: Brasiliense.

Rodrigues Brandão, C. (Ed.). (1986). *O educador: vida e morte.* Rio de Janeiro, Brazil: GRAAL.

Rodrigues Brandão, C. (2013). *Paulo Freire. A educação, a cultura e a universidade. Memória de uma história há cinquenta anos atrás.* São Paulo, Brazil: Unpublished manuscript.

Romão, J. E. (2001). Contextualización. Paulo Freire y el pacto populista. In P. Freire, *Educación y actualidad brasileña.* (pp. xiii–xlviii). Mexico City, Mexico: Siglo XXI Editores.

Romão, J. E. (2007). Sociology of education or the education of sociology. Paulo Freire and the sociology of education. In C. A. Torres & A. Teodoro (Eds.), *Critique and utopia: New developments in the sociology of education* (pp. 131–138). Lanham, MD: Rowman and Littlefield Publishers.

Rosas, P. (2002). *Paulo Freire: educação e transformação social.* Recife, Pernambuco, Brazil: Centro Paulo Freire/UFPE.

Rubel, M. (1970). *Karl Marx. Ensayo de Biografía Intelectual.* Buenos Aires, Argentina, Paidos.

Rubel, M. (1973). *Marx, theoretician of anarchism.* Retrieved from http://www.marxists.org/archive/rubel/1973/marx-anarchism.htm

Sarlo, B. (2001). *Tiempo presente: Notas sobre el cambio de una cultura.* Buenos Aires, Argentina: Siglo XXI Editores.

Sanchez, S. (1975). *Paulo Freire: Una pedagogía para el adulto.* Madrid, Spain: Zero.

Schugurensky, D. (1997, Fall). Paulo Freire: A man who lived, loved and try to know. *Taboo, 1(2),* 104–107.

Schugurensky, D. (2011). *Paulo Freire*. New York, NY: Continuum.

Scocuglia, A. C. (1999). *A história das idéias de Paulo Freire e a atual crise de paradigmas* (2nd ed.). João Pessoa, Paraíba, Brazil: Editora Universitária—UFPB.

Scocuglia, A. C. (2001). Origems e prospective do pensamiento politico-pedagógico de Paulo Freire. In C. A. Torres (Ed.), *Paulo Freire e a agenda da educação Latino-Americana No Século XXI* (pp. 323–348). Buenos Aires, Argentina: CLCSO.

Scocuglia, A. C. (2010). *A influência de Amílcar Cabral e do trabalho na África na construção da práxis de Paulo Freire*. Paper presented to Biannual Paulo Freire International Forum, Praia, Cape Verde.

Sebreli, J. J. (2003). *Crítica de las ideas políticas argentinas* (5th ed.). Buenos Aires, Argentina: Sudamericana.

Skidmore, T. (2000, April 19) Interview. *Revista Veja, 1645*, 11–15. Retrieved from http://veja.abril.com.br/acervo/home.aspx

Streck, D., Redin, E., & Zitkoski, J. J. (2012). *Paulo Freire encyclopedia*. Lanham, MD: Rowman and Littlefield.

Suárez, L. (1980). *Entre el fusil y la palabra*. Mexico City, Mexico: Universidad Nacional Autónoma de México.

Suárez-Orozco, M. M., Louie, V., & Suro, R. (2011). *Writing immigration: Scholars and journalists in dialogue*. Berkeley: University of California Press.

Tarrow, S. (2005). *The New trasnational activism*. New York, NY: Cambridge University Press.

Taylor, G. (Ed.). (1981). *Lectures on ideology and utopia*. New York, NY: Cambridge University Press.

Teodoro, A., & Torres, C. A. (2007). Introduction: Critique and utopia in the sociology of education. In C. A. Torres & A. Teodoro (Eds.), *Critique and utopia: New developments in the sociology of education* (pp. 1–8). Lanham, MD: Rowman and Littlefield.

Torres, C. A. (1976a). A dialética Hegeliana e o pensamento lógico-estrutural do Paulo Freire. Notas para uma análise e confrontação dos pressupostos filosóficos vigentes na dialética da pedagogia dos oprimidos e do pensamento freireano em geral. *Revista Síntese, 7*, 61–78.

Torres, C. A. (1976b, September–December). Servidumbre, autoconciencia y liberación. *Franciscanum: Revista de la Universidad de Buenaventura. 54*, 405–478.

Torres, C. A. (1977). Las Migraciones rurales, el proceso de urbanización y la marginalidad social en América Latina. [Rural migration, the process of urbanization, and social marginality in Latin America]. *Franciscanu:. Revista de la Universidad de San Buenaventura, 56*, 185–230.

Torres, C. A. (1980a). Las corrientes filosóficas que fecundan la filosofía de Paulo Freire. *Colección Pedagógica Universitaria, 9*, 7–25.

Torres, C. A. (1980b). *Paulo Freire: Educación y concientización*. Salamanca, Spain: Ediciones Sígueme.

Torres, C. A. (1981a). *Leitura crítica de Paulo Freire*. São Paulo, Brazil: Loyola Editores.

Torres, C. A. (1981b). La sociología de la cultura y la crítica pedagógica de Paulo Freire. In G. González Rivera & C. A. Torres (Eds.), *Sociología de la educación: Corrientes contemporáneas* (pp. 271–298). Mexico City, Mexico: Centro de Estudios Educativos.

Torres, C. A. (1989). Political culture and state bureaucracy in Mexico: The case of adult education. *International Journal of Educational Development, 9*(1), 53–68.

Torres, C. A. (1990). *The politics of nonformal education in Latin America.* New York, NY: Praeger.

Torres, C. A. (1991). The state, nonformal education, and socialism in Cuba, Nicaragua, and Grenada. *Comparative Education Review, 39*(1), 1–27.

Torres, C. A. (1992a). *The Church, Society and Hegemony: A Critical Sociology of Religion in Latin America* (Trans. R. A. Young). Westport, CT, and London, UK: Praeger.

Torres, C. A. (1992b). From the "Pedagogy of the Oppressed" to "A Luta Continua": The Political Pedagogy of Paulo Freire. In P. McLaren & P. Leonard (Eds.), *Paulo Freire: A Critical Encounter* (pp. 119–145). London, UK: Routledge.

Torres, C. A. (1992c). Participatory Action Research and Popular Education in Latin America. *International Journal of Qualitative Studies in Education, 5(1)*, 51–62.

Torres, C. A. (1994a). Education and the archeology of consciousness: Hegel and Freire. *Educational Theory, 44*(4), 429–445.

Torres, C. A. (1994b). *Estudios Freireanos.* Buenos Aires, Argentina: Ediciones del Quirquincho.

Torres, C. A. (1994c). Intellectuals and university life: Paulo Freire on higher education. In G. Guevara Niebla, A. L. Fernandez, & M. Escobar (Eds.), *Paulo Freire at the National University in Mexico: A Dialogue* (pp. 2–25). New York, NY: State University of New York Press

Torres, C. A. (1994d). A land of contrasts and a pedagogy of contradiction. In M. Gadotti, *Reading Paulo Freire: His life and work* (pp. ix–xii). Albany, New York: SUNY Press.

Torres, C. A. (1995a). Fictional dialogues on teachers, politics, and power in Latin America. In M. Ginsburg (Ed.), *The politics of educators' work and lives* (pp. 133–168). New York, NY: Garland.

Torres, C. A. (1995b). Estado, políticas públicas e educação de adultos. In M. Gadotti & J. E. Romão (Eds.), *Educação de jovens e adultos. Teoria, prática e proposta* (pp. 19–27). São Paulo, Brazil: Cortez Editora and Paulo Freire Institute.

Torres, C. A. (Ed.). (1995c). *Education and social change in Latin America.* Albert Park, Australia: James Nicholas Publishers.

Torres, C. A. (1996a). Adult education and instrumental rationality: A critique. *International Journal of Educational Development, 16*(2), 195–206.

Torres, C. A. (1996b). A voz do biógrafo Latinoamericano: Uma biografía intelectual. In M. Gadotti, M. et al. (Eds.), *Paulo Freire: Uma bio-bibliografia* (pp. 117–147). São Paulo, Brazil: Paulo Freire Institute/UNESCO.

Torres, C. A. (1996c). Dialectics, conflict and dialogue. In M. Gadotti, *Pedagogy of praxis: A Dialectical Philosophy of Education* (pp. xix-xxx). Albany: State University of New York Press.

Torres, C. A. (1996d). *Las secretas aventuras del orden. Estado y educación.* Buenos Aires, Argentina: Miño y Dávila Editores.

Torres, C. A. (1998a). *Education, democracy and multiculturalism: Dilemmas of citizenship in a global world.* Lanham, MD: Rowman and Littlefield.

Torres, C. A. (1998b). *Pedagogia da luta. Da pedagogia do oprimido à educação pública popular.* São Paulo, Brazil: Cortez Editores e IPF.

Torres, C. A. (1998c). The political pedagogy of Paulo Freire. In *Paulo Freire, politics and education.* Los Angeles, CA: Latin American Center, UCLA.

Torres, C. A. (1998d). *Education, power and personal biography: Dialogues with critical educators.* New York, NY: Routledge.

Torres, C. A. (2002). Raccomandazione finale. In F. Telleri (Ed.), *Il metodo Paulo Freire. Nuove tecnologie e sviluppo sostenibile.* Bologna, Italy: Coperative Libraria Universitaria Editrice Bologna.

Torres, C. A. (2003, April 22). Paulo Freire: Politics and education as sources of hope. Paper presented to the symposium on Dewey, Freire and Sources of Hope, AERA, Chicago, IL.

Torres, C. A. (2004). Els mons distorsionats de Paulo Freire i Ivan Illich. In P. Aparicio (Ed.), *Diàleg Paulo Freire Ivan Illich* (pp. 9–30). Valencia, Spain: Paulo Freire Institute; Xativa: Edicions del CreC.

Torres, C. A. (2005). Requiem for Paulo Reglus Neves Freire (Trans. Peter Lownds). In Torres, *Poesia perdida al atardecer* (pp. 22–24). Valencia, Spain: Germania.

Torres, C. A. (2009a). *Globalizations and education: Collected essays on class, race, gender, and the state.* New York, NY: Teachers College Press.

Torres, C. A. (2009b). *Education and Neoliberal globalization.* New York, NY: Routledge.

Torres, C. A. (2011a). Dancing in the deck of the Titanic. Adult education, the nation state and new social movements. *International Review of Education,* 57: 39–55.

Torres, C. A. (2011b). Public universities and the neoliberal common sense: Seven iconoclastic theses. *International Studies in Sociology of Education, 21*(3), 177–197.

Torres, C.A. (2013). Afterword on comparative education: The dialectics of globalization and its discontents. In R. Arnove, C. A. Torres, & S. Frantz (Eds.), *Comparative education: The dialectics of the global and the local* (4th ed.) (pp. 459–483). Lanham, MD: Rowman and Littlefield.

Torres, C. A., & Morrow, R. (2002a). *Reading Freire and Habermas.* New York, NY: Teachers College Press.

Torres, C. A., & Morrow, R. (2002b). Theory and methods of Paulo Freire: A discussion of forms and content of emancipatory learning and revolutionary pedagogy and its reception in the United States. In F. Telleri (Ed.), *Il metodo Paulo Freire. Nuove tecnologie e sviluppo sostenibile.* Bologna, Italy: Coperative Libraria Universitaria Editrice Bologna.

Torres, C. A., & Noguera, P. (Eds.). (2008). *Social justice education for teachers: Paulo Freire and the possible dream.* Rotterdam, Netherlands, and Taipei, Taiwan: Sense Publishers

Torres Novoa, C. A. (1978a). *Entrevistas con Paulo Freire.* Mexico City, Mexico: Ediciones Guernika.

Torres Novoa, C. A. (1978b). *La praxis educativa de Paulo Freire.* Mexico City, Mexico: Ediciones Guernika.

Torres Novoa, C. A. (1978c). *Paulo Freire en América Latina.* Mexico City, Mexico: Ediciones Guernika.

Tucker, R. C. (Ed.). (1978). *The Marx-Engels reader.* New York, NY: W. W. Norton.

UNESCO. (2009). Global report on adult learning and education (GRALE). Paris, France: UNESCO. Retrieved from http://www.unesco.org/en/confinteavi/grale/

Vachet, A. (1972). *La ideologia liberal.* Madrid, Spain: Ed. Fundamentos

Weber, M. (1973). *Ensayo sobre metodología sociológica.* Buenos Aires, Argentina: Amorrortu.

Welton, M. (1993). Social revolutionary learning: The new social movements as learning sites. *Adult Education Quarterly, 43*(3), 152–164.

Williamson, G. (1988). *Paulo Freire en Chile.* Campinas, Brazil: UNICAMP.

Wright Mills, C. (2008). *The Politics of Truth. Selected Writings of C. Wright Mills* (Selected and introduced by J. H. Summers). New York, NY: Oxford University Press.

Index

About the Author

Carlos Alberto Torres is distinguished professor of social sciences and comparative education; associate dean for global programs; and founding director at the Paulo Freire Institute, Graduate School of Education and Information Studies–UCLA. He is also the president of the World Council of Comparative Education Societies (WCCES). In addition, Professor Torres, along with Paulo Freire, Moacir Gadotti, José Eustaquio Romão, Walter García, and Francisco Gutierrez, founded and was a director of the Paulo Freire Institute, São Paulo, Brazil, in 1991. He is the founding director of the the Paulo Freire Institute–Argentina, established in 2003.